THEOLOGICO-POLITICAL TREATISE

Baruch Spinoza

Translated by
R. H. M. Elwes

C L A S S Y
PUBLISHING

THEOLOGICO-POLITICAL TREATISE
by Baruch Spinoza

Published by Classy Publishing, 2024

www.classypublishing.com
info@classypublishing.com

ISBN: 978-93-5522-703-4

Cover Design by Classy Publishing

CONTENTS

PREFACE

Men would never be superstitious, if they could govern all their circumstances by set rules, or if they were always favoured by fortune: but being frequently driven into straits where rules are useless, and being often kept fluctuating pitiably between hope and fear by the uncertainty of fortune's greedily coveted favours, they are consequently, for the most part, very prone to credulity. The human mind is readily swayed this way or that in times of doubt, especially when hope and fear are struggling for the mastery, though usually it is boastful, over — confident, and vain.

This as a general fact I suppose everyone knows, though few, I believe, know their own nature; no one can have lived in the world without observing that most people, when in prosperity, are so over-brimming with wisdom (however inexperienced they may be), that they take every offer of advice as a personal insult, whereas in adversity they know not where to turn, but beg and pray for counsel from every passer-by. No plan is then too futile, too absurd, or too fatuous for their adoption; the most frivolous causes will raise them to hope, or plunge them into despair — if anything happens during their fright which reminds them of some past good or ill, they think it portends a happy or unhappy issue, and therefore (though it may have proved abortive a hundred times before) style it a lucky or unlucky omen. Anything which excites their astonishment they believe to be a portent signifying the anger of the gods or of the Supreme Being, and, mistaking superstition for religion, account it impious not to avert the evil with prayer and sacrifice. Signs and wonders of this sort they conjure up perpetually, till one might think Nature as mad as themselves, they interpret her so fantastically.

Thus it is brought prominently before us, that superstition's chief victims are those persons who greedily covet temporal advantages; they it is, who (especially when they are in danger, and cannot help themselves) are wont with Prayers and womanish tears to implore help from God: upbraiding Reason as blind, because she cannot show a sure path to the shadows they pursue, and rejecting human wisdom as vain; but believing the phantoms of imagination, dreams, and other childish absurdities, to be the very oracles of Heaven. As though God had turned away from the wise, and written His decrees, not in the mind of man but in the entrails of beasts, or left them to be proclaimed by the inspiration and instinct of fools, madmen, and birds. Such is the unreason to which terror can drive mankind!

Superstition, then, is engendered, preserved, and fostered by fear. If anyone desire an example, let him take Alexander, who only began superstitiously to seek guidance from seers, when he first learnt to fear fortune in the passes of Sysis (Curtius, v. 4); whereas after he had conquered Darius he consulted prophets no more, till a second time frightened by reverses. When the Scythians were provoking a battle, the Bactrians had deserted, and he himself was lying sick of his wounds, "he once more turned to superstition, the mockery of human wisdom, and bade Aristander, to whom he confided his credulity, inquire the issue of affairs with sacrificed victims." Very numerous examples of a like nature might be cited, clearly showing the fact, that only while under the dominion of fear do men fall a prey to superstition; that all the portents ever invested with the reverence of misguided religion are mere phantoms of dejected and fearful minds; and lastly, that prophets have most power among the people, and are most formidable to rulers, precisely at those times when the state is in most peril. I think this is sufficiently plain to all, and will therefore say no more on the subject.

The origin of superstition above given affords us a clear reason for the fact, that it comes to all men naturally, though some refer its rise to a dim notion of God, universal to mankind, and also tends to show, that it is no less inconsistent and variable than other mental hallucinations and emotional impulses, and further that it can only be maintained by hope, hatred, anger, and deceit; since it springs, not from reason, but solely from the more powerful phases of emotion. Furthermore, we may readily understand how difficult it is, to maintain in the same course men prone to every form of credulity. For, as the mass of mankind remains always at about the same pitch of misery, it never assents long to any one remedy, but is always best pleased by a novelty which has not yet proved illusive.

This element of inconsistency has been the cause of many terrible wars and revolutions; for, as Curtius well says (lib. iv. chap. 10): "The mob has no ruler more potent than superstition," and is easily led, on the plea of religion, at one moment to adore its kings as gods, and anon to execrate and abjure them as humanity's common bane. Immense pains have therefore been taken to counteract this evil by investing religion, whether true or false, with such pomp and ceremony, that it may, rise superior to every shock, and be always observed with studious reverence by the whole people — a system which has been brought to great perfection by the Turks, for they consider even controversy impious, and so clog men's minds with dogmatic formulas, that they leave no room for sound reason, not even enough to doubt with.

But if, in despotic statecraft, the supreme and essential mystery be to hoodwink the subjects, and to mask the fear, which keeps them clown, with the specious garb of religion, so that men may fight as bravely for slavery as for safety, and count it not shame but highest honour to risk their blood and their lives for the vainglory of a tyrant; yet in a free state no more mischievous expedient could be planned or attempted. Wholly repugnant to the general freedom are such devices as enthralling men's minds with prejudices, forcing their judgment, or employing any of the weapons of quasi-religious sedition; indeed, such seditions only spring up, when law enters the domain of speculative thought, and opinions are put on trial and condemned on the same footing as crimes, while those who defend and follow them are sacrificed, not to public safety, but to their opponents' hatred and cruelty. If deeds only could be made the grounds of criminal charges, and words were always allowed to pass free, such seditions would be divested of every semblance of justification, and would be separated from mere controversies by a hard and fast line.

Now, seeing that we have the rare happiness of living in a republic, where everyone's judgment is free and unshackled, where each may worship God as his conscience dictates, and where freedom is esteemed before all things dear and precious, I have believed that I should be undertaking no ungrateful or unprofitable task, in demonstrating that not only can such freedom be granted without prejudice to the public peace, but also, that without such freedom, piety cannot flourish nor the public peace be secure.

Such is the chief conclusion I seek to establish in this treatise; but, in order to reach it, I must first point out the misconceptions which, like scars of our former bondage, still disfigure our notion of religion, and must expose the false views about the civil authority which many have most impudently advocated, endeavouring to turn the mind of the people, still prone to heathen superstition, away from its legitimate rulers, and so bring us again into slavery. As to the order of my treatise I will speak presently, but first I will recount the causes which led me to write.

I have often wondered, that persons who make a boast of professing the Christian religion, namely, love, joy, peace, temperance, and charity to all men, should quarrel with such rancorous animosity, and display daily towards one another such bitter hatred, that this, rather than the virtues they claim, is the readiest criterion of their faith. Matters have long since come to such a pass, that one can only pronounce a man Christian, Turk, Jew, or Heathen, by his general appearance and attire, by his frequenting this or that place of worship, or employing the phraseology of a particular sect — as for manner of life, it is in all cases the same. Inquiry into the cause of this anomaly leads me unhesitatingly to ascribe it to the fact, that the ministries of the Church are regarded by the masses merely as dignities, her offices as posts of emolument — in short, popular religion may be summed up as respect for ecclesiastics. The spread of this misconception inflamed every worthless fellow with an intense desire to enter holy orders, and thus the love of diffusing God's religion degenerated into sordid avarice and ambition. Every church became a theatre, where orators, instead of church teachers, harangued, caring not to instruct the people, but striving to attract admiration, to bring opponents to public scorn, and to preach only novelties and paradoxes, such as would tickle the ears of their congregation. This state of things necessarily stirred up an amount of controversy, envy, and hatred, which no lapse of time could appease; so that we can scarcely wonder that of the old religion nothing survives but its outward forms (even these, in the mouth of the multitude, seem rather adulation than adoration of the Deity), and that faith has become a mere compound of credulity and prejudices — aye, prejudices too, which degrade man from rational being to beast, which completely stifle the power of judgment between true and false, which seem, in fact, carefully fostered for the purpose of extinguishing the last spark of reason! Piety, great God! and religion are become a tissue of ridiculous mysteries; men, who flatly despise reason, who reject and turn away from understanding as naturally corrupt, these, I say, these of all men, are thought, 0 lie most horrible! to possess light from on High. Verily, if they had but one spark of light from on High, they would not insolently rave, but would learn to worship God more wisely, and would be as marked among their fellows for mercy as they now are for malice; if they were concerned for their opponents' souls, instead of for their own reputations, they would no longer fiercely persecute, but rather be filled with pity and compassion.

Furthermore, if any Divine light were in them, it would appear from their doctrine. I grant that they are never tired of professing their wonder at the profound mysteries of Holy Writ; still I cannot discover that they teach anything but speculations of Platonists and Aristotelians, to which (in order to save their credit for Christianity) they have made Holy Writ conform; not content to rave with the Greeks themselves, they want to make the prophets rave also; showing conclusively, that never even in sleep have they caught a glimpse of Scripture's Divine nature. The very vehemence of their admiration for the mysteries plainly attests, that their belief in the Bible is a formal assent rather than a living faith: and the fact is made still more apparent by their laying down beforehand, as a foundation for the study and true interpretation of Scripture, the principle that it is in every passage true and divine. Such a doctrine should be reached only after strict scrutiny and thorough comprehension of the Sacred Books (which would teach it much better, for they stand in need no human factions), and not be set up on the threshold, as it were, of inquiry.

As I pondered over the facts that the light of reason is not only despised, but by many even execrated as a source of impiety, that human commentaries are accepted as divine records, and that credulity is extolled as faith; as I marked the fierce controversies of philosophers raging in Church and State, the source of bitter hatred and dissension, the ready instruments of sedition and other ills innumerable, I determined to examine the Bible afresh in a careful, impartial, and unfettered spirit, making no assumptions concerning it, and attributing to it no doctrines, which I do not find clearly therein set down. With these precautions I constructed a method of Scriptural interpretation, and thus equipped proceeded to inquire — what is prophecy? In what sense did God reveal himself to the prophets, and why were these particular men — chosen by him? Was it on account of the sublimity of their thoughts about the Deity and nature, or was it solely on account of their piety? These questions being answered, I was easily able to conclude, that the authority of the prophets has weight only in matters of morality, and that their speculative doctrines affect us little.

Next I inquired, why the Hebrews were called God's chosen people, and discovering that it was only because God had chosen for them a certain strip of territory, where they might live peaceably and at ease, I learnt that the Law revealed by God to Moses was merely the law of the individual Hebrew state, therefore that it was binding on none but Hebrews, and not even on Hebrews after the downfall of their nation. Further, in order to ascertain, whether it could be concluded from Scripture, that the human understanding standing is naturally corrupt, I inquired whether the Universal Religion, the Divine Law revealed through the Prophets and Apostles to the whole human race, differs from that which is taught by the light of natural reason, whether miracles can take place in violation of the laws of nature, and if so, whether they imply the existence of God more surely and clearly than events, which we understand plainly and distinctly through their immediate natural causes.

Now, as in the whole course of my investigation I found nothing taught expressly by Scripture, which does not agree with our understanding, or which is repugnant thereto, and as I saw that the prophets taught nothing, which is not very simple and easily to be grasped by all, and further, that they clothed their leaching in the style, and confirmed it with the reasons, which would most deeply move the mind of the masses to devotion towards God, I became thoroughly convinced, that the Bible leaves reason absolutely free, that it has nothing in common with philosophy, in fact, that Revelation and Philosophy stand on different footings. In order to set this forth categorically and exhaust the whole question, I point out the way in which the Bible should be interpreted, and show that all of spiritual questions should be sought from it alone, and not from the objects of ordinary knowledge. Thence I pass on to indicate the false notions, which have from the fact that the multitude — ever prone to superstition, and caring more for the shreds of antiquity for eternal truths — pays homage to the Books of the Bible, rather than to the Word of God. I show that the Word of God has not been revealed as a certain number of books, was displayed to the prophets as a simple idea of the mind, namely, obedience to God in singleness of heart, and in the practice of justice and charity; and I further point out, that this doctrine is set forth in Scripture in accordance with the opinions and understandings of those, among whom the Apostles and Prophets preached, to the end that men might receive it willingly, and with their whole heart.

Having thus laid bare the bases of belief, I draw the conclusion that Revelation has obedience for its sole object, therefore, in purpose no less than in foundation and method, stands entirely aloof from ordinary knowledge; each has its separate province, neither can be called the handmaid of the other.

Furthermore, as men's habits of mind differ, so that some more readily embrace one form of faith, some another, for what moves one to pray may move another only to scoff, I conclude, in accordance with what has gone before, that everyone should be free to choose for himself the foundations of his creed, and that faith should be judged only by its fruits; each would then obey God freely with his whole heart, while nothing would be publicly honoured save justice and charity.

Having thus drawn attention to the liberty conceded to everyone by the revealed law of God, I pass on to another part of my subject, and prove that this same liberty can and should be accorded with safety to the state and the magisterial authority — in fact, that it cannot be withheld without great danger to peace and detriment to the community.

In order to establish my point, I start from the natural rights of the individual, which are co-extensive with his desires and power, and from the fact that no one is bound to live as another pleases, but is the guardian of his own liberty. I show that these rights can only be transferred to those whom we depute to defend us, who acquire with the duties of defence the power of ordering our lives, and I thence infer that rulers possess rights only limited by their power, that they are the sole guardians of justice and liberty, and that their subjects should act in all things as they dictate: nevertheless, since no one can so utterly abdicate his own power of self-defence as to cease to be a man, I conclude that no one can be deprived of his natural rights absolutely, but that subjects, either by tacit agreement, or by social contract, retain a certain number, which cannot be taken from them without great danger to the state.

From these considerations I pass on to the Hebrew State, which I describe at some length, in order to trace the manner in which Religion acquired the force of law, and to touch on other noteworthy points. I then prove, that the holders of sovereign power are the depositories and interpreters of religious no less than of civil ordinances, and that they alone have the right to decide what is just or unjust, pious or impious; lastly, I conclude by showing, that they best retain this right and secure safety to their state by allowing every man to think what he likes, and say what he thinks.

Such, Philosophical Reader, are the questions I submit to your notice, counting on your approval, for the subject matter of the whole book and of the several chapters is important and profitable. I would say more, but I do not want my preface to extend to a volume, especially as I know that its leading propositions are to Philosophers but common places. To the rest of mankind I care not to commend my treatise, for I cannot expect that it contains anything to please them: I know how deeply rooted are the prejudices embraced under the name of religion; I am aware that in the mind of the masses superstition is no less deeply rooted than fear; I recognize that their constancy is mere obstinacy, and that they are led to praise or blame by impulse rather than reason. Therefore the multitude, and those of like passions with the multitude, I ask not to read my book; nay, I would rather that they should utterly neglect it, than that they should misinterpret it after their wont. They would gain no good themselves, and might prove a stumbling-block to others, whose philosophy is hampered by the belief that Reason is a mere handmaid to Theology, and whom I seek in this work especially to benefit. But as there will be many who have neither the leisure, nor, perhaps, the inclination to read through all I have written, I feel bound here, as at the end of my treatise, to declare that I have written nothing, which I do not most willingly submit to the examination and judgment of my country's rulers, and that I am ready to retract anything, which they shall decide to be repugnant to the laws or prejudicial to the public good. I know that I am a man and, as a man, liable to error, but against error I have taken scrupulous care, and striven to keep in entire accordance with the laws of my country, with loyalty, and with morality.

CHAPTER I

Of Prophecy

Prophecy, or revelation is sure knowledge revealed by God to man. A prophet is one who interprets the revelations of God {insights} to those who are unable to attain to sure knowledge of the matters revealed, and therefore can only apprehend them by simple faith.

The Hebrew word for prophet is "*nabi*",[1] i.e. speaker or interpreter, but in Scripture its meaning is restricted to interpreter of God, as we may learn from Exodus vii:1, where God says to Moses, "See, I have made thee a god to Pharaoh, and Aaron thy brother shall be thy prophet;" implying that, since in interpreting Moses' words to Pharaoh, Aaron acted the part of a prophet, Moses would be to Pharaoh as a god, or in the attitude of a god.

Prophets I will treat of in the next chapter, and at present consider prophecy.

Now it is evident, from the definition above given, that prophecy really includes ordinary knowledge; for the knowledge which we acquire by our natural faculties depends on knowledge of God and His eternal laws; but ordinary knowledge is common to all men as men, and rests on foundations which all share, whereas the multitude always strains after rarities and exceptions, and thinks little of the gifts of nature; so that, when prophecy is talked of, ordinary knowledge is not supposed to be included. Nevertheless it has as much right as any other to be called Divine, for God's nature, in so far as we share therein, and God's laws, dictate it to us; nor does it suffer from that to which we give the preeminence, except in so far as the latter transcends its limits and cannot be accounted for by natural laws taken in themselves. In respect to the certainty it involves, and the source from which it is derived, i.e. God, ordinary, knowledge is no whit inferior to prophetic, unless indeed we believe, or rather dream, that

---

[1] The word *nabi* is rightly interpreted by Rabbi Salomon Jarchi, but the sense is hardly caught by Aben Ezra, who was not so good a Hebraist. We must also remark that this Hebrew word for prophecy has a universal meaning and embraces all kinds of prophecy. Other terms are more special, and denote this or that sort of prophecy, as I believe is well known to the learned.

the prophets had human bodies but superhuman minds, and therefore that their sensations and consciousness were entirely different from our own.

But, although ordinary knowledge is Divine, its professors cannot be called prophets[2], for they teach what the rest of mankind could perceive and apprehend, not merely by simple faith, but as surely and honourably as themselves.

Seeing then that our mind subjectively contains in itself and partakes of the nature of God, and solely from this cause is enabled to form notions explaining natural phenomena and inculcating morality, it follows that we may rightly assert the nature of the human mind (in so far as it is thus conceived) to be a primary cause of Divine revelation. All that we clearly and distinctly understand is dictated to us, as I have just pointed out, by the idea and nature of God; not indeed through words, but in a way far more excellent and agreeing perfectly with the nature of the mind, as all who have enjoyed intellectual certainty will doubtless attest. Here, however, my chief purpose is to speak of matters having reference to Scripture, so these few words on the light of reason will suffice.

I will now pass on to, and treat more fully, the other ways and means by which God makes revelations to mankind, both of that which transcends ordinary knowledge, and of that within its scope; for there is no reason why God should not employ other means to communicate what we know already by the power of reason.

Our conclusions on the subject must be drawn solely from Scripture; for what can we affirm about matters transcending our knowledge except what is told us by the words or writings of prophets? And since there are, so far as I know, no prophets now alive, we have no alternative but to read the books of prophets departed, taking care the while not to reason from metaphor or to ascribe anything to our authors which they do not themselves distinctly state. I must further premise that the Jews never make any mention or account of secondary, or particular causes, but in a spirit of religion, piety, and what is commonly called godliness, refer all things directly to the Deity. For instance if they make money by a transaction, they say God gave it to them; if they desire anything, they say God has disposed their hearts towards it; if they think anything, they say God told them. Hence we must not suppose that everything is

---

[2] "Although, ordinary knowledge is Divine, its professors cannot be called prophets." That is, interpreters of God. For he alone is an interpreter of God, who interprets the decrees which God has revealed to him, to others who have not received such revelation, and whose belief, therefore, rests merely on the prophet's authority and the confidence reposed in him. If it were otherwise, and all who listen to prophets became prophets themselves, as all who listen to philosophers become philosophers, a prophet would no longer be the interpreter of Divine decrees, inasmuch as his hearers would know the truth, not on the, authority of the prophet, but by means of actual Divine revelation and inward testimony. Thus the sovereign powers are the interpreters of their own rights of sway, because these are defended only by their authority and supported by their testimony.

prophecy or revelation which is described in Scripture as told by God to anyone, but only such things as are expressly announced as prophecy or revelation, or are plainly pointed to as such by the context.

A perusal of the sacred books will show us that all God's revelations to the prophets were made through words or appearances, or a combination of the two. These words and appearances were of two kinds; 1. — real when external to the mind of the prophet who heard or saw them, 2. — imaginary when the imagination of the prophet was in a state which led him distinctly to suppose that he heard or saw them.

With a real voice God revealed to Moses the laws which He wished to be transmitted to the Hebrews, as we may see from Exodus xxv:22, where God says, "And there I will meet with thee and I will commune with thee from the mercy seat which is between the Cherubim." Some sort of real voice must necessarily have been employed, for Moses found God ready to commune with him at any time. This, as I shall shortly show, is the only instance of a real voice.

We might, perhaps, suppose that the voice with which God called Samuel was real, for in 1 Sam. iii:21, we read, "And the Lord appeared again in Shiloh, for the Lord revealed Himself to Samuel in Shiloh by the word of the Lord;" implying that the appearance of the Lord consisted in His making Himself known to Samuel through a voice; in other words, that Samuel heard the Lord speaking. But we are compelled to distinguish between the prophecies of Moses and those of other prophets, and therefore must decide that this voice was imaginary, a conclusion further supported by the voice's resemblance to the voice of Eli, which Samuel was in the habit of hearing, and therefore might easily imagine; when thrice called by the Lord, Samuel supposed it to have been Eli.

The voice which Abimelech heard was imaginary, for it is written, Gen. xx:6, "And God said unto him in a dream." So that the will of God was manifest to him, not in waking, but only, in sleep, that is, when the imagination is most active and uncontrolled. Some of the Jews believe that the actual words of the Decalogue were not spoken by God, but that the Israelites heard a noise only, without any distinct words, and during its continuance apprehended the Ten Commandments by pure intuition; to this opinion I myself once inclined, seeing that the words of the Decalogue in Exodus are different from the words of the Decalogue in Deuteronomy: for the discrepancy seemed to imply (since God only spoke once) that the Ten Commandments were not intended to convey the actual words of the Lord, but only His meaning. However, unless we would do violence to Scripture, we must certainly admit that the Israelites heard a real voice, for Scripture expressly says, Deut. v:4," God spake with you face to face," i.e. as two men ordinarily interchange ideas through the instrumentality of their two bodies; and therefore it seems more consonant with Holy Writ to suppose that God really did create a voice of some kind with which the Decalogue was revealed. The discrepancy of the two versions is treated of in Chap. VIII.

Yet not even thus is all difficulty removed, for it seems scarcely reasonable to affirm that a created thing, depending on God in the same manner as other created things, would be able to express or explain the nature of God either verbally or really by means of its individual organism: for instance, by declaring in the first person, "I am the Lord your God."

Certainly when anyone says with his mouth, "I understand," we do not attribute the understanding to the mouth, but to the mind of the speaker; yet this is because the mouth is the natural organ of a man speaking, and the hearer, knowing what understanding is, easily comprehends, by a comparison with himself, that the speaker's mind is meant; but if we knew nothing of God beyond the mere name and wished to commune with Him, and be assured of His existence, I fail to see how our wish would be satisfied by the declaration of a created thing (depending on God neither more nor less than ourselves), "I am the Lord." If God contorted the lips of Moses, or, I will not say Moses, but some beast, till they pronounced the words, "I am the Lord," should we apprehend the Lord's existence therefrom?

Scripture seems clearly to point to the belief that God spoke Himself, having descended from heaven to Mount Sinai for the purpose — and not only that the Israelites heard Him speaking, but that their chief men beheld Him (Ex:xxiv.) Further the law of Moses, which might neither be added to nor curtailed, and which was set up as a national standard of right, nowhere prescribed the belief that God is without body, or even without form or figure, but only ordained that the Jews should believe in His existence and worship Him alone: it forbade them to invent or fashion any likeness of the Deity, but this was to insure purity of service; because, never having seen God, they could not by means of images recall the likeness of God, but only the likeness of some created thing which might thus gradually take the place of God as the object of their adoration. Nevertheless, the Bible clearly implies that God has a form, and that Moses when he heard God speaking was permitted to behold it, or at least its hinder parts.

Doubtless some mystery lurks in this question which we will discuss more fully below. For the present I will call attention to the passages in Scripture indicating the means by which God has revealed His laws to man.

Revelation may be through figures only, as in I Chron:xxii., where God displays his anger to David by means of an angel bearing a sword, and also in the story of Balaam.

Maimonides and others do indeed maintain that these and every other instance of angelic apparitions (e.g. to Manoah and to Abraham offering up

Isaac) occurred during sleep, for that no one with his eyes open ever could see an angel, but this is mere nonsense. The sole object of such commentators seems to be to extort from Scripture confirmations of Aristotelian quibbles and their own inventions, a proceeding which I regard as the acme of absurdity.

In figures, not real but existing only in the prophet's imagination, God revealed to Joseph his future lordship, and in words and figures He revealed to Joshua that He would fight for the Hebrews, causing to appear an angel, as it were the Captain of the Lord's host, bearing a sword, and by this means communicating verbally. The forsaking of Israel by Providence was portrayed to Isaiah by a vision of the Lord, the thrice Holy, sitting on a very lofty throne, and the Hebrews, stained with the mire of their sins, sunk as it were in uncleanness, and thus as far as possible distant from God. The wretchedness of the people at the time was thus revealed, while future calamities were foretold in words. I could cite from Holy Writ many similar examples, but I think they are sufficiently well known already.

However, we get a still more clear confirmation of our position in Num xii:6,7, as follows: "If there be any prophet among you, I the Lord will make myself known unto him in a vision" (i.e. by appearances and signs, for God says of the prophecy of Moses that it was a vision without signs), "and will speak unto him in a dream " (i.e. not with actual words and an actual voice). "My servant Moses is not so; with him will I speak mouth to mouth, even apparently, and not in dark speeches, and the similitude of the Lord he shall behold," i.e. looking on me as a friend and not afraid, he speaks with me (cf. Ex xxxiii:17).

This makes it indisputable that the other prophets did not hear a real voice, and we gather as much from Deut. xxiv:10: "And there arose not a prophet since in Israel like unto Moses whom the Lord knew face to face," which must mean that the Lord spoke with none other; for not even Moses saw the Lord's face. These are the only media of communication between God and man which I find mentioned in Scripture, and therefore the only ones which may be supposed or invented. We may be able quite to comprehend that God can communicate immediately with man, for without the intervention of bodily means He communicates to our minds His essence; still, a man who can by pure intuition comprehend ideas which are neither contained in nor deducible from the foundations of our natural knowledge, must necessarily possess a mind far superior to those of his fellow men, nor do I believe that any have been so endowed save Christ. To Him the ordinances of God leading men to salvation were revealed directly without words or visions, so that God manifested Himself to the Apostles through the mind of Christ as He formerly did to Moses through the supernatural voice. In this sense the voice of Christ, like the voice which Moses heard, may be called the voice of God, and it may be said that the wisdom of God (,i.e. wisdom more than human) took upon itself in Christ human nature, and that Christ was the way of salvation. I must at this juncture declare that those doctrines which certain churches put forward concerning Christ, I neither affirm nor deny, for I freely confess that I do not understand them. What I have just stated I gather from Scripture, where I never read that God appeared to Christ, or spoke to Christ, but that God was revealed to the Apostles through Christ; that Christ was the Way of Life, and that the old law was given through an angel, and not immediately by God; whence it follows that if Moses spoke with God face to face as a man speaks with his friend (i.e. by means of their two bodies) Christ communed with God mind to mind.

Thus we may conclude that no one except Christ received the revelations of God without the aid of imagination, whether in words or vision. Therefore the power of prophecy implies not a peculiarly perfect mind, but a peculiarly vivid imagination, as I will show more clearly in the next chapter. We will now inquire what is meant in the Bible by the Spirit of God breathed into the prophets, or by the prophets speaking with the Spirit of God; to that end we must determine the exact signification of the Hebrew word *ruagh*, commonly translated spirit.

The word *ruagh* literally means a wind, e..q. the south wind, but it is frequently employed in other derivative significations.

It is used as equivalent to,

(1.) Breath: "Neither is there any spirit in his mouth," Ps. cxxxv:17.

(2.) Life, or breathing: "And his spirit returned to him" 1 Sam. xxx:12; i.e. he breathed again.

(3.) Courage and strength: "Neither did there remain any more spirit in any man," Josh. ii:11; "And the spirit entered into me, and made me stand on my feet," Ezek. ii:2.

(4.) Virtue and fitness: "Days should speak, and multitudes of years should teach wisdom; but there is a spirit in man,"Job xxxii:7; i.e. wisdom is not always found among old men for I now discover that it depends on individual virtue and capacity. So, "A man in whom is the Spirit," Numbers xxvii:18.

(5.) Habit of mind: "Because he had another spirit with him," Numbers xiv:24; i.e. another habit of mind. "Behold I will pour out My Spirit unto you," Prov. i:23.

(6.) Will, purpose, desire, impulse: "Whither the spirit was to go, they went," Ezek. 1:12; "That cover with a covering, but not of My Spirit," Is. xxx:1; "For the Lord hath poured out on you the spirit of deep sleep," Is. xxix:10; "Then was their spirit softened," Judges viii:3; "He that ruleth his spirit, is better than he that taketh a city," Prov. xvi:32; "He that hath no ru over his own spirit," Prov. xxv:28; "Your spirit as fire shall devour you," Isaiah xxxiii:l.

From the meaning of disposition we get —

(7.) Passions and faculties. A lofty spirit means pride, a lowly spirit humility, an evil spirit hatred and melancholy. So, too, the expressions spirits of jealousy, fornication, wisdom, counsel, bravery, stand for a jealous, lascivious, wise, prudent, or brave mind (for we Hebrews use substantives in preference to adjectives), or these various qualities.

(8.) The mind itself, or the life: "Yea, they have all one spirit," Eccles. iii:19 "The spirit shall return to God Who gave it."

(9.) The quarters of the world (from the winds which blow thence), or even the side of anything turned towards a particular quarter — Ezek. xxxvii:9; xlii:16, 17, 18, 19, &c.

I have already alluded to the way in which things are referred to God, and said to be of God.

(1.) As belonging to His nature, and being, as it were, part of Him; e.g the power of God, the eyes of God.

(2.) As under His dominion, and depending on His pleasure; thus the heavens are called the heavens of the Lord, as being His chariot and habitation. So Nebuchadnezzar is called the servant of God, Assyria the scourge of God, &c.

(3.) As dedicated to Him, e.g. the Temple of God, a Nazarene of God, the Bread of God.

(4.) As revealed through the prophets and not through our natural faculties. In this sense the Mosaic law is called the law of God.

(5.) As being in the superlative degree. Very high mountains are styled the mountains of God, a very deep sleep, the sleep of God, &c. In this sense we must explain Amos iv:11: "I have overthrown you as the overthrow of the Lord came upon Sodom and Gomorrah," i.e. that memorable overthrow, for since God Himself is the Speaker, the passage cannot well be taken otherwise. The wisdom of Solomon is called the wisdom of God, or extraordinary. The size of the cedars of Lebanon is alluded to in the Psalmist's expression, "the cedars of the Lord."

Similarly, if the Jews were at a loss to understand any phenomenon, or were ignorant of its cause, they referred it to God. Thus a storm was termed the chiding of God, thunder and lightning the arrows of God, for it was thought that God kept the winds confined in caves, His treasuries; thus differing merely in name from the Greek wind-god Eolus. In like manner miracles were called works of God, as being especially marvellous; though in reality, of course, all natural events are the works of God, and take place solely by His power. The Psalmist calls the miracles in Egypt the works of God, because the Hebrews found in them a way of safety which they had not looked for, and therefore especially marvelled at.

As, then, unusual natural phenomena are called works of God, and trees of unusual size are called trees of God, we cannot wonder that very strong and tall men, though impious robbers and whoremongers, are in Genesis called sons of God.

This reference of things wonderful to God was not peculiar to the Jews. Pharaoh, on hearing the interpretation of his dream, exclaimed that the mind of the gods was in Joseph. Nebuchadnezzar told Daniel that he possessed the mind of the holy gods; so also in Latin anything well made is often said to be wrought with Divine hands, which is equivalent to the Hebrew phrase, wrought with the hand of God.

We can now very easily understand and explain those passages of Scripture which speak of the Spirit of God. In some places the expression merely means a very strong, dry, and deadly wind, as in Isaiah xl:7, "The grass withereth, the flower fadeth, because the Spirit of the Lord bloweth upon it." Similarly in Gen. i:2: "The Spirit of the Lord moved over the face of the waters." At other times it is used as equivalent to a high courage, thus the spirit of Gideon and of Samson is called the Spirit of the Lord, as being very bold, and prepared for any emergency. Any unusual virtue or power is called the Spirit or Virtue of the Lord, Ex. xxxi:3: "I will fill him (Bezaleel) with the Spirit of the Lord," i.e., as the Bible itself explains, with talent above man's usual endowment. So Isa. xi:2: "And the Spirit of the Lord shall rest upon him," is explained afterwards in the text to mean the spirit of wisdom and understanding, of counsel and might.

The melancholy of Saul is called the melancholy of the Lord, or a very deep melancholy, the persons who applied the term showing that they understood by it nothing supernatural, in that they sent for a musician to assuage it by harp-playing. Again, the "Spirit of the Lord" is used as equivalent to the mind of man, for instance, Job xxvii:3: "And the Spirit of the Lord in my nostrils," the allusion being to Gen. ii:7: "And God breathed into man's nostrils the breath of life." Ezekiel also, prophesying to the dead, says (xxvii:14), "And I will give to you My Spirit, and ye shall live;" i.e. I will restore you to life. In Job xxxiv:14, we read: "If He gather unto Himself His Spirit and breath;" in Gen. vi:3: "My Spirit shall not always strive with man, for that he also is flesh," i.e. since man acts on the dictates of his body, and not the spirit which I gave him to discern the good, I will let him alone. So, too, Ps. li:12: "Create in me a clean heart, 0 God, and renew a right spirit within me; cast me not away from Thy presence, and take not Thy Holy Spirit from me." It was supposed that sin originated only from the body, and that good impulses come from the mind; therefore the Psalmist invokes the aid of God against the bodily appetites, but prays that the spirit which the Lord, the Holy One, had given him might be renewed. Again, inasmuch as the Bible, in concession to popular ignorance, describes God as having a mind, a heart, emotions — nay, even a body and breath — the expression Spirit of the Lord is used for God's mind, disposition, emotion, strength, or breath. Thus, Isa. xl:13: "Who hath disposed the Spirit of the Lord?" i.e. who, save Himself, hath caused the mind of the Lord to will anything,? and Isa. lxiii:10: "But they rebelled, and vexed the Holy Spirit."

The phrase comes to be used of the law of Moses, which in a sense expounds God's will, Is. lxiii. 11, "Where is He that put His Holy Spirit within him?" meaning, as we clearly gather from the context, the law of Moses. Nehemiah, speaking of the giving of the law, says, i:20, "Thou gavest also thy good Spirit to instruct them." This is referred to in Deut. iv:6, "This is your wisdom and understanding," and in Ps. cxliii:10, "Thy good Spirit will lead me into the land of uprightness." The Spirit of the Lord may mean the breath of the Lord, for breath, no less than a mind, a heart, and a body are attributed to God in Scripture, as in Ps. xxxiii:6. Hence it gets to mean the power, strength, or faculty of God, as in Job xxxiii:4, "The Spirit of the Lord made me," i.e. the power, or, if you prefer, the decree of the Lord. So the Psalmist in poetic language declares, xxxiii:6, "By the word of the Lord were the heavens made, and all the host of them by the breath of His mouth," i.e. by a mandate issued, as it were, in one breath. Also Ps. cxxxix:7, "Wither shall I go from Thy Spirit, or whither shall I flee from Thy presence?" i.e. whither shall I go so as to be beyond Thy power and Thy presence?

Lastly, the Spirit of the Lord is used in Scripture to express the emotions of God, e.g. His kindness and mercy, Micah ii:7, "Is the Spirit [i.e. the mercy] of the Lord straitened? Are these cruelties His doings?" Zech. iv:6, "Not by might or by power, but My Spirit [i.e. mercy], saith the Lord of hosts." The twelfth verse of the seventh chapter of the same prophet must, I think, be interpreted in like manner: "Yea, they made their hearts as an adamant stone, lest they should hear the law, and the words which the Lord of hosts hath sent in His Spirit [i.e. in His mercy] by the former prophets." So also Haggai ii:5: "So My Spirit remaineth among you: fear not."

The passage in Isaiah xlviii:16, "And now the Lord and His Spirit hath sent me," may be taken to refer to God's mercy or His revealed law; for the prophet says, "From the beginning" (i.e. from the time when I first came to you, to preach God's anger and His sentence forth against you) "I spoke not in secret; from the time that it was, there am I," and now I am sent by the mercy of God as a joyful messenger to preach your restoration. Or we may understand him to mean by the revealed law that he had before come to warn them by the command of the law (Levit. xix:17) in the same manner under the same conditions as Moses had warned them, that now, like Moses, he ends by preaching their restoration. But the first explanation seems to me the best.

Returning, then, to the main object of our discussion, we find that the Scriptural phrases, "The Spirit of the Lord was upon a prophet," "The Lord breathed His Spirit into men," "Men were filled with the Spirit of God, with the Holy Spirit," &c., are quite clear to us, and mean that prophets were endowed with a peculiar and extraordinary power, and devoted themselves to piety with especial constancy[3]; that thus they perceived the mind or the thought of God, for we have shown that God's Spirit signifies in Hebrew God's mind or thought, and that the law which shows His mind and thought is called His Spirit; hence that the imagination of the prophets, inasmuch as through it were revealed the decrees of God, may equally be called the mind of God, and the prophets be said to have possessed the mind of God. On our minds also the mind of God and His eternal thoughts are impressed; but this being the same for all men is less taken into account, especially by the Hebrews, who claimed a pre-eminence, and despised other men and other men's knowledge.

Lastly, the prophets were said to possess the Spirit of God because men knew not the cause of prophetic knowledge, and in their wonder referred it with other marvels directly to the Deity, styling it Divine knowledge.

We need no longer scruple to affirm that the prophets only perceived God's revelation by the aid of imagination, that is, by words and figures either real or imaginary. We find no other means mentioned in Scripture, and therefore must not invent any. As to the particular law of Nature by which the communications took place, I confess my ignorance. I might, indeed, say as others do, that they took place by the power of God; but this would be mere trifling, and no better than explaining some unique specimen by a transcendental term. Everything takes place by the power of God. Nature herself is the power of God under another name, and our ignorance of the power of God is co-extensive with our ignorance of Nature. It is absolute folly, therefore, to ascribe an event to the power of God when we know not its natural cause, which is the power of God.

However, we are not now inquiring into the causes of prophetic knowledge. We are only attempting, as I have said, to examine the Scriptural documents, and to draw our conclusions from them as from ultimate natural facts; the causes of the documents do not concern us.

---

[3] "Prophets were endowed with a peculiar and extraordinary power." Though some men enjoy gifts which nature has not bestowed on their fellows, they are not said to surpass the bounds of human nature, unless their special qualities are such as cannot be said to be deducible from the definition of human nature. For instance, a giant is a rarity, but still human. The gift of composing poetry extempore is given to very few, yet it is human. The same may, therefore, be said of the faculty possessed by some of imagining things as vividly as though they saw them before them, and this not while asleep, but while awake. But if anyone could be found who possessed other means and other foundations for knowledge, he might be said to transcend the limits of human nature.

As the prophets perceived the revelations of God by the aid of imagination, they could indisputably perceive much that is beyond the boundary of the intellect, for many more ideas can be constructed from words and figures than from the principles and notions on which the whole fabric of reasoned knowledge is reared.

Thus we have a clue to the fact that the prophets perceived nearly everything in parables and allegories, and clothed spiritual truths in bodily forms, for such is the usual method of imagination.

We need no longer wonder that Scripture and the prophets speak so strangely and obscurely of God's Spirit or Mind (cf. Numbers xi:17, 1 Kings xxii:21, &c.), that the Lord was seen by Micah as sitting, by Daniel as an old man clothed in white, by Ezekiel as a fire, that the Holy Spirit appeared to those with Christ as a descending dove, to the apostles as fiery tongues, to Paul on his conversion as a great light.

All these expressions are plainly in harmony with the current ideas of God and spirits.

Inasmuch as imagination is fleeting and inconstant, we find that the power of prophecy did not remain with a prophet for long, nor manifest itself frequently, but was very rare, manifesting itself only in a few men, and in them not often.

We must necessarily inquire how the prophets became assured of the truth of what they perceived by imagination, and not by sure mental laws; but our investigation must be confined to Scripture, for the subject is one on which we cannot acquire certain knowledge, and which we cannot explain by the immediate causes. Scripture teaching about the assurance of prophets I will treat of in the next chapter.

CHAPTER II

Of Prophets

It follows from the last chapter that, as I have said, the prophets were endowed with unusually vivid imaginations, and not with unusually, perfect minds. This conclusion is amply sustained by Scripture, for we are told that Solomon was the wisest of men, but had no special faculty of prophecy. Heman, Calcol, and Dara, though men of great talent, were not prophets, whereas uneducated countrymen, nay, even women, such as Hagar, Abraham's handmaid, were thus gifted. Nor is this contrary to ordinary experience and reason. Men of great imaginative power are less fitted for abstract reasoning, whereas those who excel in intellect and its use keep their imagination more restrained and controlled, holding it in subjection, so to speak, lest it should usurp the place of reason.

Thus to suppose that knowledge of natural and spiritual phenomena can be gained from the prophetic books, is an utter mistake, which I shall endeavour to expose, as I think philosophy, the age, and the question itself demand. I care not for the girdings of superstition, for superstition is the bitter enemy, of all true knowledge and true morality. Yes; it has come to this! Men who openly confess that they can form no idea of God, and only know Him through created things, of which they know not the causes, can unblushingly, accuse philosophers of Atheism. Treating the question methodically, I will show that prophecies varied, not only according to the imagination and physical temperament of the prophet, but also according to his particular opinions; and further that prophecy never rendered the prophet wiser than he was before. But I will first discuss the assurance of truth which the prophets received, for this is akin to the subject-matter of the chapter, and will serve to elucidate somewhat our present point.

Imagination does not, in its own nature, involve any certainty of truth, such as is implied in every clear and distinct idea, but requires some extrinsic reason to assure us of its objective reality: hence prophecy cannot afford certainty, and the prophets were assured of God's revelation by some sign, and not by the fact of revelation, as we may see from Abraham, who, when he had heard the promise of God, demanded a sign, not because he did not believe in God, but because he wished to be sure that it was God Who made the promise. The fact is still more evident in the case of Gideon: "Show me," he says to God, "show me a sign, that I may know that it is Thou that talkest with me." God also says to Moses: "And let this be a sign that I have sent thee." Hezekiah, though he had long known Isaiah to be a prophet, none the less demanded a sign of the cure which he predicted. It is thus quite evident that the prophets always received some sign to certify them of their prophetic imaginings; and for this reason Moses bids the Jews (Deut. xviii.) ask of the prophets a sign, namely, the prediction of some coming event. In this respect, prophetic knowledge is inferior to natural knowledge, which needs no sign, and in itself implies certitude. Moreover, Scripture warrants the statement that the certitude of the prophets was not mathematical, but moral. Moses lays down the punishment of death for the prophet who preaches new gods, even though he confirm his doctrine by signs and wonders (Deut. xiii.); "For," he says, "the Lord also worketh signs and wonders to try His people." And Jesus Christ warns His disciples of the same thing (Matt. xxiv:24). Furthermore, Ezekiel (xiv:9) plainly states that God sometimes deceives men with false revelations; and Micaiah bears like witness in the case of the prophets of Ahab.

Although these instances go to prove that revelation is open to doubt, it nevertheless contains, as we have said, a considerable element of certainty, for God never deceives the good, nor His chosen, but (according to the ancient proverb, and as appears in the history of Abigail and her speech), God uses the good as instruments of goodness, and the wicked as means to execute His wrath. This may be seen from the case of Micaiah above quoted; for although God had determined to deceive Ahab, through prophets, He made use of lying prophets; to the good prophet He revealed the truth, and did not forbid his proclaiming it.

Still the certitude of prophecy, remains, as I have said, merely, moral; for no one can justify himself before God, nor boast that he is an instrument for God's goodness. Scripture itself teaches and shows that God led away David to number the people, though it bears ample witness to David's piety.

The whole question of the certitude of prophecy, was based on these three considerations:

1. That the things revealed were imagined very vividly, affecting the prophets in the same way as things seen when awake;
2. The presence of a sign;
3. Lastly, and chiefly, that the mind of the prophet was given wholly, to what was right and good.

Although Scripture does not always make mention of a sign, we must nevertheless suppose that a sign was always vouchsafed; for Scripture does not always relate every, condition and circumstance (as many, have remarked), but rather takes them for granted. We may, however, admit that no sign was needed when the prophecy declared nothing that was not already contained in the law of Moses, because it was confirmed by that law. For instance, Jeremiah's prophecy, of the destruction of Jerusalem was confirmed by the prophecies of other prophets, and by the threats in the law, and, therefore, it needed no sign; whereas Hananiah, who, contrary to all the prophets, foretold the speedy restoration of the state, stood in need of a sign, or he would have been in doubt as to the truth of his prophecy, until it was confirmed by facts. "The prophet which prophesieth of peace, when the word of the prophet shall come to pass, then shall the prophet be known that the Lord hath truly sent him."

As, then, the certitude afforded to the prophet by signs was not mathematical (i.e. did not necessarily follow from the perception of the thing perceived or seen), but only moral, and as the signs were only given to convince the prophet, it follows that such signs were given according to the opinions and capacity of each prophet, so that a sign which convince one prophet would fall far short of convincing another who was imbued with different opinions. Therefore the signs varied according to the individual prophet.

So also did the revelation vary, as we have stated, according to individual disposition and temperament, and according to the opinions previously held.

It varied according to disposition, in this way: if a prophet was cheerful, victories, peace, and events which make men glad, were revealed to him; in that he was naturally more likely to imagine such things. If, on the contrary, he was melancholy, wars, massacres, and calamities were revealed; and so, according as a prophet was merciful, gentle, quick to anger, or severe, he was more fitted for one kind of revelation than another. It varied according to the temper of imagination in this way: if a prophet was cultivated he perceived the mind of God in a cultivated way, if he was confused he perceived it confusedly. And so with revelations perceived through visions. If a prophet was a countryman he saw visions of oxen, cows, and the like; if he was a soldier, he saw generals and armies; if a courtier, a royal throne, and so on.

Lastly, prophecy varied according to the opinions held by the prophets; for instance, to the Magi, who believed in the follies of astrology, the birth of Christ was revealed through the vision of a star in the East. To the augurs of Nebuchadnezzar the destruction of Jerusalem was revealed through entrails, whereas the king himself inferred it from oracles and the direction of arrows which he shot into the air. To prophets who believed that man acts from free choice and by his own power, God was revealed as standing apart from and ignorant of future human actions. All of which we will illustrate from Scripture.

The first point is proved from the case of Elisha, who, in order to prophecy to Jehoram, asked for a harp, and was unable to perceive the Divine purpose till he had been recreated by its music; then, indeed, he prophesied to Jehoram and to his allies glad tidings, which previously he had been unable to attain to because he was angry with the king, and these who are angry with anyone can imagine evil of him, but not good. The theory that God does not reveal Himself to the angry or the sad, is a mere dream: for God revealed to Moses while angry, the terrible slaughter of the firstborn, and did so without the intervention of a harp. To Cain in his rage, God was revealed, and to Ezekiel, impatient with anger, was revealed the contumacy and wretchedness of the Jews. Jeremiah, miserable and weary of life, prophesied the disasters of the Hebrews, so that Josiah would not consult him, but inquired of a woman, inasmuch as it was more in accordance with womanly nature that God should reveal His mercy thereto. So, Micaiah never prophesied good to Ahab, though other true prophets had done so, but invariably evil. Thus we see that individual prophets were by temperament more fitted for one sort of revelation than another.

The style of the prophecy also varied according to the eloquence of the individual prophet. The prophecies of Ezekiel and Amos are not written in a cultivated style like those of Isaiah and Nahum, but more rudely. Any Hebrew scholar who wishes to inquire into this point more closely, and compares chapters of the different prophets treating of the same subject, will find great dissimilarity of style. Compare, for instance, chap. i. of the courtly Isaiah, verse 11 to verse 20, with chap. v. of the countryman Amos, verses 21-24. Compare also the order and reasoning of the prophecies of Jeremiah, written in Idumaea (chap. xhx.), with the order and reasoning of Obadiah. Compare, lastly, Isa. xl:19, 20, and xliv:8, with Hosea viii:6, and xiii:2. And so on.

A due consideration of these passage will clearly show us that God has no particular style in speaking, but, according to the learning and capacity of the prophet, is cultivated, compressed, severe, untutored, prolix, or obscure.

There was, moreover, a certain variation in the visions vouchsafed to the prophets, and in the symbols by which they expressed them, for Isaiah saw the glory of the Lord departing from the Temple in a different form from that presented to Ezekiel. The Rabbis, indeed, maintain that both visions were really the same, but that Ezekiel, being a countryman, was above measure impressed by it, and therefore set it forth in full detail; but unless there is a trustworthy tradition on the subject, which I do not for a moment believe, this theory is plainly an invention. Isaiah saw seraphim with six wings, Ezekiel beasts with four wings; Isaiah saw God clothed and sitting on a royal throne, Ezekiel saw Him in the likeness of a fire: each doubtless saw God under the form in which he usually imagined Him.

Further, the visions varied in clearness as well as in details; for the revelations of Zechariah were too obscure to be understood by the prophet without explanation, as appears from his narration of them; the visions of Daniel could not be understood by him even after they had been explained, and this obscurity did not arise from the difficulty of the matter revealed (for being merely human affairs, these only transcended human capacity in being future), but solely in the fact that Daniel's imagination was not so capable for prophecy while he was awake as while he was asleep; and this is further evident from the fact that at the very beginning of the vision he was so terrified that he almost despaired of his strength. Thus, on account of the inadequacy of his imagination and his strength, the things revealed were so obscure to him that he could not understand them even after they had been explained. Here we may note that the words heard by Daniel, were, as we have shown above, simply imaginary, so that it is hardly wonderful that in his frightened state he imagined them so confusedly and obscurely that afterwards he could make nothing of them. Those who say that God did not wish to make a clear revelation, do not seem to have read the words of the angel, who expressly says that he came to make the prophet understand what should befall his people in the latter days (Dan. x:14).

The revelation remained obscure because no one was found, at that time, with imagination sufficiently strong to conceive it more clearly. Lastly, the prophets, to whom it was revealed that God would take away Elijah, wished to persuade Elisha that he had been taken somewhere where they would find him; showing sufficiently clearly that they had not understood God's revelation aright.

There is no need to set this out more amply, for nothing is more plain in the Bible than that God endowed some prophets with far greater gifts of prophecy than others. But I will show in greater detail and length, for I consider the point more important, that the prophecies varied according to the opinions previously embraced by the prophets, and that the prophets held diverse and even contrary opinions and prejudices. (I speak, be it understood, solely of matters speculative, for in regard to uprightness and morality the case is widely different.) From thence I shall conclude that prophecy never rendered the prophets more learned, but left them with their former opinions, and that we are, therefore, not at all bound to trust them in matters of intellect.

Everyone has been strangely hasty in affirming that the prophets knew everything within the scope of human intellect; and, although certain passages of Scripture plainly affirm that the prophets were in certain respects ignorant, such persons would rather say that they do not understand the passages than admit that there was anything which the prophets did not know; or else they try to wrest the Scriptural words away from their evident meaning.

If either of these proceedings is allowable we may as well shut our Bibles, for vainly shall we attempt to prove anything from them if their plainest passages may be classed among obscure and impenetrable mysteries, or if we may put any interpretation on them which we fancy. For instance, nothing is more clear in the Bible than that Joshua, and perhaps also the author who wrote his history, thought that the sun revolves round the earth, and that the earth is fixed, and further that the sun for a certain period remained still. Many, who will not admit any movement in the heavenly bodies, explain away the passage till it seems to mean something quite different; others, who have learned to philosophize more correctly, and understand that the earth moves while the sun is still, or at any rate does not revolve round the earth, try with all their might to wrest this meaning from Scripture, though plainly nothing of the sort is intended. Such quibblers excite my wonder! Are we, forsooth, bound to believe that Joshua the Soldier was a learned astronomer? or that a miracle could not be revealed to him, or that the light of the sun could not remain longer than usual above the horizon, without his knowing the cause? To me both alternatives appear ridiculous, and therefore I would rather say, that Joshua was ignorant of the true cause of the lengthened day, and that he and the whole host with him thought that the sun moved round the earth every day, and that on that particular occasion it stood still for a time, thus causing the light to remain longer; and I would say, that they did not conjecture that, from the amount of snow in the air (see Josh. x:11), the refraction may have been greater than usual, or that there may have been some other cause which we will not now inquire into.

So also the sign of the shadow going back was revealed to Isaiah according to his understanding; that is, as proceeding from a going backwards of the sun; for he, too, thought that the sun moves and that the earth is still; of parhelia he perhaps never even dreamed. We may arrive at this conclusion without any, scruple, for the sign could really have come to pass, and have been predicted by Isaiah to the king, without the prophet being aware of the real cause.

With regard to the building of the Temple by Solomon, if it was really dictate by God we must maintain the same doctrine: namely, that all the measurements were revealed according to the opinions and understanding of the king; for as we are not bound to believe that Solomon was a mathematician, we may affirm that he was ignorant of the true ratio between the circumference and the diameter of a circle, and that, like the generality of workmen, he thought that it was as three to one. But if it is allowable to declare that we do not understand the passage, in good sooth I know nothing in the Bible that we can understand; for the process of building is there narrated simply and as a mere matter of history. If, again, it is permitted to pretend that the passage has another meaning, and was written as it is from some reason unknown to us, this is no less than a complete subversal of the Bible; for every absurd and evil invention of human perversity could thus, without detriment to Scriptural authority, be defended and fostered. Our conclusion is in no wise impious, for though Solomon, Isaiah, Joshua, &c. were prophets, they were none the less men, and as such not exempt from human shortcomings.

According to the understanding of Noah it was revealed to him that God as about to destroy the whole human race, for Noah thought that beyond the limits of Palestine the world was not inhabited.

Not only in matters of this kind, but in others more important, the about the Divine attributes, but held quite ordinary notions about God, and to these notions their revelations were adapted, as I will demonstrate by ample Scriptural testimony; from all which one may easily see that they were praised and commended, not so much for the sublimity and eminence of their intellect as for their piety and faithfulness.

Adam, the first man to whom God was revealed, did not know that He is omnipotent and omniscient; for he hid himself from Him, and attempted to make excuses for his fault before God, as though he had had to do with a man; therefore to him also was God revealed according to his understanding — that is, as being unaware of his situation or his sin, for Adam heard, or seemed to hear, the Lord walling, in the garden, calling him and asking him where he was; and then, on seeing his shamefacedness, asking him whether he had eaten of the forbidden fruit. Adam evidently only knew the Deity as the Creator of all things. To Cain also God was revealed, according to his understanding, as ignorant of human affairs, nor was a higher conception of the Deity required for repentance of his sin.

To Laban the Lord revealed Himself as the God of Abraham, because Laban believed that each nation had its own special divinity (see Gen. xxxi:29). Abraham also knew not that God is omnipresent, and has foreknowledge of all things; for when he heard the sentence against the inhabitants of Sodom, he prayed that the Lord should not execute it till He had ascertained whether they all merited such punishment; for he said (see Gen. xviii:24), "Peradventure there be fifty righteous within the city," and in accordance with this belief God was revealed to him; as Abraham imagined, He spake thus: "I will go down now, and see whether they have done altogether according to the cry of it which is come unto Me; and, if not, I will know." Further, the Divine testimony concerning Abraham asserts nothing but that he was obedient, and that he "commanded his household after him that they should keep the way of the Lord" (Gen. xviii:19); it does not state that he held sublime conceptions of the Deity.

Moses, also, was not sufficiently aware that God is omniscient, and directs human actions by His sole decree, for although God Himself says that the

Israelites should hearken to Him, Moses still considered the matter doubtful and repeated, "But if they will not believe me, nor hearken unto my voice." To him in like manner God was revealed as taking no part in, and as being ignorant of, future human actions: the Lord gave him two signs and said, "And it shall come to pass that if they will not believe thee, neither hearken to the voice of the first sign, that they will believe the voice of the latter sign; but if not, thou shalt take of the water of the river," &c. Indeed, if any one considers without prejudice the recorded opinions of Moses, he will plainly see that Moses conceived the Deity as a Being Who has always existed, does exist, and always will exist, and for this cause he calls Him by the name Jehovah, which in Hebrew signifies these three phases of existence: as to His nature, Moses only taught that He is merciful, gracious, and exceeding jealous, as appears from many passages in the Pentateuch. Lastly, he believed and taught that this Being was so different from all other beings, that He could not be expressed by the image of any visible thing; also, that He could not be looked upon, and that not so much from inherent impossibility as from human infirmity; further, that by reason of His power He was without equal and unique. Moses admitted, indeed, that there were beings (doubtless by the plan and command of the Lord) who acted as God's vicegerents — that is, beings to whom God had given the right, authority, and power to direct nations, and to provide and care for them; but he taught that this Being Whom they were bound to obey was the highest and Supreme God, or (to use the Hebrew phrase) God of gods, and thus in the song (Exod. xv:11) he exclaims, "Who is like unto Thee, 0 Lord, among the gods?" and Jethro says (Exod. xviii:11), "Now I know that the Lord is greater than all gods." That is to say, "I am at length compelled to admit to Moses that Jehovah is greater than all gods, and that His power is unrivalled." We must remain in doubt whether Moses thought that these beings who acted as God's vicegerents were created by Him, for he has stated nothing, so far as we know, about their creation and origin. He further taught that this Being had brought the visible world into order from Chaos, and had given Nature her germs, and therefore that He possesses supreme right and power over all things; further, that by reason of this supreme right and power He had chosen for Himself alone the Hebrew nation and a certain strip of territory, and had handed over to the care of other gods substituted by Himself the rest of the nations and territories, and that therefore He was called the God of Israel and the God of Jerusalem, whereas the other gods were called the gods of the Gentiles. For this reason the Jews believed that the strip of territory which God had chosen for Himself, demanded a Divine worship quite apart and different from the worship which obtained elsewhere, and that the Lord would not suffer the worship of other gods adapted to other countries. Thus they thought that the people whom the king of Assyria had brought into Judaea were torn in pieces by lions because they knew not the worship of the National Divinity (2 Kings xvii:25).

Jacob, according to Aben Ezra's opinion, therefore admonished his sons when he wished them to seek out a new country, that they should prepare themselves for a new worship, and lay aside the worship of strange, gods — that is, of the gods of the land where they were (Gen. xxxv:2, 3).

David, in telling Saul that he was compelled by the king's persecution to live away from his country, said that he was driven out from the heritage of the Lord, and sent to worship other gods (1 Sam. xxvi:19). Lastly, he believed that this Being or Deity had His habitation in the heavens (Deut. xxxiii:27), an opinion very common among the Gentiles.

If we now examine the revelations to Moses, we shall find that they were accommodated to these opinions; as he believed that the Divine Nature was subject to the conditions of mercy, graciousness, &c., so God was revealed to him in accordance with his idea and under these attributes (see Exodus xxxiv:6, 7, and the second commandment). Further it is related (Ex. xxxiii:18) that Moses asked of God that he might behold Him, but as Moses (as we have said) had formed no mental image of God, and God (as I have shown) only revealed Himself to the prophets in accordance with the disposition of their imagination, He did not reveal Himself in any form. This, I repeat, was because the imagination of Moses was unsuitable, for other prophets bear witness that they saw the Lord; for instance, Isaiah, Ezekiel, Daniel, &c. For this reason God answered Moses, "Thou canst not see My face;" and inasmuch as Moses believed that God can be looked upon — that is, that no contradiction of the Divine nature is therein involved (for otherwise he would never have preferred his request) — it is added, "For no one shall look on Me and live," thus giving a reason in accordance with Moses' idea, for it is not stated that a contradiction of the Divine nature would be involved, as was really the case, but that the thing would not come to pass because of human infirmity.

When God would reveal to Moses that the Israelites, because they worshipped the calf, were to be placed in the same category as other nations, He said (ch. xxxiii:2, 3), that He would send an angel (that is, a being who should have charge of the Israelites, instead of the Supreme Being), and that He Himself would no longer remain among them; thus leaving Moses no ground for supposing that the Israelites were more beloved by God than the other nations whose guardianship He had entrusted to other beings or angels (vide verse 16).

Lastly, as Moses believed that God dwelt in the heavens, God was revealed to him as coming down from heaven on to a mountain, and in order to talk with the Lord Moses went up the mountain, which he certainly need not have done if he could have conceived of God as omnipresent.

The Israelites knew scarcely anything of God, although He was revealed to them; and this is abundantly evident from their transferring, a few days afterwards, the honour and worship due to Him to a calf, which they believed to be the god who had brought them out of Egypt. In truth, it is hardly likely that men accustomed to the superstitions of Egypt, uncultivated and sunk in most abject slavery, should have held any sound notions about the Deity, or that Moses should have taught them anything beyond a rule of right living; inculcating it not like a philosopher, as the result of freedom, but like a lawgiver compelling them to be moral by legal authority. Thus the rule of right living, the worship and love of God, was to them rather a bondage than the true liberty, the gift and grace of the Deity. Moses bid them love God and keep His law, because they had in the past received benefits from Him (such as the deliverance from slavery in Egypt), and further terrified them with threats if they transgressed His commands, holding out many promises of good if they should observe them; thus treating them as parents treat irrational children. It is, therefore, certain that they knew not the excellence of virtue and the true happiness.

Jonah thought that he was fleeing from the sight of God, which seems to show that he too held that God had entrusted the care of the nations outside Judaea to other substituted powers. No one in the whole of the Old Testament speaks more rationally of God than Solomon, who in fact surpassed all the men of his time in natural ability. Yet he considered himself above the law (esteeming it only to have been given for men without reasonable and intellectual grounds for their actions), and made small account of the laws concerning kings, which are mainly three: nay, he openly violated them (in this he did wrong, and acted in a manner unworthy of a philosopher, by indulging in sensual pleasure), and taught that all Fortune's favours to mankind are vanity, that humanity has no nobler gift than wisdom, and no greater punishment than folly. See Proverbs xvi:22, 23.

But let us return to the prophets whose conflicting opinions we have undertaken to note. The expressed ideas of Ezekiel seemed so diverse from those of Moses to the Rabbis who have left us the extant prophetic books (as is told in the treatise of Sabbathus, i:13, 2), that they had serious thoughts of omitting his prophecy from the canon, and would doubtless have thus excluded it if a certain Hananiah had not undertaken to explain it; a task which (as is there narrated) he with great zeal and labour accomplished. How he did so does not sufficiently appear, whether it was by writing a commentary which has now perished, or by altering Ezekiel's words and audaciously — striking out phrases according to his fancy. However this may be, chapter xviii. certainly does not seem to agree with Exodus xxxiv:7, Jeremiah xxxii:18, &c.

Samuel believed that the Lord never repented of anything He had decreed (1 Sam. xv:29), for when Saul was sorry for his sin, and wished to worship God and ask for forgiveness, Samuel said that the Lord would not go back from his decree.

To Jeremiah, on the other hand, it was revealed that, "If that nation against whom I (the Lord) have pronounced, turn from their evil, I will repent of the evil that I thought to do unto them. If it do evil in my sight, that it obey not my voice, then I will repent of the good wherewith I said I would benefit them" (Jer. xviii:8-10). Joel (ii:13) taught that the Lord repented Him only of evil. Lastly, it is clear from Gen iv: 7 that a man can overcome the temptations of sin, and act righteously; for this doctrine is told to Cain, though, as we learn from Josephus and the Scriptures, he never did so overcome them. And this agrees with the chapter of Jeremiah just cited, for it is there said that the Lord repents of the good or the evil pronounced, if the men in question change their ways and manner of life. But, on the other hand, Paul (Rom.ix:10) teaches as plainly as possible that men have no control over the temptations of the flesh save by the special vocation and grace of God. And when (Rom. iii:5 and vi:19) he attributes righteousness to man, he corrects himself as speaking merely humanly and through the infirmity of the flesh.

We have now more than sufficiently proved our point, that God adapted revelations to the understanding and opinions of the prophets, and that in matters of theory without bearing on charity or morality the prophets could be, and, in fact, were, ignorant, and held conflicting opinions. It therefore follows that we must by no means go to the prophets for knowledge, either of natural or of spiritual phenomena.

We have determined, then, that we are only bound to believe in the prophetic writings, the object and substance of the revelation; with regard to the details, every one may believe or not, as he likes.

For instance, the revelation to Cain only teaches us that God admonished him to lead the true life, for such alone is the object and substance of the revelation, not doctrines concerning free will and philosophy. Hence, though the freedom of the will is clearly implied in the words of the admonition, we are at liberty to hold a contrary opinion, since the words and reasons were adapted to the understanding of Cain.

So, too, the revelation to Micaiah would only teach that God revealed to him the true issue of the battle between Ahab and Aram; and this is all we are bound to believe. Whatever else is contained in the revelation concerning the true and the false Spirit of God, the army of heaven standing on the right hand and on the left, and all the other details, does not affect us at all. Everyone may believe as much of it as his reason allows.

The reasonings by which the Lord displayed His power to Job (if they really were a revelation, and the author of the history is narrating, and not merely, as some suppose, rhetorically adorning his own conceptions), would come under the same category — that is, they were adapted to Job's understanding, for the purpose of convincing him, and are not universal, or for the convincing of all men.

We can come to no different conclusion with respect to the reasonings of Christ, by which He convicted the Pharisees of pride and ignorance, and exhorted His disciples to lead the true life. He adapted them to each man's opinions and principles. For instance, when He said to the Pharisees (Matt. xii:26), "And if Satan cast out devils, his house is divided against itself, how then shall his kingdom stand? "He only wished to convince the Pharisees according, to their own principles, not to teach that there are devils, or any kingdom of devils. So, too, when He said to His disciples (Matt. viii:10), "See that ye despise not one of these little ones, for I say unto you that their angels," &c., He merely desired to warn them against pride and despising any of their fellows, not to insist on the actual reason given, which was simply adopted in order to persuade them more easily.

Lastly, we should say, exactly the same of the apostolic signs and reasonings, but there is no need to go further into the subject. If I were to enumerate all the passages of Scripture addressed only to individuals, or to a particular man's understanding, and which cannot, without great danger to philosophy, be defended as Divine doctrines, I should go far beyond the brevity at which I aim. Let it suffice, then, to have indicated a few instances of general application, and let the curious reader consider others by himself. Although the points we have just raised concerning prophets and prophecy are the only ones which have any direct bearing on the end in view, namely, the separation of Philosophy from Theology, still, as I have touched on the general question, I may here inquire whether the gift of prophecy was peculiar to the Hebrews, or whether it was common to all nations. I must then come to a conclusion about the vocation of the Hebrews, all of which I shall do in the ensuing chapter.

CHAPTER III

Of the Vocation of the Hebrews, and whether the Gift of Prophecy was peculiar to them

Every man's true happiness and blessedness consist solely in the enjoyment of what is good, not in the pride that he alone is enjoying it, to the exclusion of others. He who thinks himself the more blessed because he is enjoying benefits which others are not, or because he is more blessed or more fortunate than his fellows, is ignorant of true happiness and blessedness, and the joy which he feels is either childish or envious and malicious. For instance, a man's true happiness consists only in wisdom, and the knowledge of the truth, not at all in the fact that he is wiser than others, or that others lack such knowledge: such considerations do not increase his wisdom or true happiness.

Whoever, therefore, rejoices for such reasons, rejoices in another's misfortune, and is, so far, malicious and bad, knowing neither true happiness nor the peace of the true life.

When Scripture, therefore, in exhorting the Hebrews to obey the law, says that the Lord has chosen them for Himself before other nations (Deut. x:15); that He is near them, but not near others (Deut. iv:7); that to them alone He has given just laws (Deut. iv:8); and, lastly, that He has marked them out before others (Deut. iv:32); it speaks only according to the understanding of its hearers, who, as we have shown in the last chapter, and as Moses also testifies (Deut. ix:6, 7), knew not true blessedness. For in good sooth they would have been no less blessed if God had called all men equally to salvation, nor would God have been less present to them for being equally present to others; their laws, would have been no less just if they had been ordained for all, and they themselves would have been no less wise. The miracles would have shown God's power no less by being wrought for other nations also; lastly, the Hebrews would have been just as much bound to worship God if He had bestowed all these gifts equally on all men.

When God tells Solomon (1 Kings iii:12) that no one shall be as wise as he in time to come, it seems to be only a manner of expressing surpassing wisdom;

it is little to be believed that God would have promised Solomon, for his greater happiness, that He would never endow anyone with so much wisdom in time to come; this would in no wise have increased Solomon's intellect, and the wise king would have given equal thanks to the Lord if everyone had been gifted with the same faculties.

Still, though we assert that Moses, in the passages of the Pentateuch just cited, spoke only according to the understanding of the Hebrews, we have no wish to deny that God ordained the Mosaic law for them alone, nor that He spoke to them alone, nor that they witnessed marvels beyond those which happened to any other nation; but we wish to emphasize that Moses desired to admonish the Hebrews in such a manner, and with such reasonings as would appeal most forcibly to their childish understanding, and constrain them to worship the Deity. Further, we wished to show that the Hebrews did not surpass other nations in knowledge, or in piety, but evidently in some attribute different from these; or (to speak like the Scriptures, according to their understanding), that the Hebrews were not chosen by God before others for the sake of the true life and sublime ideas, though they were often thereto admonished, but with some other object. What that object was, I will duly show.

But before I begin, I wish in a few words to explain what I mean by the guidance of God, by the help of God, external and inward, and, lastly, what I understand by fortune.

By the help of God, I mean the fixed and unchangeable order of nature or the chain of natural events: for I have said before and shown elsewhere that the universal laws of nature, according to which all things exist and are determined, are only another name for the eternal decrees of God, which always involve eternal truth and necessity.

So that to say that everything happens according to natural laws, and to say that everything is ordained by the decree and ordinance of God, is the same thing. Now since the power in nature is identical with the power of God, by which alone all things happen and are determined, it follows that whatsoever man, as a part of nature, provides himself with to aid and preserve his existence, or whatsoever nature affords him without his help, is given to him solely by the Divine power, acting either through human nature or through external circumstance. So whatever human nature can furnish itself with by its own efforts to preserve its existence, may be fitly called the inward aid of God, whereas whatever else accrues to man's profit from outward causes may be called the external aid of God.

We can now easily understand what is meant by the election of God. For since no one can do anything save by the predetermined order of nature, that is by God's eternal ordinance and decree, it follows that no one can choose a plan of life for himself, or accomplish any work save by God's vocation choosing him for the work or the plan of life in question, rather than any other. Lastly, by fortune, I mean the ordinance of God in so far as it directs human life through external and unexpected means. With these preliminaries I return to my purpose of discovering the reason why the Hebrews were said to be elected by God before other nations, and with the demonstration I thus proceed.

All objects of legitimate desire fall, generally speaking, under one of these three categories:

1.   The knowledge of things through their primary causes.
2.   The government of the passions, or the acquirement of the habit of virtue.
3.   Secure and healthy life.

The means which most directly conduce towards the first two of these ends, and which may be considered their proximate and efficient causes are contained in human nature itself, so that their acquisition hinges only on our own power, and on the laws of human nature. It may be concluded that these gifts are not peculiar to any nation, but have always been shared by the whole human race, unless, indeed, we would indulge the dream that nature formerly created men of different kinds. But the means which conduce to security and health are chiefly in external circumstance, and are called the gifts of fortune because they depend chiefly on objective causes of which we are ignorant; for a fool may be almost as liable to happiness or unhappiness as a wise man. Nevertheless, human management and watchfulness can greatly assist towards living in security and warding off the injuries of our fellow-men, and even of beasts. Reason and experience show no more certain means of attaining this object than the formation of a society with fixed laws, the occupation of a strip of territory and the concentration of all forces, as it were, into one body, that is the social body. Now for forming and preserving a society, no ordinary ability and care is required: that society will be most secure, most stable, and least liable to reverses, which is founded and directed by far-seeing and careful men; while, on the other hand, a society constituted by men without trained skill, depends in a great measure on fortune, and is less constant. If, in spite of all, such a society lasts a long time, it is owing to some other directing influence than its own; if it overcomes great perils and its affairs prosper, it will perforce marvel at and adore the guiding Spirit of God (in so far, that is, as God works through hidden means, and not through the nature and mind of man), for everything happens to it unexpectedly and contrary to anticipation, it may even be said and thought to be by miracle. Nations, then, are distinguished from one another in respect to the social organization and the laws under which they live and are governed; the Hebrew nation was not chosen by God in respect to its wisdom nor its tranquillity of mind, but in respect to its social organization and the good fortune with which it obtained supremacy and kept it so many years. This is abundantly clear from Scripture. Even a cursory perusal will show us that the only respects in which the Hebrews surpassed other nations, are in their successful conduct of matters relating to government, and in their surmounting great perils solely by God's external aid; in other ways they were on a par with their fellows, and God was equally gracious to all. For in respect to intellect (as we have shown in the last chapter) they held very ordinary ideas about God and nature, so that they cannot have been God's chosen in this respect; nor were they so chosen in respect of virtue and the true life, for here again they, with the exception of a very few elect, were on an equality with other nations: therefore their choice and vocation consisted only in the temporal happiness and advantages of independent rule. In fact, we do not see that God promised anything beyond this to the patriarchs[4] or their successors; in the law no other reward is offered for obedience than the continual happiness of an independent commonwealth and other goods of this life; while, on the other hand, against contumacy and the breaking of the covenant is threatened the downfall of the commonwealth and great hardships. Nor is this to be wondered at; for the ends of every social organization and commonwealth are (as appears from what we have said, and as we will explain more at length hereafter) security and comfort; a commonwealth can only exist by the laws being binding on all. If all the members of a state wish to disregard the law, by that very fact they dissolve the state and destroy the commonwealth. Thus, the only reward which could be promised to the Hebrews for continued obedience to the law was security[5] and its attendant advantages, while no surer punishment could be threatened for disobedience, than the ruin of the state and the evils which generally follow therefrom, in addition to such further consequences as might accrue to the Jews in particular from the ruin of their especial state. But there is no need here to go into this point at more length. I will only add that the laws of the Old Testament were revealed and ordained to the Jews only, for as God chose them in respect to the special constitution of their society and government, they must, of course, have had special laws. Whether God ordained special laws for other nations also, and revealed Himself to their lawgivers prophetically, that is, under the attributes by which the latter were accustomed to imagine Him,

---

[4] In Gen. xv. it is written that God promised Abraham to protect him, and to grant him ample rewards. Abraham answered that he could expect nothing which could be of any value to him, as he was childless and well stricken in years.

[5] That a keeping of the commandments of the old Testament is not sufficient for eternal life, appears from Mark x:21.

I cannot sufficiently determine. It is evident from Scripture itself that other nations acquired supremacy and particular laws by the external aid of God; witness only the two following passages:

In Genesis xiv:18, 19, 20, it is related that Melchisedek was king of Jerusalem and priest of the Most High God, that in exercise of his priestly functions he blessed Abraham, and that Abraham the beloved of the Lord gave to this priest of God a tithe of all his spoils. This sufficiently shows that before He founded the Israelitish nation God constituted kings and priests in Jerusalem, and ordained for them rites and laws. Whether He did so prophetically is, as I have said, not sufficiently clear; but I am sure of this, that Abraham, whilst he sojourned in the city, lived scrupulously according to these laws, for Abraham had received no special rites from God; and yet it is stated (Gen. xxvi:5), that he observed the worship, the precepts, the statutes, and the laws of God, which must be interpreted to mean the worship, the statutes, the precepts, and the laws of king Melchisedek. Malachi chides the Jews as follows (i:10-11.): "Who is there among you that will shut the doors? [of the Temple]; neither do ye kindle fire on mine altar for nought. I have no pleasure in you, saith the Lord of Hosts. For from the rising of the sun, even until the going down of the same My Name shall be great among the Gentiles; and in every place incense shall be offered in My Name, and a pure offering; for My Name is great among the heathen, saith the Lord of Hosts." These words, which, unless we do violence to them, could only refer to the current period, abundantly testify that the Jews of that time were not more beloved by God than other nations, that God then favoured other nations with more miracles than He vouchsafed to the Jews, who had then partly recovered their empire without miraculous aid; and, lastly, that the Gentiles possessed rites and ceremonies acceptable to God. But I pass over these points lightly: it is enough for my purpose to have shown that the election of the Jews had regard to nothing but temporal physical happiness and freedom, in other words, autonomous government, and to the manner and means by which they obtained it; consequently to the laws in so far as they were necessary to the preservation of that special government; and, lastly, to the manner in which they were revealed. In regard to other matters, wherein man's true happiness consists, they were on a par with the rest of the nations.

When, therefore, it is said in Scripture (Deut. iv:7) that the Lord is not so nigh to any other nation as He is to the Jews, reference is only made to their government, and to the period when so many miracles happened to them, for in respect of intellect and virtue — that is, in respect of blessedness — God was, as we have said already, and are now demonstrating, equally gracious to all. Scripture itself bears testimony to this fact, for the Psalmist says (cxlv:18), "The Lord is near unto all them that call upon Him, to all that call upon Him in truth." So in the same Psalm, verse 9, "The Lord is good to all, and His tender mercies are over all His works." In Ps. xxxiii:16, it is clearly stated that God has granted to all men the same intellect, in these words, He fashioneth their hearts alike." The heart was considered by the Hebrews, as I suppose everyone knows, to be the seat of the soul and the intellect.

Lastly, from Job xxxviii:28, it is plain that God had ordained for the whole human race the law to reverence God, to keep from evil doing, or to do well, and that Job, although a Gentile, was of all men most acceptable to God, because he exceeded all in piety and religion. Lastly, from Jonah iv:2, it is very evident that, not only to the Jews but to all men, God was gracious, merciful, long — suffering, and of great goodness, and repented Him of the evil, for Jonah says: "Therefore I determined to flee before unto Tarshish, for I know that Thou art a gracious God, and merciful, slow to anger, and of great kindness," &c., and that, therefore, God would pardon the Ninevites. We conclude, therefore (inasmuch as God is to all men equally gracious, and the Hebrews were only, chosen by him in respect to their social organization and government), that the individual Jew, taken apart from his social organization and government, possessed no gift of God above other men, and that there was no difference between Jew and Gentile. As it is a fact that God is equally gracious, merciful, and the rest, to all men; and as the function of the prophet was to teach men not so much the laws of their country, as true virtue, and to exhort them thereto, it is not to be doubted that all nations possessed prophets, and that the prophetic gift was not peculiar to the Jews. Indeed, history, both profane and sacred, bears witness to the fact. Although, from the sacred histories of the Old Testament, it is not evident that the other nations had as many prophets as the Hebrews, or that any Gentile prophet was expressly sent by God to the nations, this does not affect the question, for the Hebrews were careful to record their own affairs, not those of other nations. It suffices, then, that we find in the Old Testament Gentiles, and uncircumcised, as Noah, Enoch, Abimelech, Balaam, &c., exercising prophetic gifts; further, that Hebrew prophets were sent by God, not only to their own nation but to many others also. Ezekiel prophesied to all the nations then known; Obadiah to none, that we are aware of, save the Idumeans; and Jonah was chiefly the prophet to the Ninevites. Isaiah bewails and predicts the calamities, and hails the restoration not only of the Jews but also of other nations, for he says (chap. xvi:9), "Therefore I will bewail Jazer with weeping;" and in chap. xix. he foretells first the calamities and then the restoration of the Egyptians (see verses 19, 20, 21, 25), saying that God shall send them a Saviour to free them, that the Lord shall be known in Egypt, and, further, that the Egyptians shall worship God with sacrifice and oblation; and, at last, he calls that nation the blessed Egyptian people of God; all of which particulars are specially noteworthy.

Jeremiah is called, not the prophet of the Hebrew nation, but simply the prophet of the nations (see Jer:i.5). He also mournfully foretells the calamities of the nations, and predicts their restoration, for he says (xlviii:31) of the Moabites, "Therefore will I howl for Moab, and I will cry out for all Moab" (verse 36), "and therefore mine heart shall sound for Moab like pipes;" in the end he prophesies their restoration, as also the restoration of the Egyptians, Ammonites, and Elamites. Wherefore it is beyond doubt that other nations also, like the Jews, had their prophets, who prophesied to them.

Although Scripture only, makes mention of one man, Balaam, to whom the future of the Jews and the other nations was revealed, we must not suppose that Balaam prophesied only once, for from the narrative itself it is abundantly clear that he had long previously been famous for prophesy and other Divine gifts. For when Balak bade him to come to him, he said (Num. xxii:6), "For I know that he whom thou blessest is blessed, and he whom thou cursest is cursed." Thus we see that he possessed the gift which God had bestowed on Abraham. Further, as accustomed to prophesy, Balaam bade the messengers wait for him till the will of the Lord was revealed to him. When he prophesied, that is, when he interpreted the true mind of God, he was wont to say this of himself: "He hath said, which heard the words of God and knew the knowledge of the Most High, which saw the vision of the Almighty falling into a trance, but having his eyes open." Further, after he had blessed the Hebrews by the command of God, he began (as was his custom) to prophesy to other nations, and to predict their future; all of which abundantly shows that he had always been a prophet, or had often prophesied, and (as we may also remark here) possessed that which afforded the chief certainty to prophets of the truth of their prophecy, namely, a mind turned wholly to what is right and good, for he did not bless those whom he wished to bless, nor curse those whom he wished to curse, as Balak supposed, but only those whom God wished to be blessed or cursed. Thus he answered Balak: "If Balak should give me his house full of silver and gold, I cannot go beyond the commandment of the Lord to do either good or bad of my own mind; but what the Lord saith, that will I speak." As for God being angry with him in the way, the same happened to Moses when he set out to Egypt by the command of the Lord; and as to his receiving money for prophesying, Samuel did the same (1 Sam. ix:7, 8); if in anyway he sinned, "there is not a just man upon earth that doeth good and sinneth not," Eccles. vii:20. (Vide 2 Epist. Peter ii:15, 16, and Jude 5:11.)

His speeches must certainly have had much weight with God, and His power for cursing must assuredly have been very great from the number of times that we find stated in Scripture, in proof of God's great mercy to the Jews, that God would not hear Balaam, and that He changed the cursing to blessing (see Deut. xxiii:6, Josh. xxiv:10, Neh. xiii:2). Wherefore he was without doubt most acceptable to God, for the speeches and cursings of the wicked move God not at all. As then he was a true prophet, and nevertheless Joshua calls him a soothsayer or augur, it is certain that this title had an honourable signification, and that those whom the Gentiles called augurs and soothsayers were true prophets, while those whom Scripture often accuses and condemns were false soothsayers, who deceived the Gentiles as false prophets deceived the Jews; indeed, this is made evident from other passages in the Bible, whence we conclude that the gift of prophecy was not peculiar to the Jews, but common to all nations. The Pharisees, however, vehemently contend that this Divine gift was peculiar to their nation, and that the other nations foretold the future (what will superstition invent next?) by some unexplained diabolical faculty. The principal passage of Scripture which they cite, by way of confirming their theory with its authority, is Exodus xxxiii:16, where Moses says to God, "For wherein shall it be known here that I and Thy people have found grace in Thy sight? is it not in that Thou goest with us? so shall we be separated, I and Thy people, from all the people that are upon the face of the earth." From this they would infer that Moses asked of God that He should be present to the Jews, and should reveal Himself to them prophetically; further, that He should grant this favour to no other nation. It is surely absurd that Moses should have been jealous of God's presence among the Gentiles, or that he should have dared to ask any such thing. The act is, as Moses knew that the disposition and spirit of his nation was rebellious, he clearly saw that they could not carry out what they had begun without very great miracles and special external aid from God; nay, that without such aid they must necessarily perish: as it was evident that God wished them to be preserved, he asked for this special external aid. Thus he says (Ex. xxxiv:9), "If now I have found grace in Thy sight, 0 Lord, let my Lord, I pray Thee, go among us; for it is a stiffnecked people." The reason, therefore, for his seeking special external aid from God was the stiffneckedness of the people, and it is made still more plain, that he asked for nothing beyond this special external aid by God's answer — for God answered at once (verse 10 of the same chapter) — "Behold, I make a covenant: before all Thy people I will do marvels, such as have not been done in all the earth, nor in any nation." Therefore Moses had in view nothing beyond the special election of the Jews, as I have explained it, and made no other request to God. I confess that in Paul's Epistle to the Romans, I find another text which carries more weight, namely, where Paul seems to teach a different doctrine from that here set down, for he there says (Rom. iii:1): "What advantage then hath the Jew? or what profit is there of circumcision? Much every way: chiefly, because that unto them were committed the oracles of God."

But if we look to the doctrine which Paul especially desired to teach, we shall find nothing repugnant to our present contention; on the contrary, his doctrine is the same as ours, for he says (Rom. iii:29) "that God is the God of the Jews and of the Gentiles, and" (ch. ii:25, 26) "But, if thou be a breaker of the law, thy circumcision is made uncircumcision. Therefore if the uncircumcision keep the righteousness of the law, shall not his uncircumcision be counted for circumcision?" Further, in chap. iv:verse 9, he says that all alike, Jew and Gentile, were under sin, and that without commandment and law there is no sin. Wherefore it is most evident that to all men absolutely was revealed the law under which all lived — namely, the law which has regard only to true virtue, not the law established in respect to, and in the formation of a particular state and adapted to the disposition of a particular people. Lastly, Paul concludes that since God is the God of all nations, that is, is equally gracious to all, and since all men equally live under the law and under sin, so also to all nations did God send His Christ, to free all men equally from the bondage of the law, that they should no more do right by the command of the law, but by the constant determination of their hearts. So that Paul teaches exactly the same as ourselves. When, therefore, he says "To the Jews only were entrusted the oracles of God," we must either understand that to them only were the laws entrusted in writing, while they were given to other nations merely in revelation and conception, or else (as none but Jews would object to the doctrine he desired to advance) that Paul was answering only in accordance with the understanding and current ideas of the Jews, for in respect to teaching things which he had partly seen, partly heard, he was to the Greeks a Greek, and to the Jews a Jew.

It now only remains to us to answer the arguments of those who would persuade themselves that the election of the Jews was not temporal, and merely in respect of their commonwealth, but eternal; for, they say, we see the Jews after the loss of their commonwealth, and after being scattered so many years and separated from all other nations, still surviving, which is without parallel among other peoples, and further the Scriptures seem to teach that God has chosen for Himself the Jews for ever, so that though they have lost their commonwealth, they still nevertheless remain God's elect.

The passages which they think teach most clearly this eternal election, are chiefly:

(1.) Jer. xxxi:36, where the prophet testifies that the seed of Israel shall for ever remain the nation of God, comparing them with the stability of the heavens and nature;

(2.) Ezek. xx:32, where the prophet seems to intend that though the Jews wanted after the help afforded them to turn their backs on the worship of the Lord, that God would nevertheless gather them together again from all the lands in which they were dispersed, and lead them to the wilderness of the peoples — as He had led their fathers to the wilderness of the land of Egypt — and would at length, after purging out from among them the rebels and transgressors, bring them thence to his Holy mountain, where the whole house of Israel should worship Him. Other passages are also cited, especially by the Pharisees, but I think I shall satisfy everyone if I answer these two, and this I shall easily accomplish after showing from Scripture itself that God chose not the Hebrews for ever, but only on the condition under which He had formerly chosen the Canaanites, for these last, as we have shown, had priests who religiously worshipped God, and whom God at length rejected because of their luxury, pride, and corrupt worship.

Moses (Lev. xviii:27) warned the Israelites that they be not polluted with whoredoms, lest the land spue them out as it had spued out the nations who had dwelt there before, and in Deut. viii:19, 20, in the plainest terms He threatens their total ruin, for He says, "I testify against you that ye shall surely perish. As the nations which the Lord destroyeth before your face, so shall ye perish." In like manner many other passages are found in the law which expressly show that God chose the Hebrews neither absolutely nor for ever. If, then, the prophets foretold for them a new covenant of the knowledge of God, love, and grace, such a promise is easily proved to be only made to the elect, for Ezekiel in the chapter which we have just quoted expressly says that God will separate from them the rebellious and transgressors, and Zephaniah (iii:12, 13), says that "God will take away the proud from the midst of them, and leave the poor." Now, inasmuch as their election has regard to true virtue, it is not to be thought that it was promised to the Jews alone to the exclusion of others, but we must evidently believe that the true Gentile prophets (and every nation, as we have shown, possessed such) promised the same to the faithful of their own people, who were thereby comforted. Wherefore this eternal covenant of the knowledge of God and love is universal, as is clear, moreover, from Zeph. iii:10, 11: no difference in this respect can be admitted between Jew and Gentile, nor did the former enjoy any special election beyond that which we have pointed out.

When the prophets, in speaking of this election which regards only true virtue, mixed up much concerning sacrifices and ceremonies, and the rebuilding of the temple and city, they wished by such figurative expressions, after the manner and nature of prophecy, to expound matters spiritual, so as at the same time to show to the Jews, whose prophets they were, the true restoration of the state and of the temple to be expected about the time of Cyrus.

At the present time, therefore, there is absolutely nothing which the Jews can arrogate to themselves beyond other people.

As to their continuance so long after dispersion and the loss of empire, there is nothing marvellous in it, for they so separated themselves from every other nation as to draw down upon themselves universal hate, not only by their outward rites, rites conflicting with those of other nations, but also by the sign of circumcision which they most scrupulously observe.

That they have been preserved in great measure by Gentile hatred, experience demonstrates. When the king of Spain formerly compelled the Jews to embrace the State religion or to go into exile, a large number of Jews accepted Catholicism. Now, as these renegades were admitted to all the native privileges of Spaniards, and deemed worthy of filling all honourable offices, it came to pass that they straightway became so intermingled with the Spaniards as to leave of themselves no relic or remembrance. But exactly the opposite happened to those whom the king of Portugal compelled to become Christians, for they always, though converted, lived apart, inasmuch as they were considered unworthy of any civic honours.

The sign of circumcision is, as I think, so important, that I could persuade myself that it alone would preserve the nation for ever. Nay, I would go so far as to believe that if the foundations of their religion have not emasculated their minds they may even, if occasion offers, so changeable are human affairs, raise up their empire afresh, and that God may a second time elect them.

Of such a possibility we have a very famous example in the Chinese. They, too, have some distinctive mark on their heads which they most scrupulously observe, and by which they keep themselves apart from everyone else, and have thus kept themselves during so many thousand years that they far surpass all other nations in antiquity. They have not always retained empire, but they have recovered it when lost, and doubtless will do so again after the spirit of the Tartars becomes relaxed through the luxury of riches and pride.

Lastly, if any one wishes to maintain that the Jews, from this or from any other cause, have been chosen by God for ever, I will not gainsay him if he will admit that this choice, whether temporary or eternal, has no regard, in so far as it is peculiar to the Jews, to aught but dominion and physical advantages (for by such alone can one nation be distinguished from another), whereas in regard to intellect and true virtue, every nation is on a par with the rest, and God has not in these respects chosen one people rather than another.

CHAPTER IV

Of the Divine Law

The word law, taken in the abstract, means that by which an individual, or all things, or as many things as belong to a particular species, act in one and the same fixed and definite manner, which manner depends either on natural necessity or on human decree. A law which depends on natural necessity is one which necessarily follows from the nature, or from the definition of the thing in question; a law which depends on human decree, and which is more correctly called an ordinance, is one which men have laid down for themselves and others in order to live more safely or conveniently, or from some similar reason.

For example, the law that all bodies impinging on lesser bodies, lose as much of their own motion as they communicate to the latter is a universal law of all bodies, and depends on natural necessity. So, too, the law that a man in remembering one thing, straightway remembers another either like it, or which he had perceived simultaneously with it, is a law which necessarily follows from the nature of man. But the law that men must yield, or be compelled to yield, somewhat of their natural right, and that they bind themselves to live in a certain way, depends on human decree. Now, though I freely admit that all things are predetermined by universal natural laws to exist and operate in a given, fixed, and definite manner, I still assert that the laws I have just mentioned depend on human decree.

(1.) Because man, in so far as he is a part of nature, constitutes a part of the power of nature. Whatever, therefore, follows necessarily from the necessity of human nature (that is, from nature herself, in so far as we conceive of her as acting through man) follows, even though it be necessarily, from human power. Hence the sanction of such laws may very well be said to depend on man's decree, for it principally depends on the power of the human mind; so that the human mind in respect to its perception of things as true and false, can readily be conceived as without such laws, but not without necessary law as we have just defined it.

(2.) I have stated that these laws depend on human decree because it is well to define and explain things by their proximate causes. The general consideration of fate and the concatenation of causes would aid us very little in forming and arranging our ideas concerning particular questions. Let us add that as to the actual coordination and concatenation of things, that is how things are ordained and linked together, we are obviously ignorant; therefore, it is more profitable for right living, nay, it is necessary for us to consider things as contingent. So much about law in the abstract.

Now the word law seems to be only applied to natural phenomena by analogy, and is commonly taken to signify a command which men can either obey or neglect, inasmuch as it restrains human nature within certain originally exceeded limits, and therefore lays down no rule beyond human strength. Thus it is expedient to define law more particularly as a plan of life laid down by man for himself or others with a certain object.

However, as the true object of legislation is only perceived by a few, and most men are almost incapable of grasping it, though they live under its conditions, legislators, with a view to exacting general obedience, have wisely put forward another object, very different from that which necessarily follows from the nature of law: they promise to the observers of the law that which the masses chiefly desire, and threaten its violators with that which they chiefly fear: thus endeavouring to restrain the masses, as far as may be, like a horse with a curb; whence it follows that the word law is chiefly applied to the modes of life enjoined on men by the sway of others; hence those who obey the law are said to live under it and to be under compulsion. In truth, a man who renders everyone their due because he fears the gallows, acts under the sway and compulsion of others, and cannot be called just. But a man who does the same from a knowledge of the true reason for laws and their necessity, acts from a firm purpose and of his own accord, and is therefore properly called just. This, I take it, is Paul's meaning when he says, that those who live under the law cannot be justified through the law, for justice, as commonly defined, is the constant and perpetual will to render every man his due. Thus Solomon says (Prov. xxi:15), "It is a joy to the just to do judgment," but the wicked fear.

Law, then, being a plan of living which men have for a certain object laid down for themselves or others, may, as it seems, be divided into human law and Divine law. {But both are opposite sides of the same coin}

By human law I mean a plan of living which serves only to render life and the state secure. By Divine law I mean that which only regards the highest good, in other words, the true knowledge of God and love.

I call this law Divine because of the nature of the highest good, which I will here shortly explain as clearly as I can.

Inasmuch as the intellect is the best part of our being, it is evident that we should make every effort to perfect it as far as possible if we desire to search for what is really profitable to us. For in intellectual perfection the highest good should consist. Now, since all our knowledge, and the certainty which removes every doubt, depend solely on the knowledge of God; — firstly, because without God nothing can exist or be conceived; secondly, because so long as we have no clear and distinct idea of God we may remain in universal doubt — it follows that our highest good and perfection also depend solely on the knowledge of God. Further, since without God nothing can exist or be conceived, it is evident that all natural phenomena involve and express the conception of God as far as their essence and perfection extend, so that we have greater and more perfect knowledge of God in proportion to our knowledge of natural phenomena: conversely (since the knowledge of an effect through its cause is the same thing as the knowledge of a particular property of a cause) the greater our knowledge of natural phenomena, the more perfect is our knowledge of the essence of God (which is the cause of all things). So, then, our highest good not only depends on the knowledge of God, but wholly consists therein; and it further follows that man is perfect or the reverse in proportion to the nature and perfection of the object of his special desire; hence the most perfect and the chief sharer in the highest blessedness is he who prizes above all else, and takes especial delight in, the intellectual knowledge of God, the most perfect Being.

Hither, then, our highest good and our highest blessedness aim — namely, to the knowledge and love of God; therefore the means demanded by this aim of all human actions, that is, by God in so far as the idea of him is in us, may be called the commands of God, because they proceed, as it were, from God Himself, inasmuch as He exists in our minds, and the plan of life which has regard to this aim may be fitly called the law of God.

The nature of the means, and the plan of life which this aim demands, how the foundations of the best states follow its lines, and how men's life is conducted, are questions pertaining to general ethics. Here I only proceed to treat of the Divine law in a particular application.

As the love of God is man's highest happiness and blessedness, and the ultimate end and aim of all human actions, it follows that he alone lives by the Divine law who loves God not from fear of punishment, or from love of any other object, such as sensual pleasure, fame, or the like; but solely because he has knowledge of God, or is convinced that the knowledge and love of God is the highest good. The sum and chief precept, then, of the Divine law is to love God as the highest good, namely, as we have said, not from fear of any pains and penalties, or from the love of any other object in which we desire to take pleasure. The idea of God lays down the rule that God is our highest good — in other words, that the knowledge and love of God is the ultimate aim to which all our actions should be directed. The worldling cannot understand these things, they appear foolishness to him. because he has too meager a knowledge of God, and also because in this highest good he can discover nothing which he can handle or eat, or which affects the fleshly appetites wherein he chiefly delights, for it consists solely in thought and the pure reason. They, on the other hand, who know that they possess no greater gift than intellect and sound reason, will doubtless accept what I have said without question.

We have now explained that wherein the Divine law chiefly consists, and what are human laws, namely, all those which have a different aim unless they have been ratified by revelation, for in this respect also things are referred to God (as we have shown above) and in this sense the law of Moses, although it was not universal, but entirely adapted to the disposition and particular preservation of a single people, may yet be called a law of God or Divine law, inasmuch as we believe that it was ratified by prophetic insight. If we consider the nature of natural Divine law as we have just explained it, we shall see:

I. — That it is universal or common to all men, for we have deduced it from universal human nature.

II. That it does not depend on the truth of any historical narrative whatsoever, for inasmuch as this natural Divine law is comprehended solely by the consideration of human nature, it is plain that we can conceive it as existing as well in Adam as in any other man, as well in a man living among his fellows, as in a man who lives by himself.

The truth of a historical narrative, however assured, cannot give us the knowledge nor consequently the love of God, for love of God springs from knowledge of Him, and knowledge of Him should be derived from general ideas, in themselves certain and known, so that the truth of a historical narrative is very far from being a necessary requisite for our attaining our highest good.

Still, though the truth of histories cannot give us the knowledge and love of God, I do not deny that reading them is very useful with a view to life in the world, for the more we have observed and known of men's customs and circumstances, which are best revealed by their actions, the more warily we shall be able to order our lives among them, and so far as reason dictates to adapt our actions to their dispositions.

III. We see that this natural Divine law does not demand the performance of ceremonies — that is, actions in themselves indifferent, which are called good from the fact of their institution, or actions symbolizing something profitable for salvation, or (if one prefers this definition) actions of which the meaning surpasses human understanding. The natural light of reason does not demand anything which it is itself unable to supply, but only such as it can very clearly show to be good, or a means to our blessedness. Such things as are good simply because they have been commanded or instituted, or as being symbols of something good, are mere shadows which cannot be reckoned among actions that are the offsprings as it were, or fruit of a sound mind and of intellect. There is no need for me to go into this now in more detail.

IV. Lastly, we see that the highest reward of the Divine law is the law itself, namely, to know God and to love Him of our free choice, and with an undivided and fruitful spirit; while its penalty is the absence of these things, and being in bondage to the flesh — that is, having an inconstant and wavering spirit.

These points being noted, I must now inquire:

I. Whether by the natural light of reason we can conceive of God as a law-giver or potentate ordaining laws for men?

II. What is the teaching of Holy Writ concerning this natural light of reason and natural law?

III. With what objects were ceremonies formerly instituted?

IV. Lastly, what is the good gained by knowing the sacred histories and believing them?

Of the first two I will treat in this chapter, of the remaining two in the following one.

Our conclusion about the first is easily deduced from the nature of God's will, which is only distinguished from His understanding in relation to our intellect — that is, the will and the understanding of God are in reality one and the same, and are only distinguished in relation to our thoughts which we form concerning God's understanding. For instance, if we are only looking to the fact that the nature of a triangle is from eternity contained in the Divine nature as an eternal verity, we say that God possesses the idea of a triangle, or that He understands the nature of a triangle; but if afterwards we look to the fact that the nature of a triangle is thus contained in the Divine nature, solely by the necessity of the Divine nature, and not by the necessity of the nature and essence of a triangle — in fact, that the necessity of a triangle's essence and nature, in so far as they are conceived of as eternal verities, depends solely on the necessity of the Divine nature and intellect, we then style God's will or decree, that which before we styled His intellect. Wherefore we make one and the same affirmation concerning God when we say that He has from eternity decreed that three angles of a triangle are equal to two right angles, as when we say that He has understood it.

Hence the affirmations and the negations of God always involve necessity or truth; so that, for example, if God said to Adam that He did not wish him to eat of the tree of knowledge of good and evil, it would have involved a contradiction that Adam should have been able to eat of it, and would therefore have been impossible that he should have so eaten, for the Divine command would have involved an eternal necessity and truth. But since Scripture nevertheless narrates that God did give this command to Adam, and yet that none the less Adam ate of the tree, we must perforce say that God revealed to Adam the evil which would surely follow if he should eat of the tree, but did not disclose that such evil would of necessity come to pass. Thus it was that Adam took the revelation to be not an eternal and necessary truth, but a law — that is, an ordinance followed by gain or loss, not depending necessarily on the nature of the act performed, but solely on the will and absolute power of some potentate, so that the revelation in question was solely in relation to Adam, and solely through his lack of knowledge a law, and God was, as it were, a lawgiver and potentate. From the same cause, namely, from lack of knowledge, the Decalogue in relation to the Hebrews was a law, for since they knew not the existence of God as an eternal truth, they must have taken as a law that which was revealed to them in the Decalogue, namely, that God exists, and that God only should be worshipped. But if God had spoken to them without the intervention of any bodily means, immediately they would have perceived it not as a law, but as an eternal truth.

What we have said about the Israelites and Adam, applies also to all the prophets who wrote laws in God's name — they did not adequately conceive God's decrees as eternal truths. For instance, we must say of Moses that from revelation, from the basis of what was revealed to him, he perceived the method by which the Israelitish nation could best be united in a particular territory, and could form a body politic or state, and further that he perceived the method by which that nation could best be constrained to obedience; but he did not perceive, nor was it revealed to him, that this method was absolutely the best, nor that the obedience of the people in a certain strip of territory would necessarily imply the end he had in view. Wherefore he perceived these things not as eternal truths, but as precepts and ordinances, and he ordained them as laws of God, and thus it came to be that he conceived God as a ruler, a legislator, a king, as merciful, just, &c., whereas such qualities are simply attributes of human nature, and utterly alien from the nature of the Deity. Thus much we may affirm of the prophets who wrote laws in the name of God; but we must not affirm it of Christ, for Christ, although He too seems to have written laws in the name of God, must be taken to have had a clear and adequate perception, for Christ was not so much a prophet as the mouthpiece of God. For God made revelations to mankind through Christ as He had before done through angels — that is, a created voice, visions, &c. It would be as unreasonable to say that God had accommodated his revelations to the opinions of Christ as that He had before accommodated them to the opinions of angels (that is, of a created voice or visions) as matters to be revealed to the prophets, a wholly absurd hypothesis.

Moreover, Christ was sent to teach not only the Jews but the whole human race, and therefore it was not enough that His mind should be accommodated to the opinions the Jews alone, but also to the opinion and fundamental teaching common to the whole human race — in other words, to ideas universal and true. Inasmuch as God revealed Himself to Christ, or to Christ's mind immediately, and not as to the prophets through words and symbols, we must needs suppose that Christ perceived truly what was revealed, in other words, He understood it, for a, matter is understood when it is perceived simply by the mind without words or symbols.

Christ, then, perceived (truly and adequately) what was revealed, and if He ever proclaimed such revelations as laws, He did so because of the ignorance and obstinacy of the people, acting in this respect the part of God; inasmuch as He accommodated Himself to the comprehension of the people, and though He spoke somewhat more clearly than the other prophets, yet He taught what was revealed obscurely, and generally through parables, especially when He was speaking to those to whom it was not yet given to understand the kingdom of heaven. (See Matt. xiii:10, &c.) To those to whom it was given to understand the mysteries of heaven, He doubtless taught His doctrines as eternal truths, and did not lay them down as laws, thus freeing the minds of His hearers from the bondage of that law which He further confirmed and established. Paul apparently points to this more than once (e.g. Rom. vii:6, and iii:28), though he never himself seems to wish to speak openly, but, to quote his own words (Rom. iii:6, and vi:19), "merely humanly." This he expressly states when he calls God just, and it was doubtless in concession to human weakness that he attributes mercy, grace, anger, and similar qualities to God, adapting his language to the popular mind, or, as he puts it (1 Cor. iii:1, 2), to carnal men. In Rom. ix:18, he teaches undisguisedly that God's auger and mercy depend not on the actions of men, but on God's own nature or will; further, that no one is justified by the works of the law, but only by faith, which he seems to identify with the full assent of the soul; lastly, that no one is blessed unless he have in him the mind of Christ (Rom. viii:9), whereby he perceives the laws of God as eternal truths. We conclude, therefore, that God is described as a lawgiver or prince, and styled just, merciful, &c., merely in concession to popular understanding, and the imperfection of popular knowledge; that in reality God acts and directs all things simply by the necessity of His nature and perfection, and that His decrees and volitions are eternal truths, and always involve necessity. So much for the first point which I wished to explain and demonstrate.

Passing on to the second point, let us search the sacred pages for their teaching concerning the light of nature and this Divine law. The first doctrine we find in the history of the first man, where it is narrated that God commanded Adam not to eat of the fruit of the tree of the knowledge of good and evil; this seems to mean that God commanded Adam to do and to seek after righteousness because it was good, not because the contrary was evil: that is, to seek the good for its own sake, not from fear of evil. We have seen that he who acts rightly from the true knowledge and love of right, acts with freedom and constancy, whereas he who acts from fear of evil, is under the constraint of evil, and acts in bondage under external control. So that this commandment of God to Adam comprehends the whole Divine natural law, and absolutely agrees with the dictates of the light of nature; nay, it would be easy to explain on this basis the whole history or allegory of the first man. But I prefer to pass over the subject in silence, because, in the first place, I cannot be absolutely certain that my explanation would be in accordance with the intention of the sacred writer; and, secondly, because many do not admit that this history is an allegory, maintaining it to be a simple narrative of facts. It will be better, therefore, to adduce other passages of Scripture, especially such as were written by him, who speaks with all the strength of his natural understanding, in which he surpassed all his contemporaries, and whose sayings are accepted by the people as of equal weight with those of the prophets. I mean Solomon, whose prudence and wisdom are commended in Scripture rather than his piety and gift of prophecy. Life being taken to mean the true life (as is evident from Deut. xxx:19), the fruit of the understanding consists only in the true life, and its absence constitutes punishment. All this absolutely agrees with what was set out in our fourth point concerning natural law. Moreover our position that it is the well-spring of life, and that the intellect alone lays down laws for the wise, is plainly taught by, the sage, for he says (Prov. xiii14): "The law of the wise is a fountain of life " — that is, as we gather from the preceding text, the understanding. In chap. iii:13, he expressly teaches that the understanding renders man blessed and happy, and gives him true peace of mind. "Happy is the man that findeth wisdom, and the man that getteth understanding," for "Wisdom gives length of days, and riches and honour; her ways are ways of pleasantness, and all her paths peace" (xiiii6, 17). According to Solomon, therefore, it is only, the wise who live in peace and equanimity, not like the wicked whose minds drift hither and thither, and (as Isaiah says, chap. lvii:20) "are like the troubled sea, for them there is no peace."

Lastly, we should especially note the passage in chap. ii. of Solomon's proverbs which most clearly confirms our contention: "If thou criest after knowledge, and liftest up thy voice for understanding . . . then shalt thou understand the fear of the Lord, and find the knowledge of God; for the Lord giveth wisdom; out of His mouth cometh knowledge and understanding." These words clearly enunciate, that wisdom or intellect alone teaches us to fear God wisely — that is, to worship Him truly;, that wisdom and knowledge flow from God's mouth, and that God bestows on us this gift; this we have already shown in proving that our understanding and our knowledge depend on, spring from, and are perfected by the idea or knowledge of God, and nothing else. Solomon goes on to say in so many words that this knowledge contains and involves the true principles of ethics and politics: "When wisdom entereth into thy heart, and knowledge is pleasant to thy soul, discretion shall preserve thee, understanding shall keep thee, then shalt thou understand righteousness, and judgment, and equity, yea every good path." All of which is in obvious agreement with natural knowledge: for after we have come to the understanding of things, and have tasted the excellence of knowledge, she teaches us ethics and true virtue.

Thus the happiness and the peace of him who cultivates his natural understanding lies, according to Solomon also, not so much under the dominion of fortune (or God's external aid) as in inward personal virtue (or God's internal aid), for the latter can to a great extent be preserved by vigilance, right action, and thought.

Lastly, we must by no means pass over the passage in Paul's Epistle to the Romans, i:20, in which he says: "For the invisible things of God from the creation of the world are clearly seen, being understood by the things that are made, even His eternal power and Godhead; so that they are without excuse, because, when they knew God, they glorified Him not as God, neither were they thankful." These words clearly show that everyone can by the light of nature clearly understand the goodness and the eternal divinity of God, and can thence know and deduce what they should seek for and what avoid; wherefore the Apostle says that they are without excuse and cannot plead ignorance, as they certainly might if it were a question of supernatural light and the incarnation, passion, and resurrection of Christ. "Wherefore," he goes on to say (ib. 24), "God gave them up to uncleanness through the lusts of their own hearts;" and so on, through the rest of the chapter, he describes the vices of ignorance, and sets them forth as the punishment of ignorance. This obviously agrees with the verse of Solomon, already quoted, "The instruction of fools is folly," so that it is easy to understand why Paul says that the wicked are without excuse. As every man sows so shall he reap: out of evil, evils necessarily spring, unless they be wisely counteracted.

Thus we see that Scripture literally approves of the light of natural reason and the natural Divine law, and I have fulfilled the promises made at the beginning of this chapter.

CHAPTER V

Of the Ceremonial Law

In the foregoing chapter we have shown that the Divine law, which renders men truly blessed, and teaches them the true life, is universal to all men; nay, we have so intimately deduced it from human nature that it must be esteemed innate, and, as it were, ingrained in the human mind.

But with regard to the ceremonial observances which were ordained in the Old Testament for the Hebrews only, and were so adapted to their state that they could for the most part only be observed by the society as a whole and not by each individual, it is evident that they formed no part of the Divine law, and had nothing to do with blessedness and virtue, but had reference only to the election of the Hebrews, that is (as I have shown in Chap. II.), to their temporal bodily happiness and the tranquillity of their kingdom, and that therefore they were only valid while that kingdom lasted. If in the Old Testament they are spoken of as the law of God, it is only because they were founded on revelation, or a basis of revelation. Still as reason, however sound, has little weight with ordinary theologians, I will adduce the authority of Scripture for what I here assert, and will further show, for the sake of greater clearness, why and how these ceremonials served to establish and preserve the Jewish kingdom. Isaiah teaches most plainly that the Divine law in its strict sense signifies that universal law which consists in a true manner of life, and does not signify ceremonial observances. In chapter i:10, the prophet calls on his countrymen to hearken to the Divine law as he delivers it, and first excluding all kinds of sacrifices and all feasts, he at length sums up the law in these few words, "Cease to do evil, learn to do well: seek judgment, relieve the oppressed." Not less striking testimony is given in Psalm xl:7 — 9, where the Psalmist addresses God: "Sacrifice and offering Thou didst not desire; mine ears hast Thou opened; burnt offering and sin-offering hast Thou not required; I delight to do Thy will, 0 my God; yea, Thy law is within my heart." Here the Psalmist reckons as the law of God only that which is inscribed in his heart, and excludes ceremonies therefrom, for the latter are good and inscribed on the heart only from the fact of their institution, and not because of their intrinsic value.

Other passages of Scripture testify to the same truth, but these two will suffice. We may also learn from the Bible that ceremonies are no aid to blessedness, but only have reference to the temporal prosperity of the kingdom; for the rewards promised for their observance are merely temporal advantages and delights, blessedness being reserved for the universal Divine law. In all the five books commonly attributed to Moses nothing is promised, as I have said, beyond temporal benefits, such as honours, fame, victories, riches, enjoyments, and health. Though many moral precepts besides ceremonies are contained in these five books, they appear not as moral doctrines universal to all men, but as commands especially adapted to the understanding and character of the Hebrew people, and as having reference only to the welfare of the kingdom. For instance, Moses does not teach the Jews as a prophet not to kill or to steal, but gives these commandments solely as a lawgiver and judge; he does not reason out the doctrine, but affixes for its non-observance a penalty which may and very properly does vary in different nations. So, too, the command not to commit adultery is given merely with reference to the welfare of the state; for if the moral doctrine had been intended, with reference not only to the welfare of the state, but also to the tranquillity and blessedness of the individual, Moses would have condemned not merely the outward act, but also the mental acquiescence, as is done by Christ, Who taught only universal moral precepts, and for this cause promises a spiritual instead of a temporal reward. Christ, as I have said, was sent into the world, not to preserve the state nor to lay down laws, but solely to teach the universal moral law, so we can easily understand that He wished in nowise to do away with the law of Moses, inasmuch as He introduced no new laws of His own — His sole care was to teach moral doctrines, and distinguish them from the laws of the state; for the Pharisees, in their ignorance, thought that the observance of the state law and the Mosaic law was the sum total of morality; whereas such laws merely had reference to the public welfare, and aimed not so much at instructing the Jews as at keeping them under constraint. But let us return to our subject, and cite other passages of Scripture which set forth temporal benefits as rewards for observing the ceremonial law, and blessedness as reward for the universal law.

None of the prophets puts the point more clearly than Isaiah. (18.) After condemning hypocrisy he commends liberty and charity towards one's self and one's neighbours, and promises as a reward: "Then shall thy light break forth as the morning, and thy health shall spring forth speedily, thy righteousness shall go before thee, and the glory of the Lord shall be thy reward" (chap. lviii:8). Shortly afterwards he commends the Sabbath, and for a due observance of it, promises: "Then shalt thou delight thyself in the Lord, and I will cause thee to ride upon the high places of the earth, and feed thee with the heritage of Jacob thy father: for the mouth of the Lord has spoken it." Thus the prophet for liberty bestowed, and charitable works, promises a healthy mind in a healthy body, and the glory of the Lord even after death; whereas, for ceremonial exactitude, he only promises security of rule, prosperity, and temporal happiness.

In Psalms xv. and xxiv. no mention is made of ceremonies, but only of moral doctrines, inasmuch as there is no question of anything but blessedness, and blessedness is symbolically promised: it is quite certain that the expressions, "the hill of God," and "His tents and the dwellers therein," refer to blessedness and security of soul, not to the actual mount of Jerusalem and the tabernacle of Moses, for these latter were not dwelt in by anyone, and only the sons of Levi ministered there. Further, all those sentences of Solomon to which I referred in the last chapter, for the cultivation of the intellect and wisdom, promise true blessedness, for by wisdom is the fear of God at length understood, and the knowledge of God found.

That the Jews themselves were not bound to practise their ceremonial observances after the destruction of their kingdom is evident from Jeremiah. For when the prophet saw and foretold that the desolation of the city was at hand, he said that God only delights in those who know and understand that He exercises loving-kindness, judgment, and righteousness in the earth, and that such persons only are worthy of praise. (Jer. ix:23.) As though God had said that, after the desolation of the city, He would require nothing special from the Jews beyond the natural law by which all men are bound.

The New Testament also confirms this view, for only moral doctrines are therein taught, and the kingdom of heaven is promised as a reward, whereas ceremonial observances are not touched on by the Apostles, after they began to preach the Gospel to the Gentiles. The Pharisees certainly continued to practise these rites after the destruction of the kingdom, but more with a view of opposing the Christians than of pleasing God: for after the first destruction of the city, when they were led captive to Babylon, not being then, so far as I am aware, split up into sects, they straightway neglected their rites, bid farewell to the Mosaic law, buried their national customs in oblivion as being plainly superfluous, and began to mingle with other nations, as we may abundantly learn from Ezra and Nehemiah. We cannot, therefore, doubt that they were no more bound by the law of Moses, after the destruction of their kingdom, than they had been before it had been begun, while they were still living among other peoples before the exodus from Egypt, and were subject to no special law beyond the natural law, and also, doubtless, the law of the state in which they were living, in so far as it was consonant with the Divine natural law.

As to the fact that the patriarchs offered sacrifices, I think they did so for the purpose of stimulating their piety, for their minds had been accustomed from childhood to the idea of sacrifice, which we know had been universal from the time of Enoch; and thus they found in sacrifice their most powerful incentive. The patriarchs, then, did not sacrifice to God at the bidding of a Divine right, or as taught by the basis of the Divine law, but simply in accordance with the custom of the time; and, if in so doing they followed any ordinance, it was simply the ordinance of the country they were living in, by which (as we have seen before in the case of Melchisedek) they were bound.

I think that I have now given Scriptural authority for my view: it remains to show why and how the ceremonial observances tended to preserve and confirm the Hebrew kingdom; and this I can very briefly do on grounds universally accepted.

The formation of society serves not only for defensive purposes, but is also very useful, and, indeed, absolutely necessary, as rendering possible the division of labour. If men did not render mutual assistance to each other, no one would have either the skill or the time to provide for his own sustenance and preservation: for all men are not equally apt for all work, and no one would be capable of preparing all that he individually stood in need of. Strength and time, I repeat, would fail, if every one had in person to plough, to sow, to reap, to grind corn, to cook, to weave, to stitch, and perform the other numerous functions required to keep life going; to say nothing of the arts and sciences which are also entirely necessary to the perfection and blessedness of human nature. We see that peoples living, in uncivilized barbarism lead a wretched and almost animal life, and even they would not be able to acquire their few rude necessaries without assisting one another to a certain extent.

Now if men were so constituted by nature that they desired nothing but what is designated by true reason, society would obviously have no need of laws: it would be sufficient to inculcate true moral doctrines; and men would freely, without hesitation, act in accordance with their true interests. But human nature is framed in a different fashion: every one, indeed, seeks his own interest, but does not do so in accordance with the dictates of sound reason, for most men's ideas of desirability and usefulness are guided by their fleshly instincts and emotions, which take no thought beyond the present and the immediate object. Therefore, no society can exist without government, and force, and laws to restrain and repress men's desires and immoderate impulses. Still human nature will not submit to absolute repression. Violent governments, as Seneca says, never last long; the moderate governments endure. So long as men act simply from fear they act contrary to their inclinations, taking no thought for the advantages or necessity of their actions, but simply endeavouring to escape punishment or loss of life. They must needs rejoice in any evil which befalls their ruler, even if it should involve themselves; and must long for and bring about such evil by every means in their power. Again, men are especially intolerant of serving and being ruled by their equals. Lastly, it is exceedingly difficult to revoke liberties once granted.

From these considerations it follows, firstly, that authority should either be vested in the hands of the whole state in common, so that everyone should be bound to serve, and yet not be in subjection to his equals; or else, if power be in the hands of a few, or one man, that one man should be something above average humanity, or should strive to get himself accepted as such. Secondly, laws should in every government be so arranged that people should be kept in bounds by the hope of some greatly desired good, rather than by fear, for then everyone will do his duty willingly.

Lastly, as obedience consists in acting at the bidding of external authority, it would have no place in a state where the government is vested in the whole people, and where laws are made by common consent. In such a society the people would remain free, whether the laws were added to or diminished, inasmuch as it would not be done on external authority, but their own free consent. The reverse happens when the sovereign power is vested in one man, for all act at his bidding; and, therefore, unless they had been trained from the first to depend on the words of their ruler, the latter would find it difficult, in case of need, to abrogate liberties once conceded, and impose new laws.

From these universal considerations, let us pass on to the kingdom of the Jews. The Jews when they first came out of Egypt were not bound by any national laws, and were therefore free to ratify any laws they liked, or to make new ones, and were at liberty to set up a government and occupy a territory wherever they chose. However, they, were entirely unfit to frame a wise code of laws and to keep the sovereign power vested in the community; they were all uncultivated and sunk in a wretched slavery, therefore the sovereignty was bound to remain vested in the hands of one man who would rule the rest and keep them under constraint, make laws and interpret them. This sovereignty was easily retained by Moses, because he surpassed the rest in virtue and persuaded the people of the fact, proving it by many testimonies (see Exod. chap. xiv., last verse, and chap. xix:9). He then, by the Divine virtue he possessed, made laws and ordained them for the people, taking the greatest care that they should be obeyed willingly and not through fear, being specially induced to adopt this course by the obstinate nature of the Jews, who would not have submitted to be ruled solely by constraint; and also by the imminence of war, for it is always better to inspire soldiers with a thirst for glory than to terrify them with threats; each man will then strive to distinguish himself by valour and courage, instead of merely trying to escape punishment. Moses, therefore, by his virtue and the Divine command, introduced a religion, so that the people might do their duty from devotion rather than fear. Further, he bound them over by benefits, and prophesied many advantages in the future; nor were his laws very severe, as anyone may see for himself, especially if he remarks the number of circumstances necessary in order to procure the conviction of an accused person.

Lastly, in order that the people which could not govern itself should be entirely dependent on its ruler, he left nothing to the free choice of individuals (who had hitherto been slaves); the people could do nothing but remember the law, and follow the ordinances laid down at the good pleasure of their ruler; they were not allowed to plough, to sow, to reap, nor even to eat; to clothe themselves, to shave, to rejoice, or in fact to do anything whatever as they liked, but were bound to follow the directions given in the law; and not only this, but they were obliged to have marks on their door-posts, on their hands, and between their eyes to admonish them to perpetual obedience.

This, then, was the object of the ceremonial law, that men should do nothing of their own free will, but should always act under external authority, and should continually confess by their actions and thoughts that they were not their own masters, but were entirely under the control of others.

From all these considerations it is clearer than day that ceremonies have nothing to do with a state of blessedness, and that those mentioned in the Old Testament, i.e. the whole Mosaic Law, had reference merely to the government of the Jews, and merely temporal advantages.

As for the Christian rites, such as baptism, the Lord's Supper, festivals, public prayers, and any other observances which are, and always have been, common to all Christendom, if they were instituted by Christ or His Apostles (which is open to doubt), they were instituted as external signs of the universal church, and not as having anything to do with blessedness, or possessing any sanctity in themselves. Therefore, though such ceremonies were not ordained for the sake of upholding a government, they were ordained for the preservation of a society, and accordingly he who lives alone is not bound by them: nay, those who live in a country where the Christian religion is forbidden, are bound to abstain from such rites, and can none the less live in a state of blessedness. We have an example of this in Japan, where the Christian religion is forbidden, and the Dutch who live there are enjoined by their East India Company not to practise any outward rites of religion. I need not cite other examples, though it would be easy to prove my point from the fundamental principles of the New Testament, and to adduce many confirmatory instances; but I pass on the more willingly, as

I am anxious to proceed to my next proposition. I will now, therefore, pass on to what I proposed to treat of in the second part of this chapter, namely, what persons are bound to believe in the narratives contained in Scripture, and how far they are so bound. Examining this question by the aid of natural reason, I will proceed as follows.

If anyone wishes to persuade his fellows for or against anything which is not self-evident[6], he must deduce his contention from their admissions, and convince them either by experience or by ratiocination; either by appealing to facts of natural experience, or to self-evident intellectual axioms. Now unless the experience be of such a kind as to be clearly and distinctly understood, though it may convince a man, it will not have the same effect on his mind and disperse the clouds of his doubt so completely as when the doctrine taught is deduced entirely from intellectual axioms — that is, by the mere power of the understanding and logical order, and this is especially the case in spiritual matters which have nothing to do with the senses.

But the deduction of conclusions from general truths . priori, usually requires a long chain of arguments, and, moreover, very great caution, acuteness, and self-restraint — qualities which are not often met with; therefore people prefer to be taught by experience rather than deduce their conclusion from a few axioms, and set them out in logical order. Whence it follows, that if anyone wishes to teach a doctrine to a whole nation (not to speak of the whole human race), and to be understood by all men in every particular, he will seek to support his teaching with experience, and will endeavour to suit his reasonings and the definitions of his doctrines as far as possible to the understanding of the common people, who form the majority of mankind, and he will not set them forth in logical sequence nor adduce the definitions which serve to establish them. Otherwise he writes only for the learned — that is, he will be understood by only a small proportion of the human race.

All Scripture was written primarily for an entire people, and secondarily for the whole human race; therefore its contents must necessarily be adapted as

---

[6] We doubt of the existence of God, and consequently of all else, so long as we have no clear and distinct idea of God, but only a confused one. For as he who knows not rightly the nature of a triangle, knows not that its three angles are equal to two right angles, so he who conceives the Divine nature confusedly, does not see that it pertains to the nature of God to exist. Now, to conceive the nature of God clearly and distinctly, it is necessary to pay attention to a certain number of very simple notions, called general notions, and by their help to associate the conceptions which we form of the attributes of the Divine nature. It then, for the first time, becomes clear to us, that God exists necessarily, that He is omnipresent, and that all our conceptions involve in themselves the nature of God and are conceived through it. Lastly, we see that all our adequate ideas are true. Compare on this point the prolegomena to book, "Principles of Descartes's philosophy set forth geometrically."

far as possible to the understanding of the masses, and proved only by examples drawn from experience. We will explain ourselves more clearly. The chief speculative doctrines taught in Scripture are the existence of God, or a Being Who made all things, and Who directs and sustains the world with consummate wisdom; furthermore, that God takes the greatest thought for men, or such of them as live piously and honourably, while He punishes, with various penalties, those who do evil, separating them from the good. All this is proved in Scripture entirely through experience-that is, through the narratives there related. No definitions of doctrine are given, but all the sayings and reasonings are adapted to the understanding of the masses. Although experience can give no clear knowledge of these things, nor explain the nature of God, nor how He directs and sustains all things, it can nevertheless teach and enlighten men sufficiently to impress obedience and devotion on their minds.

It is now, I think, sufficiently clear what persons are bound to believe in the Scripture narratives, and in what degree they are so bound, for it evidently follows from what has been said that the knowledge of and belief in them is particularly necessary to the masses whose intellect is not capable of perceiving things clearly and distinctly. Further, he who denies them because he does not believe that God exists or takes thought for men and the world, may be accounted impious; but a man who is ignorant of them, and nevertheless knows by natural reason that God exists, as we have said, and has a true plan of life, is altogether blessed — yes, more blessed than the common herd of believers, because besides true opinions he possesses also a true and distinct conception. Lastly, he who is ignorant of the Scriptures and knows nothing by the light of reason, though he may not be impious or rebellious, is yet less than human and almost brutal, having none of God's gifts.

We must here remark that when we say that the knowledge of the sacred narrative is particularly necessary to the masses, we do not mean the knowledge of absolutely all the narratives in the Bible, but only of the principal ones, those which, taken by themselves, plainly display the doctrine we have just stated, and have most effect over men's minds.

If all the narratives in Scripture were necessary for the proof of this doctrine, and if no conclusion could be drawn without the general consideration of every one of the histories contained in the sacred writings, truly the conclusion and demonstration of such doctrine would overtask the understanding and strength not only of the masses, but of humanity; who is there who could give attention to all the narratives at once, and to all the circumstances, and all the scraps of doctrine to be elicited from such a host of diverse histories? I cannot believe that the men who have left us the Bible as we have it were so abounding in talent that they attempted setting about such a method of demonstration, still less can I suppose that we cannot understand Scriptural doctrine till we have given heed to the quarrels of Isaac, the advice of Achitophel to Absalom, the civil war between Jews and Israelites, and other similar chronicles; nor can I think that it was more difficult to teach such doctrine by means of history to the Jews of early times, the contemporaries of Moses, than it was to the contemporaries of Esdras. But more will be said on this point hereafter, we may now only note that the masses are only bound to know those histories which can most powerfully dispose their mind to obedience and devotion. However, the masses are not sufficiently skilled to draw conclusions from what they read, they take more delight in the actual stories, and in the strange and unlooked-for issues of events than in the doctrines implied; therefore, besides reading these narratives, they are always in need of pastors or church ministers to explain them to their feeble intelligence.

But not to wander from our point, let us conclude with what has been our principal object — namely, that the truth of narratives, be they what they may, has nothing to do with the Divine law, and serves for nothing except in respect of doctrine, the sole element which makes one history better than another. The narratives in the Old and New Testaments surpass profane history, and differ among themselves in merit simply by reason of the salutary doctrines which they inculcate. Therefore, if a man were to read the Scripture narratives believing the whole of them, but were to give no heed to the doctrines they contain, and make no amendment in his life, he might employ himself just as profitably in reading the Koran or the poetic drama, or ordinary chronicles, with the attention usually given to such writings; on the other hand, if a man is absolutely ignorant of the Scriptures, and none the less has right opinions and a true plan of life, he is absolutely blessed and truly possesses in himself the spirit of Christ.

The Jews are of a directly contrary way of thinking, for they hold that true opinions and a true plan of life are of no service in attaining blessedness, if their possessors have arrived at them by the light of reason only, and not like the documents prophetically revealed to Moses. Maimonides ventures openly to make this assertion: "Every man who takes to heart the seven precepts and diligently follows them, is counted with the pious among the nation, and an heir of the world to come; that is to say, if he takes to heart and follows them because God ordained them in the law, and revealed them to us by Moses, because they were of aforetime precepts to the sons of Noah: but he who follows them as led thereto by reason, is not counted as a dweller among the pious or among the wise of the nations." Such are the words Of Maimonides, to which R. Joseph, the son of Shem Job, adds in his book which he calls "Kebod Elohim, or God's Glory," that although Aristotle (whom he considers to have written the best ethics and to be above everyone else) has not omitted anything that concerns true ethics, and which he has adopted in his own book, carefully following the lines laid down, yet this was not able to suffice for his salvation, inasmuch as he embraced his doctrines in accordance with the dictates of reason and not as Divine documents prophetically revealed.

However, that these are mere figments, and are not supported by Scriptural authority will, I think, be sufficiently evident to the attentive reader, so that an examination of the theory will be sufficient for its refutation. It is not my purpose here to refute the assertions of those who assert that the natural light of reason can teach nothing, of any value concerning the true way of salvation. People who lay no claims to reason for themselves, are not able to prove by reason this their assertion; and if they hawk about something superior to reason, it is a mere figment, and far below reason, as their general method of life sufficiently shows. But there is no need to dwell upon such persons. I will merely add that we can only judge of a man by his works. If a man abounds in the fruits of the Spirit, charity, joy, peace, long-suffering, kindness, goodness, faith, gentleness, chastity, against which, as Paul says (Gal. v:22), there is no law, such an one, whether he be taught by reason only or by the Scripture only, has been in very truth taught by God, and is altogether blessed. Thus have I said all that I undertook to say concerning Divine law.

CHAPTER VI

Of Miracles

As men are accustomed to call Divine the knowledge which transcends human understanding, so also do they style Divine, or the work of God, anything of which the cause is not generally known: for the masses think that the power and providence of God are most clearly displayed by events that are extraordinary and contrary to the conception they have formed of nature, especially if such events bring them any profit or convenience: they think that the clearest possible proof of God's existence is afforded when nature, as they suppose, breaks her accustomed order, and consequently they believe that those who explain or endeavour to understand phenomena or miracles through their natural causes are doing away with God and His providence. They suppose, forsooth, that God is inactive so long as nature works in her accustomed order, and vice versa, that the power of nature and natural causes are idle so long as God is acting: thus they imagine two powers distinct one from the other, the power of God and the power of nature, though the latter is in a sense determined by God, or (as most people believe now) created by Him. What they mean by either, and what they understand by God and nature they do not know, except that they imagine the power of God to be like that of some royal potentate, and nature's power to consist in force and energy.

The masses then style unusual phenomena, "miracles," and partly from piety, partly for the sake of opposing the students of science, prefer to remain in ignorance of natural causes, and only to hear of those things which they know least, and consequently admire most. In fact, the common people can only adore God, and refer all things to His power by removing natural causes, and conceiving things happening out of their due course, and only admires the power of God when the power of nature is conceived of as in subjection to it.

This idea seems to have taken its rise among the early Jews who saw the Gentiles round them worshipping visible gods such as the sun, the moon, the earth, water, air, &c., and in order to inspire the conviction that such divinities were weak and inconstant, or changeable, told how they themselves were under the sway of an invisible God, and narrated their miracles, trying further to show that the God whom they worshipped arranged the whole of nature for their sole benefit: this idea was so pleasing to humanity that men go on to this day imagining miracles, so that they may believe themselves God's favourites, and the final cause for which God created and directs all things.

What pretension will not people in their folly advance! They have no single sound idea concerning either God or nature, they confound God's decrees with human decrees, they conceive nature as so limited that they believe man to be its chief part! I have spent enough space in setting forth these common ideas and prejudices concerning nature and miracles, but in order to afford a regular demonstration I will show —

I.   That nature cannot be contravened, but that she preserves a fixed and immutable order, and at the same time I will explain what is meant by a miracle.

II. That God's nature and existence, and consequently His providence cannot be known from miracles, but that they can all be much better perceived from the fixed and immutable order of nature.

III. That by the decrees and volitions, and consequently the providence of God, Scripture (as I will prove by Scriptural examples) means nothing but nature's order following necessarily from her eternal laws.

IV. Lastly, I will treat of the method of interpreting Scriptural miracles, and the chief points to be noted concerning the narratives of them.

Such are the principal subjects which will be discussed in this chapter, and which will serve, I think, not a little to further the object of this treatise.

Our first point is easily proved from what we showed in Chap. IV. about Divine law — namely, that all that God wishes or determines involves eternal necessity, and truth, for we demonstrated that God's understanding is identical with His will, and that it is the same thing to say that God wills a thing, as to say, that He understands it; hence, as it follows necessarily, from the Divine nature and perfection that God understands a thing as it is, it follows no less necessarily that He wills it as it is. Now, as nothing is necessarily true save only by, Divine decree, it is plain that the universal laws of nature are decrees of God following from the necessity and perfection of the Divine nature. Hence, any event happening in nature which contravened nature's universal laws, would necessarily also contravene the Divine decree, nature, and understanding; or if anyone asserted that God acts in contravention to the laws of nature, he, ipso facto, would be compelled to assert that God acted against His own nature — an evident absurdity. One might easily show from the same premises that the power and efficiency, of nature are in themselves the Divine power and efficiency, and that the Divine power is the very essence of God, but this I gladly pass over for the present.

Nothing, then, comes to pass in nature (N.B. I do not mean here by "nature," merely matter and its modifications, but infinite other things besides matter.) in contravention to her universal laws, nay, everything agrees with them and follows from them, for whatsoever comes to pass, comes to pass by the will and eternal decree of God; that is, as we have just pointed out, whatever comes to pass, comes to pass according to laws and rules which involve eternal necessity and truth; nature, therefore, always observes laws and rules which involve eternal necessity, and truth, although they may not all be known to us, and therefore she keeps a fixed and mutable order. Nor is there any sound reason for limiting the power and efficacy of nature, and asserting that her laws are fit for certain purposes, but not for all; for as the efficacy, and power of nature, are the very, efficacy and power of God, and as the laws and rules of nature are the decrees of God, it is in every way to be believed that the power of nature is infinite, and that her laws are broad enough to embrace everything conceived by, the Divine intellect; the only alternative is to assert that God has created nature so weak, and has ordained for her laws so barren, that He is repeatedly compelled to come afresh to her aid if He wishes that she should be preserved, and that things should happen as He desires: a conclusion, in My opinion, very far removed from reason. Further, as nothing happens in nature which does not follow from her laws, and as her laws embrace everything conceived by the Divine intellect, and lastly, as nature preserves a fixed and immutable order; it most clearly follows that miracles are only intelligible as in relation to human opinions, and merely mean events of which the natural cause cannot be explained by a reference to any ordinary occurrence, either by us, or at any rate, by the writer and narrator of the miracle.

We may, in fact, say that a miracle is an event of which the causes annot be explained by the natural reason through a reference to ascertained workings of nature; but since miracles were wrought according to the understanding of the masses, who are wholly ignorant of the workings of nature, it is certain that the ancients took for a miracle whatever they could not explain by the method adopted by the unlearned in such cases, namely, an appeal to the memory, a recalling of something similar, which is ordinarily regarded without wonder; for most people think they sufficiently understand a thing when they have ceased to wonder at it. The ancients, then, and indeed most men up to the present day, had no other criterion for a miracle; hence we cannot doubt that many things are narrated in Scripture as miracles of which the causes could easily be explained by reference to ascertained workings of nature. We have hinted as much in Chap. II., in speaking of the sun standing still in the time of Joshua, and to say on the subject when we come to treat of the interpretation of miracles later on in this chapter.

It is now time to pass on to the second point, and show that we cannot gain an understanding of God's essence, existence, or providence by means of miracles, but that these truths are much better perceived through the fixed and immutable order of nature. I thus proceed with the demonstration. As God's existence is not self-evident it must necessarily be inferred from ideas so firmly and incontrovertibly true, that no power can be postulated or conceived sufficient to impugn them. They ought certainly so to appear to us when we infer from them God's existence, if we wish to place our conclusion beyond the reach of doubt; for if we could conceive that such ideas could be impugned by any power whatsoever, we should doubt of their truth, we should doubt of our conclusion, namely, of God's existence, and should never be able to be certain of anything. Further, we know that nothing either agrees with or is contrary to nature, unless it agrees with or is contrary to these primary ideas; wherefore if we would conceive that anything could be done in nature by any power whatsoever which would be contrary to the laws of nature, it would also be contrary to our primary ideas, and we should have either to reject it as absurd, or else to cast doubt (as just shown) on our primary ideas, and consequently on the existence of God, and on everything howsoever perceived. Therefore miracles, in the sense of events contrary to the laws of nature, so far from demonstrating to us the existence of God, would, on the contrary, lead us to doubt it, where, otherwise, we might have been absolutely certain of it, as knowing that nature follows a fixed and immutable order.

Let us take miracle as meaning that which cannot be explained through natural causes. This may be interpreted in two senses: either as that which has natural causes, but cannot be examined by the human intellect; or as that which has no cause save God and God's will. But as all things which come to pass through natural causes, come to pass also solely through the will and power of God, it comes to this, that a miracle, whether it has natural causes or not, is a result which cannot be explained by its cause, that is a phenomenon which surpasses human understanding; but from such a phenomenon, and certainly from a result surpassing our understanding, we can gain no knowledge. For whatsoever we understand clearly and distinctly should be plain to us either in itself or by means of something else clearly and distinctly understood; wherefore from a miracle or a phenomenon which we cannot understand, we can gain no knowledge of God's essence, or existence, or indeed anything about God or nature; whereas when we know that all things are ordained and ratified by God, that the operations of nature follow from the essence of God, and that the laws of nature are eternal decrees and volitions of God, we must perforce conclude that our knowledge of God, and of God's will increases in proportion to our knowledge and clear understanding of nature, as we see how she depends on her primal cause, and how she works according to eternal law. Wherefore so far as our understanding goes, those phenomena which we clearly and distinctly understand have much better right to be called works of God, and to be referred to the will of God than those about which we are entirely ignorant, although they appeal powerfully to the imagination, and compel men's admiration.

It is only phenomena that we clearly and distinctly understand, which heighten our knowledge of God, and most clearly indicate His will and decrees. Plainly, they are but triflers who, when they cannot explain a thing, run back to the will of God; this is, truly, a ridiculous way of expressing ignorance. Again, even supposing that some conclusion could be drawn from miracles, we could not possibly infer from them the existence of God: for a miracle being an event under limitations is the expression of a fixed and limited power; therefore we could not possibly infer from an effect of this kind the existence of a cause whose power is infinite, but at the utmost only of a cause whose power is greater than that of the said effect. I say at the utmost, for a phenomenon may be the result of many concurrent causes, and its power may be less than the power of the sum of such causes, but far greater than that of any one of them taken individually. On the other hand, the laws of nature, as we have shown, extend over infinity, and are conceived by us as, after a fashion, eternal, and nature works in accordance with them in a fixed and immutable order; therefore, such laws indicate to us in a certain degree the infinity, the eternity, and the immutability of God.

We may conclude, then, that we cannot gain knowledge of the existence and providence of God by means of miracles, but that we can far better infer them from the fixed and immutable order of nature. By miracle, I here mean an event which surpasses, or is thought to surpass, human comprehension: for in so far as it is supposed to destroy or interrupt the order of nature or her laws, it not only can give us no knowledge of God, but, contrariwise, takes away that which we naturally have, and makes us doubt of God and everything else.

Neither do I recognize any difference between an event against the laws of nature and an event beyond the laws of nature (that is, according to some, an event which does not contravene nature, though she is inadequate to produce or effect it) — for a miracle is wrought in, and not beyond nature, though it may be said in itself to be above nature, and, therefore, must necessarily interrupt the order of nature, which otherwise we conceive of as fixed and unchangeable, according to God's decrees. If, therefore, anything should come to pass in nature which does not follow from her laws, it would also be in contravention to the order which God has established in nature for ever through universal natural laws: it would, therefore, be in contravention to God's nature and laws, and, consequently, belief in it would throw doubt upon everything, and lead to Atheism.

I think I have now sufficiently established my second point, so that we can again conclude that a miracle, whether in contravention to, or beyond, nature, is a mere absurdity; and, therefore, that what is meant in Scripture by a miracle can only be a work of nature, which surpasses, or is believed to surpass, human comprehension. Before passing on to my third point, I will adduce Scriptural authority for my assertion that God cannot be known from miracles. Scripture nowhere states the doctrine openly, but it can readily be inferred from several passages. Firstly, that in which Moses commands (Deut. xiii.) that a false prophet should be put to death, even though he work miracles: "If there arise a prophet among you, and giveth thee a sign or wonder, and the sign or wonder come to pass, saying, Let us go after other gods . . . thou shalt not hearken unto the voice of that prophet; for the Lord your God proveth you, and that prophet shall be put to death." From this it clearly follows that miracles could be wrought even by false prophets; and that, unless men are honestly endowed with the true knowledge and love of God, they may be as easily led by miracles to follow false gods as to follow the true God; for these words are added: "For the Lord your God tempts you, that He may know whether you love Him with all your heart and with all your mind."

Further, the Israelites, from all their miracles, were unable to form a sound conception of God, as their experience testified: for when they had persuaded themselves that Moses had departed from among them, they petitioned Aaron to give them visible gods; and the idea of God they had formed as the result of all their miracles was — a calf!

Asaph, though he had heard of so many miracles, yet doubted of the providence of God, and would have turned himself from the true way, if he had not at last come to understand true blessedness. (See Ps. lxxxiii.) Solomon, too, at a time when the Jewish nation was at the height of its prosperity, suspects that all things happen by chance. (See Eccles. iii:19, 20, 21; and chap. ix:2, 3, &c.)

Lastly, nearly all the prophets found it very hard to reconcile the order of nature and human affairs with the conception they had formed of God's providence, whereas philosophers who endeavour to understand things by clear conceptions of them, rather than by miracles, have always found the task extremely easy — at least, such of them as place true happiness solely in virtue and peace of mind, and who aim at obeying nature, rather than being obeyed by her. Such persons rest assured that God directs nature according to the requirements of universal laws, not according to the requirements of the particular laws of human nature, and trial, therefore, God's scheme comprehends, not only the human race, but the whole of nature.

It is plain, then, from Scripture itself, that miracles can give no knowledge of God, nor clearly teach us the providence of God. As to the frequent statements in Scripture, that God wrought miracles to make Himself plain to man — as in Exodus x:2, where He deceived the Egyptians, and gave signs of Himself, that the Israelites might know that He was God — it does not, therefore, follow that miracles really taught this truth, but only that the Jews held opinions which laid them easily open to conviction by miracles. We have shown in Chap. II. that the reasons assigned by the prophets, or those which are formed from revelation, are not assigned in accordance with ideas universal and common to all, but in accordance with the accepted doctrines, however absurd, and with the opinions of those to whom the revelation was given, or those whom the Holy Spirit wished to convince.

This we have illustrated by many Scriptural instances, and can further cite Paul, who to the Greeks was a Greek, and to the Jews a Jew. But although these miracles could convince the Egyptians and Jews from their standpoint, they could not give a true idea and knowledge of God, but only cause them to admit that there was a Deity more powerful than anything known to them, and that this Deity took special care of the Jews, who had just then an unexpectedly happy issue of all their affairs. They could not teach them that God cares equally for all, for this can be taught only by philosophy: the Jews, and all who took their knowledge of God's providence from the dissimilarity of human conditions of life and the inequalities of fortune, persuaded themselves that God loved the Jews above all men, though they did not surpass their fellows in true human perfection.

I now go on to my third point, and show from Scripture that the decrees and mandates of God, and consequently His providence, are merely the order of nature — that is, when Scripture describes an event as accomplished by God or God's will, we must understand merely that it was in accordance with the law and order of nature, not, as most people believe, that nature had for a season ceased to act, or that her order was temporarily interrupted. But Scripture does not directly teach matters unconnected with its doctrine, wherefore it has no care to explain things by their natural causes, nor to expound matters merely speculative. Wherefore our conclusion must be gathered by inference from those Scriptural narratives which happen to be written more at length and circumstantially than usual. Of these I will cite a few.

In the first book of Samuel, ix:15, 16, it is related that God revealed to Samuel that He would send Saul to him, yet God did not send Saul to Samuel as people are wont to send one man to another. His "sending" was merely the ordinary course of nature. Saul was looking for the asses he had lost, and was meditating a return home without them, when, at the suggestion of his servant, he went to the prophet Samuel, to learn from him where he might find them.

From no part of the narrative does it appear that Saul had any command from God to visit Samuel beyond this natural motive.

In Psalm cv. 24 it is said that God changed the hearts of the Egyptians, so that they hated the Israelites. This was evidently a natural change, as appears from Exodus, chap.i., where we find no slight reason for the Egyptians reducing the Israelites to slavery.

In Genesis ix:13, God tells Noah that He will set His bow in the cloud; this action of God's is but another way of expressing the refraction and reflection which the rays of the sun are subjected to in drops of water.

In Psalm cxlvii:18, the natural action and warmth of the wind, by which hoar frost and snow are melted, are styled the word of the Lord, and in verse 15 wind and cold are called the commandment and word of God.

In Psalm civ:4, wind and fire are called the angels and ministers of God, and various other passages of the same sort are found in Scripture, clearly showing that the decree, commandment, fiat, and word of God are merely expressions for the action and order of nature.

Thus it is plain that all the events narrated in Scripture came to pass naturally, and are referred directly to God because Scripture, as we have shown, does not aim at explaining things by their natural causes, but only at narrating what appeals to the popular imagination, and doing so in the manner best calculated to excite wonder, and consequently to impress the minds of the masses with devotion. If, therefore, events are found in the Bible which we cannot refer to their causes, nay, which seem entirely to contradict the order of nature, we must not come to a stand, but assuredly believe that whatever did really happen happened naturally. This view is confirmed by the fact that in the case of every miracle there were many attendant circumstances, though these were not always related, especially where the narrative was of a poetic character.

The circumstances of the miracles clearly show, I maintain, that natural causes were needed. For instance, in order to infect the Egyptians with blains, it was necessary that Moses should scatter ashes in the air (Exod. ix: 10); the locusts also came upon the land of Egypt by a command of God in accordance with nature, namely, by an east wind blowing for a whole day and night; and they departed by a very strong west wind (Exod. x:14, 19). By a similar Divine mandate the sea opened a way for the Jews (Exo. xiv:21), namely, by an east wind which blew very strongly all night.

So, too, when Elisha would revive the boy who was believed to be dead, he was obliged to bend over him several times until the flesh of the child waxed warm, and at last he opened his eyes (2 Kings iv:34, 35).

Again, in John's Gospel (chap. ix.) certain acts are mentioned as performed by Christ preparatory to healing the blind man, and there are numerous other instances showing that something further than the absolute fiat of God is required for working a miracle.

Wherefore we may believe that, although the circumstances attending miracles are not related always or in full detail, yet a miracle was never performed without them.

This is confirmed by Exodus xiv:27, where it is simply stated that "Moses stretched forth his hand, and the waters of the sea returned to their strength in the morning," no mention being made of a wind; but in the song of Moses (Exod. xv:10) we read, "Thou didst blow with Thy wind (i.e. with a very strong wind), and the sea covered them." Thus the attendant circumstance is omitted in the history, and the miracle is thereby enhanced.

But perhaps someone will insist that we find many things in Scripture which seem in nowise explicable by natural causes, as for instance, that the sins of men and their prayers can be the cause of rain and of the earth's fertility, or that faith can heal the blind, and so on. But I think I have already made sufficient answer: I have shown that Scripture does not explain things by their secondary causes, but only narrates them in the order and the style which has most power to move men, and especially uneducated men, to devotion; and therefore it speaks inaccurately of God and of events, seeing that its object is not to convince the reason, but to attract and lay hold of the imagination. If the Bible were to describe the destruction of an empire in the style of political historians, the masses would remain unstirred, whereas the contrary is the case when it adopts the method of poetic description, and refers all things immediately to God. When, therefore, the Bible says that the earth is barren because of men's sins, or that the blind were healed by faith, we ought to take no more notice than when it says that God is angry at men's sins, that He is sad, that He repents of the good He has promised and done; or that on seeing a sign he remembers something He had promised, and other similar expressions, which are either thrown out poetically or related according to the opinion and prejudices of the writer.

We may, then, be absolutely certain that every event which is truly described in Scripture necessarily happened, like everything else, according to natural laws; and if anything is there set down which can be proved in set terms to contravene the order of nature, or not to be deducible therefrom, we must believe it to have been foisted into the sacred writings by irreligious hands; for whatsoever is contrary to nature is also contrary to reason, and whatsoever is contrary to reason is absurd, and, ipso facto, to be rejected.

There remain some points concerning the interpretation of miracles to be noted, or rather to be recapitulated, for most of them have been already stated. These I proceed to discuss in the fourth division of my subject, and I am led to do so lest anyone should, by wrongly interpreting a miracle, rashly suspect that he has found something in Scripture contrary to human reason.

It is very rare for men to relate an event simply as it happened, without adding any element of their own judgment. When they see or hear anything new, they are, unless strictly on their guard, so occupied with their own preconceived opinions that they perceive something quite different from the plain facts seen or heard, especially if such facts surpass the comprehension of the beholder or hearer, and, most of all, if he is interested in their happening in a given way.

Thus men relate in chronicles and histories their own opinions rather than actual events, so that one and the same event is so differently related by two men of different opinions, that it seems like two separate occurrences; and, further, it is very easy from historical chronicles to gather the personal opinions of the historian.

I could cite many instances in proof of this from the writings both of natural philosophers and historians, but I will content myself with one only from Scripture, and leave the reader to judge of the rest.

In the time of Joshua the Hebrews held the ordinary opinion that the sun moves with a daily motion, and that the earth remains at rest; to this preconceived opinion they adapted the miracle which occurred during their battle with the five kings. They did not simply relate that that day was longer than usual, but asserted that the sun and moon stood still, or ceased from their motion — a statement which would be of great service to them at that time in convincing and proving by experience to the Gentiles, who worshipped the sun, that the sun was under the control of another deity who could compel it to change its daily course. Thus, partly through religious motives, partly through preconceived opinions, they conceived of and related the occurrence as something quite different from what really happened.

Thus in order to interpret the Scriptural miracles and understand from the narration of them how they really happened, it is necessary to know the opinions of those who first related them, and have recorded them for us in writing, and to distinguish such opinions from the actual impression made upon their senses, otherwise we shall confound opinions and judgments with the actual miracle as it really occurred: nay, further, we shall confound actual events with symbolical and imaginary ones. For many things are narrated in Scripture as real, and were believed to be real, which were in fact only symbolical and imaginary. As, for instance, that God came down from heaven (Exod. xix:28, Deut. v:28), and that Mount Sinai smoked because God descended upon it surrounded with fire; or, again that Elijah ascended into heaven in a chariot of fire, with horses of fire; all these things were assuredly merely symbols adapted to the opinions of those who have handed them down to us as they were represented to them, namely, as real. All who have any education know that God has no right hand nor left; that He is not moved nor at rest, nor in a particular place, but that He is absolutely infinite and contains in Himself all perfections.

These things, I repeat, are known to whoever judges of things by the perception of pure reason, and not according as his imagination is affected by his outward senses. Following the example of the masses who imagine a bodily Deity, holding a royal court with a throne on the convexity of heaven, above the stars, which are believed to be not very, far off from the earth.

To these and similar opinions very many narrations in Scripture are adapted, and should not, therefore, be mistaken by philosophers for realities.

Lastly, in order to understand, in the case of miracles, what actually took place, we ought to be familiar with Jewish phrases and metaphors; anyone who did not make sufficient allowance for these, would be continually seeing miracles in Scripture where nothing of the kind is intended by the writer; he would thus miss the knowledge not only of what actually happened, but also of the mind of the writers of the sacred text. For instance, Zechariah speaking of some future war says (chap. xiv;7): "It shall be one day which shall be known to the Lord, not day, nor night; but at even time it shall be light." In these words he seems to predict a great miracle, yet he only means that the battle will be doubtful the whole day, that the issue will be known only to God, but that in the evening they will gain the victory: the prophets frequently used to predict victories and defeats of the nations in similar phrases. Thus Isaiah, describing the destruction of Babylon, says (chap. xiii.): "The stars of heaven, and the constellations thereof, shall not give their light; the sun shall be darkened in his going forth, and the moon shall not cause her light to shine." Now I suppose no one imagines that at the destruction of Babylon these phenomena actually occurred any more than that which the prophet adds, "For I will make the heavens to tremble, and remove the earth out of her place."

So, too, Isaiah in foretelling to the Jews that they would return from Babylon to Jerusalem in safety, and would not suffer from thirst on their journey, says: "And they thirsted not when He led them through the deserts; He caused the waters to flow out of the rocks for them; He clave the rocks, and the waters gushed out." These words merely mean that the Jews, like other people, found springs in the desert, at which they quenched their thirst; for when the Jews returned to Jerusalem with the consent of Cyrus, it is admitted that no similar miracles befell them.

In this way many occurrences in the Bible are to be regarded merely as Jewish expressions. There is no need for me to go through them in detail; but I will call attention generally to the fact that the Jews employed such phrases not only rhetorically, but also, and indeed chiefly, from devotional motives. Such is the reason for the substitution of "bless God" for "curse God" in 1 Kings xxi:10, and Job ii:9, and for all things being referred to God, whence it appears that the Bible seems to relate nothing but miracles, even when speaking of the most ordinary occurrences, as in the examples given above.

Hence we must believe that when the Bible says that the Lord hardened Pharaoh's heart, it only means that Pharaoh was obstinate; when it says that God opened the windows of heaven, it only means that it rained very hard, and so on. When we reflect on these peculiarities, and also on the fact that most things are related very shortly, with very little details and almost in abridgments, we shall see that there is hardly anything in Scripture which can be proved contrary to natural reason, while, on the other hand, many things which before seemed obscure, will after a little consideration be understood and easily explained.

I think I have now very clearly explained all that I proposed to explain, but before I finish this chapter I would call attention to the fact that I have adopted a different method in speaking of miracles to that which I employed in treating of prophecy. Of prophecy I have asserted nothing which could not be inferred from promises revealed in Scripture, whereas in this chapter I have deduced my conclusions solely from the principles ascertained by the natural light of reason. I have proceeded in this way advisedly, for prophecy, in that it surpasses human knowledge, is a purely theological question; therefore, I knew that I could not make any assertions about it, nor learn wherein it consists, except through deductions from premises that have been revealed; therefore I was compelled to collate the history of prophecy, and to draw therefrom certain conclusions which would teach me, in so far as such teaching is possible, the nature and properties of the gift. But in the case of miracles, as our inquiry is a question purely philosophical (namely, whether anything can happen which contravenes or does not follow from the laws of nature), I was not under any such necessity: I therefore thought it wiser to unravel the difficulty through premises ascertained and thoroughly known by could also easily have solved the problem merely from the doctrines and fundamental principles of Scripture: in order that everyone may acknowledge this, I will briefly show how it could be done.

Scripture makes the general assertion in several passages that nature's course is fixed and unchangeable. In Ps. cxlviii:6, for instance, and Jer. xxxi:35. The wise man also, in Eccles. i:10, distinctly teaches that "there is nothing new under the sun," and in verses 11, 12, illustrating the same idea, he adds that although something occasionally happens which seems new, it is not really new, but "hath been already of old time, which was before us, whereof there is no remembrance, neither shall there be any remembrance of things that are to come with those that come after." Again in chap. iii:11, he says, "God hath made everything beautiful in his time," and immediately afterwards adds, "I know that whatsoever God doeth, it shall be for ever; nothing can be put to it, nor anything taken from it."

Now all these texts teach most distinctly that nature preserves a fixed and unchangeable order, and that God in all ages, known and unknown, has been the same; further, that the laws of nature are so perfect, that nothing can be added thereto nor taken therefrom; and, lastly, that miracles only appear as something new because of man's ignorance.

Such is the express teaching of Scripture: nowhere does Scripture assert that anything happens which contradicts, or cannot follow from the laws of nature; and, therefore, we should not attribute to it such a doctrine.

To these considerations we must add, that miracles require causes and attendant circumstances, and that they follow, not from some mysterious royal power which the masses attribute to God, but from the Divine rule and decree, that is (as we have shown from Scripture itself) from the laws and order of nature; lastly, that miracles can be wrought even by false prophets, as is proved from Deut. xiii. and Matt. xxiv:24.

The conclusion, then, that is most plainly put before us is, that miracles were natural occurrences, and must therefore be so explained as to appear neither new (in the words of Solomon) nor contrary to nature, but, as far as possible, in complete agreement with ordinary events. This can easily be done by anyone, now that I have set forth the rules drawn from Scripture. Nevertheless, though I maintain that Scripture teaches this doctrine, I do not assert that it teaches it as a truth necessary to salvation, but only that the prophets were in agreement with ourselves on the point; therefore everyone is free to think on the subject as he likes, according as he thinks it best for himself, and most likely to conduce to the worship of God and to singlehearted religion.

This is also the opinion of Josephus, for at the conclusion of the second book of his "Antiquities," he writes: Let no man think this story incredible of the sea's dividing to save these people, for we find it in ancient records that this hath been seen before, whether by God's extraordinary will or by the course of nature it is indifferent. The same thing happened one time to the Macedonians, under the command of Alexander, when for want of another passage the Pamphylian Sea divided to make them way; God's Providence making use of Alexander at that time as His instrument for destroying the Persian Empire. This is attested by all the historians who have pretended to write the Life of that Prince. But people are at liberty to think what they please."

Such are the words of Josephus, and such is his opinion on faith in miracles.

CHAPTER VII

Of the Interpretation of Scripture

When people declare, as all are ready, to do, that the Bible is the Word of God teaching man true blessedness and the way of salvation, they evidently do not mean what they, say; for the masses take no pains at all to live according to Scripture, and we see most people endeavouring to hawk about their own commentaries as the word of God, and giving their best efforts, under the guise of religion, to compelling others to think as they do: we generally see, I say, theologians anxious to learn how to wring their inventions and sayings out of the sacred text, and to fortify, them with Divine authority. Such persons never display, less scruple or more zeal than when they, are interpreting Scripture or the mind of the Holy Ghost; if we ever see them perturbed, it is not that they fear to attribute some error to the Holy Spirit, and to stray from the right path, but that they are afraid to be convicted of error by, others, and thus to overthrow and bring into contempt their own authority. But if men really believed what they verbally testify of Scripture, they would adopt quite a different plan of life: their minds would not be agitated by so many contentions, nor so many hatreds, and they would cease to be excited by such a blind and rash passion for interpreting the sacred writings, and excogitating novelties in religion. On the contrary, they would not dare to adopt, as the teaching of Scripture, anything which they could not plainly deduce therefrom: lastly, those sacrilegious persons who have dared, in several passages, to interpolate the Bible, would have shrunk from so great a crime, and would have stayed their sacrilegious hands.

Ambition and unscrupulousness have waxed so powerful, that religion is thought to consist, not so much in respecting the writings of the Holy Ghost, as in defending human commentaries, so that religion is no longer identified with charity, but with spreading discord and propagating insensate hatred disguised under the name of zeal for the Lord, and eager ardour.

To these evils we must add superstition, which teaches men to despise reason and nature, and only to admire and venerate that which is repugnant to both: whence it is not wonderful that for the sake of increasing the admiration and veneration felt for Scripture, men strive to explain it so as to make it appear to contradict, as far as possible, both one and the other: thus they dream that most profound mysteries lie hid in the Bible, and weary themselves out in the investigation of these absurdities, to the neglect of what is useful. Every result of their diseased imagination they attribute to the Holy Ghost, and strive to defend with the utmost zeal and passion; for it is an observed fact that men employ their reason to defend conclusions arrived at by reason, but conclusions arrived at by the passions are defended by the passions.

If we would separate ourselves from the crowd and escape from theological prejudices, instead of rashly accepting human commentaries for Divine documents, we must consider the true method of interpreting Scripture and dwell upon it at some length: for if we remain in ignorance of this we cannot know, certainly, what the Bible and the Holy Spirit wish to teach.

I may sum up the matter by saying that the method of interpreting Scripture does not widely differ from the method of interpreting nature — in fact, it is almost the same. For as the interpretation of nature consists in the examination of the history of nature, and therefrom deducing definitions of natural phenomena on certain fixed axioms, so Scriptural interpretation proceeds by the examination of Scripture, and inferring the intention of its authors as a legitimate conclusion from its fundamental principles. By working in this manner everyone will always advance without danger of error — that is, if they admit no principles for interpreting Scripture, and discussing its contents save such as they find in Scripture itself — and will be able with equal security to discuss what surpasses our understanding, and what is known by the natural light of reason.

In order to make clear that such a method is not only correct, but is also the only one advisable, and that it agrees with that employed in interpreting nature, I must remark that Scripture very often treats of matters which cannot be deduced from principles known to reason: for it is chiefly made up of narratives and revelation: the narratives generally contain miracles — that is, as we have shown in the last chapter, relations of extraordinary natural occurrences adapted to the opinions and judgment of the historians who recorded them: the revelations also were adapted to the opinions of the prophets, as we showed in Chap. II., and in themselves surpassed human comprehension. Therefore the knowledge of all these — that is, of nearly the whole contents of Scripture, must be sought from Scripture alone, even as the knowledge of nature is sought from nature. As for the moral doctrines which are also contained in the Bible, they may be demonstrated from received axioms, but we cannot prove in the same manner that Scripture intended to teach them, this can only be learned from Scripture itself.

If we would bear unprejudiced witness to the Divine origin of Scripture, we must prove solely on its own authority that it teaches true moral doctrines, for by such means alone can its Divine origin be demonstrated: we have shown that the certitude of the prophets depended chiefly on their having minds turned towards what is just and good, therefore we ought to have proof of their possessing this quality before we repose faith in them. From miracles God's divinity cannot be proved, as I have already shown, and need not now repeat, for miracles could be wrought by false prophets. Wherefore the Divine origin of Scripture must consist solely in its teaching true virtue. But we must come to our conclusion simply on Scriptural grounds, for if we were unable to do so we could not, unless strongly prejudiced accept the Bible and bear witness to its Divine origin.

Our knowledge of Scripture must then be looked for in Scripture only.

Lastly, Scripture does not give us definition of things any more than nature does: therefore, such definitions must be sought in the latter case from the diverse workings of nature: in the former case, from the various narratives about the given subject which occur in the Bible.

The universal rule, then, in interpreting Scripture is to accept nothing as an authoritative Scriptural statement which we do not perceive very clearly when we examine it in the light of its history. What I mean by its history, and what should be the chief points elucidated, I will now explain.

The history of a Scriptural statement comprises —

I. The nature and properties of the language in which the books of the Bible were written, and in which their authors were, accustomed to speak. We shall thus be able to investigate every expression by comparison with common conversational usages.

Now all the writers both of the Old Testament and the New were Hebrews: therefore, a knowledge of the Hebrew language is before all things necessary, not only for the comprehension of the Old Testament, which was written in that tongue, but also of the New: for although the latter was published in other languages, yet its characteristics are Hebrew.

II. An analysis of each book and arrangement of its contents under heads; so that we may have at hand the various texts which treat of a given subject. Lastly, a note of all the passages which are ambiguous or obscure, or which seem mutually contradictory.

I call passages clear or obscure according as their meaning is inferred easily or with difficulty in relation to the context, not according as their truth is perceived easily or the reverse by reason. We are at work not on the truth of passages, but solely on their meaning. We must take especial care, when we are in search of the meaning of a text, not to be led away by our reason in so far as it is founded on principles of natural knowledge (to say nothing of prejudices): in order not to confound the meaning of a passage with its truth, we must examine it solely by means of the signification of the words, or by a reason acknowledging no foundation but Scripture.

I will illustrate my meaning by an example. The words of Moses, "God is a fire" and "God is jealous," are perfectly clear so long as we regard merely the signification of the words, and I therefore reckon them among the clear passages, though in relation to reason and truth they are most obscure: still, although the literal meaning is repugnant to the natural light of reason, nevertheless, if it cannot be clearly overruled on grounds and principles derived from its Scriptural "history," it, that is, the literal meaning, must be the one retained: and contrariwise if these passages literally interpreted are found to clash with principles derived from Scripture, though such literal interpretation were in absolute harmony with reason, they must be interpreted in a different manner, i.e. metaphorically.

If we would know whether Moses believed God to be a fire or not, we must on no account decide the question on grounds of the reasonableness or the reverse of such an opinion, but must judge solely by the other opinions of Moses which are on record.

In the present instance, as Moses says in several other passages that God has no likeness to any visible thing, whether in heaven or in earth, or in the water, either all such passages must be taken metaphorically, or else the one before us must be so explained. However, as we should depart as little as possible from the literal sense, we must first ask whether this text, God is a fire, admits of any but the literal meaning — that is, whether the word fire ever means anything besides ordinary natural fire. If no such second meaning can be found, the text must be taken literally, however repugnant to reason it may be: and all the other passages, though in complete accordance with reason, must be brought into harmony with it. If the verbal expressions would not admit of being thus harmonized, we should have to set them down as irreconcilable, and suspend our judgment concerning them. However, as we find the name fire applied to anger and jealousy (see Job xxxi:12) we can thus easily reconcile the words of Moses, and legitimately conclude that the two propositions God is a fire, and God is jealous, are in meaning identical.

Further, as Moses clearly teaches that God is jealous, and nowhere states that God is without passions or emotions, we must evidently infer that Moses held this doctrine himself, or at any rate, that he wished to teach it, nor must we refrain because such a belief seems contrary to reason: for as we have shown, we cannot wrest the meaning of texts to suit the dictates of our reason, or our preconceived opinions. The whole knowledge of the Bible must be sought solely from itself.

III. Lastly, such a history should relate the environment of all the prophetic books extant; that is, the life, the conduct, and the studies of the author of each book, who he was, what was the occasion, and the epoch of his writing, whom did he write for, and in what language. Further, it should inquire into the fate of each book: how it was first received, into whose hands it fell, how many different versions there were of it, by whose advice was it received into the Bible, and, lastly, how all the books now universally accepted as sacred, were united into a single whole.

All such information should, as I have said, be contained in the "history" of Scripture. For, in order to know what statements are set forth as laws, and what as moral precepts, it is important to be acquainted with the life, the conduct, and the pursuits of their author: moreover, it becomes easier to explain a man's writings in proportion as we have more intimate knowledge of his genius and temperament.

Further, that we may not confound precepts which are eternal with those which served only a temporary purpose, or were only meant for a few, we should know what was the occasion, the time, the age, in which each book was written, and to what nation it was addressed.Lastly, we should have knowledge on the other points I have mentioned, in order to be sure, in addition to the authenticity of the work, that it has not been tampered with by sacrilegious hands, or whether errors can have crept in, and, if so, whether they have been corrected by men sufficiently skilled and worthy of credence. All these things should be known, that we may not be led away by blind impulse to accept whatever is thrust on our notice, instead of only that which is sure and indisputable.

Now when we are in possession of this history of Scripture, and have finally decided that we assert nothing as prophetic doctrine which does not directly follow from such history, or which is not clearly deducible from it, then, I say, it will be time to gird ourselves for the task of investigating the mind of the prophets and of the Holy Spirit. But in this further arguing, also, we shall require a method very like that employed in interpreting nature from her history. As in the examination of natural phenomena we try first to investigate what is most universal and common to all nature — such, for instance, as motion and rest, and their laws and rules, which nature always observes, and through which she continually works — and then we proceed to what is less universal; so, too, in the history of Scripture, we seek first for that which is most universal, and serves for the basis and foundation of all Scripture, a doctrine, in fact, that is commended by all the prophets as eternal and most profitable to all men. For example, that God is one, and that He is omnipotent, that He alone should be worshipped, that He has a care for all men, and that He especially loves those who adore Him and love their neighbour as themselves, &c. These and similar doctrines, I repeat, Scripture everywhere so clearly and expressly teaches, that no one was ever in doubt of its meaning concerning them.

The nature of God, His manner of regarding and providing for things, and similar doctrines, Scripture nowhere teaches professedly, and as eternal doctrine; on the contrary, we have shown that the prophets themselves did not agree on the subject; therefore, we must not lay down any doctrine as Scriptural on such subjects, though it may appear perfectly clear on rational grounds.

From a proper knowledge of this universal doctrine of Scripture, we must then proceed to other doctrines less universal, but which, nevertheless, have regard to the general conduct of life, and flow from the universal doctrine like rivulets from a source; such are all particular external manifestations of true virtue, which need a given occasion for their exercise; whatever is obscure or ambiguous on such points in Scripture must be explained and defined by its universal doctrine; with regard to contradictory instances, we must observe the occasion and the time in which they were written. For instance, when Christ says, "Blessed are they that mourn, for they shall be comforted" we do not know, from the actual passage, what sort of mourners are meant; as, however, Christ afterwards teaches that we should have care for nothing, save only for the kingdom of God and His righteousness, which is commended as the highest good (see Matt. vi;33), it follows that by mourners He only meant those who mourn for the kingdom of God and righteousness neglected by man: for this would be the only cause of mourning to those who love nothing but the Divine kingdom and justice, and who evidently despise the gifts of fortune. So, too, when Christ says: "But if a man strike you on the right cheek, turn to him the left also," and the words which follow.

If He had given such a command, as a lawgiver, to judges, He would thereby have abrogated the law of Moses, but this He expressly says He did not do (Matt. v:17). Wherefore we must consider who was the speaker, what was the occasion, and to whom were the words addressed. Now Christ said that He did not ordain laws as a legislator, but inculcated precepts as a teacher: inasmuch as He did not aim at correcting outward actions so much as the frame of mind. Further, these words were spoken to men who were oppressed, who lived in a corrupt commonwealth on the brink of ruin, where justice was utterly neglected. The very doctrine inculcated here by Christ just before the destruction of the city was also taught by Jeremiah before the first destruction of Jerusalem, that is, in similar circumstances, as we see from Lamentations iii:25-30.

Now as such teaching was only set forth by the prophets in times of oppression, and was even then never laid down as a law; and as, on the other hand, Moses (who did not write in times of oppression, but — mark this — strove to found a well-ordered commonwealth), while condemning envy and hatred of one's neighbour, yet ordained that an eye should be given for an eye, it follows most clearly from these purely Scriptural grounds that this precept of Christ and Jeremiah concerning submission to injuries was only valid in places where justice is neglected, and in a time of oppression, but does not hold good in a well-ordered state.

In a well-ordered state where justice is administered every one is bound, if he would be accounted just, to demand penalties before the judge (see Lev:1), not for the sake of vengeance (Lev. xix:17, 18), but in order to defend justice and his country's laws, and to prevent the wicked rejoicing in their wickedness. All this is plainly in accordance with reason. I might cite many other examples in the same manner, but I think the foregoing are sufficient to explain my meaning and the utility of this method, and this is all my present purpose. Hitherto we have only shown how to investigate those passages of Scripture which treat of practical conduct, and which, therefore, are more easily examined, for on such subjects there was never really any controversy among the writers of the Bible.

The purely speculative passages cannot be so easily, traced to their real meaning: the way becomes narrower, for as the prophets differed in matters speculative among themselves, and the narratives are in great measure adapted to the prejudices of each age, we must not, on any, account infer the intention of one prophet from clearer passages in the writings of another; nor must we so explain his meaning, unless it is perfectly plain that the two prophets were at one in the matter.

How we are to arrive at the intention of the prophets in such cases I will briefly explain. Here, too, we must begin from the most universal proposition, inquiring first from the most clear Scriptural statements what is the nature of prophecy or revelation, and wherein does it consist; then we must proceed to miracles, and so on to whatever is most general till we come to the opinions of a particular prophet, and, at last, to the meaning of a particular revelation, prophecy, history, or miracle. We have already pointed out that great caution is necessary not to confound the mind of a prophet or historian with the mind of the Holy Spirit and the truth of the matter; therefore I need not dwell further on the subject. I would, however, here remark concerning the meaning of revelation, that the present method only teaches us what the prophets really saw or heard, not what they desired to signify or represent by symbols. The latter may be guessed at but cannot be inferred with certainty from Scriptural premises.

We have thus shown the plan for interpreting Scripture, and have, at the same time, demonstrated that it is the one and surest way of investigating its true meaning. I am willing indeed to admit that those persons (if any such there be) would be more absolutely certainly right, who have received either a trustworthy tradition or an assurance from the prophets themselves, such as is claimed by the Pharisees; or who have a pontiff gifted with infallibility in the interpretation of Scripture, such as the Roman Catholics boast. But as we can never be perfectly sure, either of such a tradition or of the authority of the pontiff, we cannot found any certain conclusion on either: the one is denied by the oldest sect of Christians, the other by the oldest sect of Jews. Indeed, if we consider the series of years (to mention no other point) accepted by the Pharisees from their Rabbis, during which time they say they have handed down the tradition from Moses, we shall find that it is not correct, as I show elsewhere. Therefore such a tradition should be received with extreme suspicion; and although, according to our method, we are bound to consider as uncorrupted the tradition of the Jews, namely, the meaning of the Hebrew words which we received from them, we may accept the latter while retaining our doubts about the former.

No one has ever been able to change the meaning of a word in ordinary use, though many have changed the meaning of a particular sentence. Such a proceeding would be most difficult; for whoever attempted to change the meaning of a word, would be compelled, at the same time, to explain all the authors who employed it, each according to his temperament and intention, or else, with consummate cunning, to falsify them.

Further, the masses and the learned alike preserve language, but it is only the learned who preserve the meaning of particular sentences and books: thus, we may easily imagine that the learned having a very rare book in their power, might change or corrupt the meaning of a sentence in it, but they could not alter the signification of the words; moreover, if anyone wanted to change the meaning of a common word he would not be able to keep up the change among posterity, or in common parlance or writing.

For these and such-like reasons we may readily conclude that it would never enter into the mind of anyone to corrupt a language, though the intention of a writer may often have been falsified by changing his phrases or interpreting them amiss. As then our method (based on the principle that the knowledge of Scripture must be sought from itself alone) is the sole true one, we must evidently renounce any knowledge which it cannot furnish for the complete understanding of Scripture. I will now point out its difficulties and shortcomings, which prevent our gaining a complete and assured knowledge of the Sacred Text.

Its first great difficulty consists in its requiring a thorough knowledge of the Hebrew language. Where is such knowledge to be obtained? The men of old who employed the Hebrew tongue have left none of the principles and bases of their language to posterity; we have from them absolutely nothing in the way of dictionary, grammar, or rhetoric.

Now the Hebrew nation has lost all its grace and beauty (as one would expect after the defeats and persecutions it has gone through), and has only retained certain fragments of its language and of a few books. Nearly all the names of fruits, birds, and fishes, and many other words have perished in the wear and tear of time. Further, the meaning of many nouns and verbs which occur in the Bible are either utterly lost, or are subjects of dispute. And not only are these gone, but we are lacking in a knowledge of Hebrew phraseology. The devouring tooth of time has destroyed turns of expression peculiar to the Hebrews, so that we know them no more.

Therefore we cannot investigate as we would all the meanings of a sentence by the uses of the language; and there are many phrases of which the meaning is most obscure or altogether inexplicable, though the component words are perfectly plain.

To this impossibility of tracing the history of the Hebrew language must be added its particular nature and composition: these give rise to so many ambiguities that it is impossible to find a method which would enable us to gain a certain knowledge of all the statements in Scripture[7]. In addition to the sources of ambiguities common to all languages, there are many peculiar to Hebrew. These, I think, it worth while to mention.

Firstly, an ambiguity often arises in the Bible from our mistaking one letter for another similar one. The Hebrews divide the letters of the alphabet into five classes, according to the five organs of the month employed in pronouncing them, namely, the lips, the tongue, the teeth, the palate, and the throat. For instance, Alpha, Ghet, Hgain, He, are called gutturals, and are barely distinguishable, by any sign that we know, one from the other. El, which signifies to, is often taken for hgal, which signifies above, and vice versa. Hence sentences are often rendered rather ambiguous or meaningless.

A second difficulty arises from the multiplied meaning of conjunctions and adverbs. For instance, vau serves promiscuously for a particle of union or of separation, meaning, and, but, because, however, then: ki, has seven or eight meanings, namely, wherefore, although, if, when, inasmuch as, because, a burning, &c., and so on with almost all particles.

The third very fertile source of doubt is the fact that Hebrew verbs in the indicative mood lack the present, the past imperfect, the pluperfect, the future perfect, and other tenses most frequently employed in other languages; in the imperative and infinitive moods they are wanting in all except the present, and a

---

[7] "It is impossible to find a method which would enable us to gain a certain knowledge of all the statements in Scripture." I mean impossible for us who have not the habitual use of the language, and have lost the precise meaning of its phraseology.

subjunctive mood does not exist. Now, although all these defects in moods and tenses may be supplied by certain fundamental rules of the language with ease and even elegance, the ancient writers evidently neglected such rules altogether, and employed indifferently future for present and past, and vice versa past for future, and also indicative for imperative and subjunctive, with the result of considerable confusion.

Besides these sources of ambiguity there are two others, one very important. Firstly, there are in Hebrew no vowels; secondly, the sentences are not separated by any marks elucidating the meaning or separating the clauses. Though the want of these two has generally been supplied by points and accents, such substitutes cannot be accepted by us, inasmuch as they were invented and designed by men of an after age whose authority should carry no weight. The ancients wrote without points (that is, without vowels and accents), as is abundantly testified; their descendants added what was lacking, according to their own ideas of Scriptural interpretation; wherefore the existing accents and points are simply current interpretations, and are no more authoritative than any other commentaries.

Those who are ignorant of this fact cannot justify the author of the Epistle to the Hebrews for interpreting (chap. xi;21) Genesis (xlvii:31) very differently from the version given in our Hebrew text as at present pointed, as though the Apostle had been obliged to learn the meaning of Scripture from those who added the points. In my opinion the latter are clearly wrong. In order that everyone may judge for himself, and also see how the discrepancy arose simply from the want of vowels, I will give both interpretations. Those who pointed our version read, "And Israel bent himself over, or (changing Hqain into Aleph, a similar letter) towards, the head of the bed." The author of the Epistle reads, "And Israel bent himself over the head of his staff," substituting mate for mita, from which it only differs in respect of vowels. Now as in this narrative it is Jacob's age only that is in question, and not his illness, which is not touched on till the next chapter, it seems more likely that the historian intended to say that Jacob bent over the head of his staff (a thing commonly used by men of advanced age for their support) than that he bowed himself at the head of his bed, especially as for the former reading no substitution of letters is required. In this example I have desired not only to reconcile the passage in the Epistle with the passage in Genesis, but also and chiefly to illustrate how little trust should be placed in the points and accents which are found in our present Bible, and so to prove that he who would be without bias in interpreting Scripture should hesitate about accepting them, and inquire afresh for himself. Such being the nature and structure of the Hebrew language, one may easily understand that many difficulties are likely to arise, and that no possible method could solve all of them. It is useless to hope for a way out of our difficulties in the comparison of various parallel passages (we have shown that the only method of discovering the true sense of a passage out of many alternative ones is to see what are the usages of the language), for this comparison of parallel passages can only accidentally throw light on a difficult point, seeing that the prophets never wrote with the express object of explaining their own phrases or those of other people, and also because we cannot infer the meaning of one prophet or apostle by the meaning of another, unless on a purely practical question, not when the matter is speculative, or if a miracle, or history is being narrated. I might illustrate my point with instances, for there are many inexplicable phrases in Scripture, but I would rather pass on to consider the difficulties and imperfections of the method under discussion.

A further difficulty attends the method, from the fact that it requires the history of all that has happened to every book in the Bible; such a history we are often quite unable to furnish. Of the authors, or (if the expression be preferred), the writers of many of the books, we are either in complete ignorance, or at any rate in doubt, as I will point out at length. Further, we do not know either the occasions or the epochs when these books of unknown authorship were written; we cannot say into what hands they fell, nor how the numerous varying versions originated; nor, lastly, whether there were not other versions, now lost. I have briefly shown that such knowledge is necessary, but I passed over certain considerations which I will now draw attention to.

If we read a book which contains incredible or impossible narratives, or is written in a very obscure style, and if we know nothing of its author, nor of the time or occasion of its being written, we shall vainly endeavour to gain any certain knowledge of its true meaning. For being in ignorance on these points we cannot possibly know the aim or intended aim of the author; if we are fully informed, we so order our thoughts as not to be in any way prejudiced either in ascribing to the author or him for whom the author wrote either more or less than his meaning, and we only take into consideration what the author may have had in his mind, or what the time and occasion demanded. I think this must be tolerably evident to all.

It often happens that in different books we read histories in themselves similar, but which we judge very differently, according to the opinions we have formed of the authors. I remember once to have read in some book that a man named Orlando Furioso used to drive a kind of winged monster through the air, fly over any countries he liked, kill unaided vast numbers of men and giants, and such like fancies, which from the point of view of reason are obviously absurd. A very similar story I read in Ovid of Perseus, and also in the books of Judges and Kings of Samson, who alone and unarmed killed thousands of men, and of Elijah, who flew through the air, said at last went up to heaven in a chariot of fire, with horses of fire. All these stories are obviously alike, but we judge them very differently. The first only sought to amuse, the second had a political object, the third a religious object.We gather this simply from the opinions we had previously formed of the authors. Thus it is evidently necessary to know something of the authors of writings which are obscure or unintelligible, if we would interpret their meaning; and for the same reason, in order to choose the proper reading from among a great variety, we ought to have information as to the versions in which the differences are found, and as to the possibility of other readings having been discovered by persons of greater authority.

A further difficulty attends this method in the case of some of the books of Scripture, namely, that they are no longer extant in their original language. The Gospel according to Matthew, and certainly the Epistle to the Hebrews, were written, it is thought, in Hebrew, though they no longer exist in that form. Aben Ezra affirms in his commentaries that the book of Job was translated into Hebrew out of another language, and that its obscurity arises from this fact. I say nothing of the apocryphal books, for their authority stands on very inferior ground.

The foregoing difficulties in this method of interpreting Scripture from its own history, I conceive to be so great that I do not hesitate to say that the true meaning of Scripture is in many places inexplicable, or at best mere subject for guesswork; but I must again point out, on the other hand, that such difficulties only arise when we endeavour to follow the meaning of a prophet in matters which cannot be perceived, but only imagined, not in things, whereof the understanding can give a clear idea, and which are conceivable through themselves:,[8], matters which by their nature are easily perceived cannot be expressed so obscurely as to be unintelligible; as the proverb says, "a word is enough to the wise." Euclid, who only wrote of matters very simple and easily understood, can easily be comprehended by anyone in any language; we can follow his intention perfectly, and be certain of his true meaning, without having a thorough knowledge of the language in which he wrote; in fact, a quite rudimentary acquaintance is sufficient. We need make no researches concerning

---

[8] "Not in things whereof the understanding can gain a clear and distinct idea, and which are conceivable through themselves." By things conceivable I mean not only those which are rigidly proved, but also those whereof we are morally certain, and are wont to hear without wonder, though they are incapable of proof. Everyone can see the truth of Euclid's propositions before they are proved. So also the histories of things both future and past which do not surpass human credence, laws, institutions, manners, I call conceivable and clear, though they cannot be proved mathematically. But hieroglyphics and histories which seem to pass the bounds of belief I call inconceivable; yet even among these last there are many which our method enables us to investigate, and to discover the meaning of their narrator.

the life, the pursuits, or the habits of the author; nor need we inquire in what language, nor when he wrote, nor the vicissitudes of his book, nor its various readings, nor how, nor by whose advice it has been received.

What we here say of Euclid might equally be said of any book which treats of things by their nature perceptible: thus we conclude that we can easily follow the intention of Scripture in moral questions, from the history we possess of it, and we can be sure of its true meaning.

The precepts of true piety are expressed in very ordinary language, and are equally simple and easily understood. Further, as true salvation and blessedness consist in a true assent of the soul — and we truly assent only to what we clearly understand — it is most plain that we can follow with certainty the intention of Scripture in matters relating to salvation and necessary to blessedness; therefore, we need not be much troubled about what remains: such matters, inasmuch as we generally cannot grasp them with our reason and understanding, are more curious than profitable.

I think I have now set forth the true method of Scriptural interpretation, and have sufficiently explained my own opinion thereon. Besides, I do not doubt that everyone will see that such a method only requires the aid of natural reason. The nature and efficacy of the natural reason consists in deducing and proving the unknown from the known, or in carrying premises to their legitimate conclusions; and these are the very processes which our method desiderates. Though we must admit that it does not suffice to explain everything in the Bible, such imperfection does not spring from its own nature, but from the fact that the path which it teaches us, as the true one, has never been tended or trodden by men, and has thus, by the lapse of time, become very difficult, and almost impassable, as, indeed, I have shown in the difficulties I draw attention to.

There only remains to examine the opinions of those who differ from me. The first which comes under our notice is, that the light of nature has no power to interpret Scripture, but that a supernatural faculty is required for the task. What is meant by this supernatural faculty I will leave to its propounders to explain. Personally, I can only suppose that they have adopted a very obscure way of stating their complete uncertainty about the true meaning of Scripture. If we look at their interpretations, they contain nothing supernatural, at least nothing but the merest conjectures.

Let them be placed side by side with the interpretations of those who frankly confess that they have no faculty beyond their natural ones; we shall see that the two are just alike — both human, both long pondered over, both laboriously invented. To say that the natural reason is insufficient for such results is plainly untrue, firstly, for the reasons above stated, namely, that the difficulty of interpreting Scripture arises from no defect in human reason, but simply from the carelessness (not to say malice) of men who neglected the history of the Bible while there were still materials for inquiry; secondly, from the fact (admitted, I think, by all) that the supernatural faculty is a Divine gift granted only to the faithful. But the prophets and apostles did not preach to the faithful only, but chiefly to the unfaithful and wicked. Such persons, therefore, were able to understand the intention of the prophets and apostles, otherwise the prophets and apostles would have seemed to be preaching to little boys and infants, not to men endowed with reason. Moses, too, would have given his laws in vain, if they could only be comprehended by the faithful, who need no law. Indeed, those who demand supernatural faculties for comprehending the meaning of the prophets and apostles seem truly lacking in natural faculties, so that we should hardly suppose such persons the possessors of a Divine supernatural gift.

The opinion of Maimonides was widely different. He asserted that each passage in Scripture admits of various, nay, contrary, meanings; but that we could never be certain of any particular one till we knew that the passage, as we interpreted it, contained nothing contrary or repugnant to reason. If the literal meaning clashes with reason, though the passage seems in itself perfectly clear, it must be interpreted in some metaphorical sense. This doctrine he lays down very plainly in chap. xxv. part ii. of his book, "More Nebuchim," for he says: "Know that we shrink not from affirming that the world hath existed from eternity, because of what Scripture saith concerning the world's creation. For the texts which teach that the world was created are not more in number than those which teach that God hath a body; neither are the approaches in this matter of the world's creation closed, or even made hard to us: so that we should not be able to explain what is written, as we did when we showed that God hath no body, nay, peradventure, we could explain and make fast the doctrine of the world's eternity more easily than we did away with the doctrines that God hath a beatified body. Yet two things hinder me from doing as I have said, and believing that the world is eternal. As it hath been clearly shown that God hath not a body, we must perforce explain all those passages whereof the literal sense agreeth not with the demonstration, for sure it is that they can be so explained. But the eternity of the world hath not been so demonstrated, therefore it is not necessary to do violence to Scripture in support of some common opinion, whereof we might, at the bidding of reason, embrace the contrary."

Such are the words of Maimonides, and they are evidently sufficient to establish our point: for if he had been convinced by reason that the world is eternal, he would not have hesitated to twist and explain away the words of Scripture till he made them appear to teach this doctrine. He would have felt quite sure that Scripture, though everywhere plainly denying the eternity of the world, really intends to teach it. So that, however clear the meaning of Scripture may be, he would not feel certain of having grasped it, so long as he remained doubtful of the truth of what, was written. For we are in doubt whether a thing is in conformity with reason, or contrary thereto, so long as we are uncertain of its truth, and, consequently, we cannot be sure whether the literal meaning of a passage be true or false.

If such a theory as this were sound, I would certainly grant that some faculty beyond the natural reason is required for interpreting Scripture. For nearly all things that we find in Scripture cannot be inferred from known principles of the natural reason, and, therefore, we should be unable to come to any conclusion about their truth, or about the real meaning and intention of Scripture, but should stand in need of some further assistance.

Further, the truth of this theory would involve that the masses, having generally no comprehension of, nor leisure for, detailed proofs, would be reduced to receiving all their knowledge of Scripture on the authority and testimony of philosophers, and, consequently, would be compelled to suppose that the interpretations given by philosophers were infallible.

Truly this would be a new form of ecclesiastical authority, and a new sort of priests or pontiffs, more likely to excite men's ridicule than their veneration. Certainly our method demands a knowledge of Hebrew for which the masses have no leisure; but no such objection as the foregoing can be brought against us. For the ordinary Jews or Gentiles, to whom the prophets and apostles preached and wrote, understood the language, and, consequently, the intention of the prophet or apostle addressing them; but they did not grasp the intrinsic reason of what was preached, which, according to Maimonides, would be necessary for an understanding of it.

There is nothing, then, in our method which renders it necessary that the masses should follow the testimony of commentators, for I point to a set of unlearned people who understood the language of the prophets and apostles; whereas Maimonides could not point to any such who could arrive at the prophetic or apostolic meaning through their knowledge of the causes of things.

As to the multitude of our own time, we have shown that whatsoever is necessary to salvation, though its reasons may be unknown, can easily be understood in any language: because it is thoroughly ordinary and usual; it is in such understanding as this that the masses acquiesce, not in the testimony of commentators; with regard to other questions, the ignorant and the learned fare alike.

But let us return to the opinion of Maimonides, and examine it more closely. In the first place, he supposes that the prophets were in entire agreement one with another, and that they were consummate philosophers and theologians;

for he would have them to have based their conclusions on the absolute truth. Further, he supposes that the sense of Scripture cannot be made plain from Scripture itself, for the truth of things is not made plain therein (in that it does not prove any thing, nor teach the matters of which it speaks through their definitions and first causes), therefore, according to Maimonides, the true sense of Scripture cannot be made plain from itself, and must not be there sought.

The falsity of such a doctrine is shown in this very chapter, for we have shown both by reason and examples that the meaning of Scripture is only made plain through Scripture itself, and even in questions deducible from ordinary knowledge should be looked for from no other source.

Lastly, such a theory supposes that we may explain the words of Scripture according to our preconceived opinions, twisting them about, and reversing or completely changing the literal sense, however plain it may be. Such licence is utterly opposed to the teaching of this and the preceding chapters, and, moreover, will be evident to everyone as rash and excessive.

But if we grant all this licence, what can it effect after all? Absolutely nothing. Those things which cannot be demonstrated, and which make up the greater part of Scripture, cannot be examined by reason, and cannot therefore be explained or interpreted by this rule; whereas, on the contrary, by following our own method, we can explain many questions of this nature, and discuss them on a sure basis, as we have already shown, by reason and example. Those matters which are by their nature comprehensible we can easily explain, as has been pointed out, simply by means of the context.

Therefore, the method of Maimonides is clearly useless: to which we may add, that it does away with all the certainty which the masses acquire by candid reading, or which is gained by any other persons in any other way. In conclusion, then, we dismiss Maimonides' theory as harmful, useless, and absurd.

As to the tradition of the Pharisees, we have already shown that it is not consistent, while the authority of the popes of Rome stands in need of more credible evidence; the latter, indeed, I reject simply on this ground, for if the popes could point out to us the meaning of Scripture as surely as did the high priests of the Jews, I should not be deterred by the fact that there have been heretic and impious Roman pontiffs; for among the Hebrew high-priests of old there were also heretics and impious men who gained the high — priesthood by improper means, but who, nevertheless, had Scriptural sanction for their supreme power of interpreting the law. (See Deut. xvii:11, 12, and xxxiii:10, also Malachi ii:8.)

However, as the popes can show no such sanction, their authority remains open to very grave doubt, nor should anyone be deceived by the example of the Jewish high-priests and think that the Catholic religion also stands in need of a pontiff; he should bear in mind that the laws of Moses being also the ordinary laws of the country, necessarily required some public authority to insure their observance; for, if everyone were free to interpret the laws of his country as he pleased, no state could stand, but would for that very reason be dissolved at once, and public rights would become private rights.

With religion the case is widely different. Inasmuch as it consists not so much in outward actions as in simplicity and truth of character, it stands outside the sphere of law and public authority. Simplicity and truth of character are not produced by the constraint of laws, nor by the authority of the state, no one the whole world over can be forced or legislated into a state of blessedness; the means required for such a consummation are faithful and brotherly admonition, sound education, and, above all, free use of the individual judgment.

Therefore, as the supreme right of free thinking, even on religion, is in every man's power, and as it is inconceivable that such power could be alienated, it is also in every man's power to wield the supreme right and authority of free judgment in this behalf, and to explain and interpret religion for himself.

The only reason for vesting the supreme authority in the interpretation of law, and judgment on public affairs in the hands of the magistrates, is that it concerns questions of public right. Similarly the supreme authority in explaining religion, and in passing judgment thereon, is lodged with the individual because it concerns questions of individual right. So far, then, from the authority of the Hebrew high-priests telling in confirmation of the authority of the Roman pontiffs to interpret religion, it would rather tend to establish individual freedom of judgment.

Thus in this way also, we have shown that our method of interpreting Scripture is the best. For as the highest power of Scriptural interpretation belongs to every man, the rule for such interpretation should be nothing but the natural light of reason which is common to all — not any supernatural light nor any external authority; moreover, such a rule ought not to be so difficult that it can only be applied by very skilful philosophers, but should be adapted to the natural and ordinary faculties and capacity of mankind. And such I have shown our method to be, for such difficulties as it has arise from men's carelessness, and are no part of its nature.

CHAPTER VIII

Of the authorship of the Pentateuch and the other historical books of the Old Testament

In the former chapter we treated of the foundations and principles of Scriptural knowledge, and showed that it consists solely in a trustworthy history of the sacred writings; such a history, in spite of its indispensability, the ancients neglected, or at any rate, whatever they may have written or handed down has perished in the lapse of time, consequently the groundwork for such an investigation is to a great extent, cut from under us. This might be put up with if succeeding generations had confined themselves within the limits of truth, and had handed down conscientiously what few particulars they had received or discovered without any additions from their own brains: as it is, the history of the Bible is not so much imperfect as untrustworthy: the foundations are not only too scanty for building upon, but are also unsound. It is part of my purpose to remedy these defects, and to remove common theological prejudices. But I fear that I am attempting my task too late, for men have arrived at the pitch of not suffering contradiction, but defending obstinately whatever they have adopted under the name of religion. So widely have these prejudices taken possession of men's minds, that very few, comparatively speaking, will listen to reason. However, I will make the attempt, and spare no efforts, for there is no positive reason for despairing of success.

In order to treat the subject methodically, I will begin with the received opinions concerning the true authors of the sacred books, and in the first place, speak of the author of the Pentateuch, who is almost universally supposed to have been Moses. The Pharisees are so firmly convinced of his identity, that they account as a heretic anyone who differs from them on the subject. Wherefore, Aben Ezra, a man of enlightened intelligence, and no small learning, who was the first, so far as I know, to treat of this opinion, dared not express his meaning openly, but confined himself to dark hints which I shall not scruple to elucidate, thus throwing, full light on the subject.

The words of Aben Ezra which occur in his commentary on Deuteronomy are as follows: "Beyond Jordan, &c . . . If so be that thou understandest the mystery of the twelve . . . moreover Moses wrote the law . . . The Canaanite was then in the land . . . . it shall be revealed on the mount of God . . . . then also behold his bed, his iron bed, then shalt thou know the truth." In these few words he hints, and also shows that it was not Moses who wrote the Pentateuch, but someone who lived long after him, and further, that the book which Moses wrote was something different from any now extant.

To prove this, I say, he draws attention to the facts:

I. That the preface to Deuteronomy could not have been written by Moses, inasmuch as he ad never crossed the Jordan.

II. That the whole book of Moses was written at full length on the circumference of a single altar (Deut. xxvii, and Josh. viii:37), which altar, according to the Rabbis, consisted of only twelve stones: therefore the book of Moses must have been of far less extent than the Pentateuch. This is what our author means, I think, by the mystery of the twelve, unless he is referring to the twelve curses contained in the chapter of Deuteronomy above cited, which he thought could not have been contained in the law, because Moses bade the Levites read them after the recital of the law, and so bind the people to its observance. Or again, he may have had in his mind the last chapter of Deuteronomy which treats of the death of Moses, and which contains twelve verses. But there is no need to dwell further on these and similar conjectures.

III. That in Deut. xxxi:9, the expression occurs, "and Moses wrote the law:" words that cannot be ascribed to Moses, but must be those of some other writer narrating the deeds and writings of Moses.

IV. That in Genesis xii:6, the historian, after narrating that Abraham journeyed through the and of Canaan, adds, "and the Canaanite was then in the land," thus clearly excluding the time at which he wrote. So that this passage must have been written after the death of Moses, when the Canaanites had been driven out, and no longer possessed the land.

Aben Ezra, in his commentary on the passage, alludes to the difficulty as follows:— "And the Canaanite was then in the land: it appears that Canaan, the grandson of Noah, took from another the land which bears his name; if this be not the true meaning, there lurks some mystery in the passage, and let him who understands it keep silence." That is, if Canaan invaded those regions, the sense will be, the Canaanite was then in the land, in contradistinction to the time when it had been held by another: but if, as follows from Gen. chap. x. Canaan was the first to inhabit the land, the text must mean to exclude the time present, that is the time at which it was written; therefore it cannot be the work of Moses, in whose time the Canaanites still possessed those territories: this is the mystery concerning which silence is recommended.

V. That in Genesis xxii:14 Mount Moriah is called the mount of God,[9] , a name which it did not acquire till after the building of the Temple; the choice of the mountain was not made in the time of Moses, for Moses does not point out any spot as chosen by God; on the contrary, he foretells that God will at some future time choose a spot to which this name will be given.

VI. Lastly, that in Deut. chap. iii., in the passage relating to Og, king of Bashan, these words are inserted: "For only Og king of Bashan remained of the remnant of giants: behold, his bedstead was a bedstead of iron: is it not in Rabbath of the children of Ammon? nine cubits was the length thereof, and four cubits the breadth of it, after the cubit of a man." This parenthesis most plainly shows that its writer lived long after Moses; for this mode of speaking is only employed by one treating of things long past, and pointing to relics for the sake of gaining credence: moreover, this bed was almost certainly first discovered by David, who conquered the city of Rabbath (2 Sam. xii:30.) Again, the historian a little further on inserts after the words of Moses, "Jair, the son of Manasseh, took all the country of Argob unto the coasts of Geshuri and Maachathi; and called them after his own name, Bashan-havoth-jair, unto this day." This passage, I say, is inserted to explain the words of Moses which precede it. "And the rest of Gilead, and all Bashan, being the kingdom of Og, gave I unto the half tribe of Manasseh; all the region of Argob, with all Bashan, which is called the land of the giants." The Hebrews in the time of the writer indisputably knew what territories belonged to the tribe of Judah, but did not know them under the name of the jurisdiction of Argob, or the land of the giants. Therefore the writer is compelled to explain what these places were which were anciently so styled, and at the same time to point out why they were at the time of his writing known by the name of Jair, who was of the tribe of Manasseh, not of Judah. We have thus made clear the meaning of Aben Ezra and also the passages of the Pentateuch which he cites in proof of his contention. However, Aben Ezra does not call attention to every instance, or even the chief ones; there remain many of greater importance, which may be cited. Namely (I.), that the writer of the books in question not only speaks of Moses in the third person, but also bears witness to many details concerning him; for instance, "Moses talked with God;" "The Lord spoke with Moses face to face; " "Moses was the meekest of men" (Numb. xii:3); "Moses was wrath with the captains of the host; "Moses, the man

---

[9] "Mount Moriah is called the mount of God." That is by the historian, not by Abraham, for he says that the place now called "In the mount of the Lord it shall be revealed," was called by Abraham, "the Lord shall provide."

of God, "Moses, the servant of the Lord, died;" "There was never a prophet in Israel like unto Moses," &c. On the other hand, in Deuteronomy, where the law which Moses had expounded to the people and written is set forth, Moses speaks and declares what he has done in the first person: "God spake with me" (Deut. ii:1, 17, &c.), "I prayed to the Lord," &c. Except at the end of the book, when the historian, after relating the words of Moses, begins again to speak in the third person, and to tell how Moses handed over the law which he had expounded to the people in writing, again admonishing them, and further, how Moses ended his life. All these details, the manner of narration, the testimony, and the context of the whole story lead to the plain conclusion that these books were written by another, and not by Moses in person.

III. We must also remark that the history relates not only the manner of Moses' death and burial, and the thirty days' mourning of the Hebrews, but further compares him with all the prophets who came after him, and states that he surpassed them all. "There was never a prophet in Israel like unto Moses, whom the Lord knew face to face." Such testimony cannot have been given of Moses by, himself, nor by any who immediately succeeded him, but it must come from someone who lived centuries afterwards, especially, as the historian speaks of past times. "There was never a prophet," &c. And of the place of burial, "No one knows it to this day."

III. We must note that some places are not styled by the names they bore during Moses' lifetime, but by others which they obtained subsequently. For instance, Abraham is said to have pursued his enemies even unto Dan, a name not bestowed on the city till long after the death of Joshua (Gen. xiv;14, Judges xviii;29).

IV. The narrative is prolonged after the death of Moses, for in Exodus xvi:34 we read that "the children of Israel did eat manna forty years until they came to a land inhabited, until they came unto the borders of the land of Canaan." In other words, until the time alluded to in Joshua vi:12.

So, too, in Genesis xxxvi:31 it is stated, "These are the kings that reigned in Edom before there reigned any king over the children of Israel." The historian, doubtless, here relates the kings of Idumaea before that territory was conquered by David[10] and garrisoned, as we read in 2 Sam. viii:14. From what has been

---

[10] "Before that territory [Idumoea] was conquered by David." From this time to the reign of Jehoram when they again separated from the Jewish kingdom (2 Kings viii:20), the Idumaeans had no king, princes appointed by the Jews supplied the place of kings (1 Kings xxii:48), in fact the prince of Idumaea is called a king (2 Kings iii:9).

It may be doubted whether the last of the Idumaean kings had begun to reign before the accession of Saul, or whether Scripture in this chapter of Genesis wished to enumerate only such kings as were independent. It is evidently mere trifling to wish to enrol among Hebrew kings the name of Moses, who set up a dominion entirely different from a monarchy.

said, it is thus clearer than the sun at noonday that the Pentateuch was not written by Moses, but by someone who lived long after Moses. Let us now turn our attention to the books which Moses actually did write, and which are cited in the Pentateuch; thus, also, shall we see that they were different from the Pentateuch. Firstly, it appears from Exodus xvii:14 that Moses, by the command of God, wrote an account of the war against Amalek. The book in which he did so is not named in the chapter just quoted, but in Numb. xxi:12 a book is referred to under the title of the wars of God, and doubtless this war against Amalek and the castrametations said in Numb. xxxiii:2 to have been written by Moses are therein described. We hear also in Exod. xxiv:4 of another book called the Book of the Covenant, which Moses read before the Israelites when they first made a covenant with God. But this book or this writing contained very little, namely, the laws or commandments of God which we find in Exodus xx:22 to the end of chap. xxiv., and this no one will deny who reads the aforesaid chapter rationally and impartially. It is there stated that as soon as Moses had learnt the feeling of the people on the subject of making a covenant with God, he immediately wrote down God's laws and utterances, and in the morning, after some ceremonies had been performed, read out the conditions of the covenant to an assembly of the whole people. When these had been gone through, and doubtless understood by all, the whole people gave their assent.

Now from the shortness of the time taken in its perusal and also from its nature as a compact, this document evidently contained nothing more than that which we have just described. Further, it is clear that Moses explained all the laws which he had received in the fortieth year after the exodus from Egypt; also that he bound over the people a second time to observe them, and that finally he committed them to writing (Deut. i:5; xxix:14; xxxi:9), in a book which contained these laws explained, and the new covenant, and this book was therefore called the book of the law of God: the same which was afterwards added to by Joshua when he set forth the fresh covenant with which he bound over the people and which he entered into with God (Josh. xxiv:25, 26).

Now, as we have extent no book containing this covenant of Moses and also the covenant of Joshua, we must perforce conclude that it has perished, unless, indeed, we adopt the wild conjecture of the Chaldean paraphrast Jonathan, and twist about the words of Scripture to our heart's content. This commentator, in the face of our present difficulty, preferred corrupting the sacred text to confessing his own ignorance. The passage in the book of Joshua which runs, "and Joshua wrote these words in the book of the law of God," he changes into "and Joshua wrote these words and kept them with the book of the law of God." What is to be done with persons who will only see what pleases them? What is such a proceeding if it is not denying Scripture, and inventing another Bible out of our own heads? We may therefore conclude that the book of the law of God which Moses wrote was not the Pentateuch, but something quite different, which the author of the Pentateuch duly inserted into his book. So much is abundantly plain both from what I have said and from what I am about to add. For in the passage of Deuteronomy above quoted, where it is related that Moses wrote the book of the law, the historian adds that he handed it over to the priests and bade them read it out at a stated time to the whole people. This shows that the work was of much less length than the Pentateuch, inasmuch as it could be read through at one sitting so as to be understood by all; further, we must not omit to notice that out of all the books which Moses wrote, this one book of the second covenant and the song (which latter he wrote afterwards so that all the people might learn it), was the only one which he caused to be religiously guarded and preserved. In the first covenant he had only bound over those who were present, but in the second covenant he bound over all their descendants also (Dent. xxix:14), and therefore ordered this covenant with future ages to be religiously preserved, together with the Song, which was especially addressed to posterity: as, then, we have no proof that Moses wrote any book save this of the covenant, and as he committed no other to the care of posterity; and, lastly, as there are many passages in the Pentateuch which Moses could not have written, it follows that the belief that Moses was the author of the Pentateuch is ungrounded and even irrational. Someone will perhaps ask whether Moses did not also write down other laws when they were first revealed to him — in other words, whether, during the course of forty years, he did not write down any of the laws which he promulgated, save only those few which I have stated to be contained in the book of the first covenant. To this I would answer, that although it seems reasonable to suppose that Moses wrote down the laws at the time when he wished to communicate them to the people, yet we are not warranted to take it as proved, for I have shown above that we must make no assertions in such matters which we do not gather from Scripture, or which do not flow as legitimate consequences from its fundamental principles. We must not accept whatever is reasonably probable. However even reason in this case would not force such a conclusion upon us: for it may be that the assembly of elders wrote down the decrees of Moses and communicated them to the people, and the historian collected them, and duly set them forth in his narrative of the life of Moses. So much for the five books of Moses: it is now time for us to turn to the other sacred writings.

The book of Joshua may be proved not to be an autograph by reasons similar to those we have just employed: for it must be some other than Joshua who testifies that the fame of Joshua was spread over the whole world; that he omitted nothing of what Moses had taught (Josh. vi:27; viii. last verse; xi:15);

that he grew old and summoned an assembly of the whole people, and finally that he departed this life. Furthermore, events are related which took place after Joshua's death. For instance, that the Israelites worshipped God, after his death, so long as there were any old men alive who remembered him; and in chap. xvi:10, we read that "Ephraim and Manasseh did not drive out the Canaanites which dwelt in Gezer, but the Canaanite dwelt in the land of Ephraim unto this day, and was tributary to him." This is the same statement as that in Judges, chap. i., and the phrase "unto this day" shows that the writer was speaking of ancient times. With these texts we may compare the last verse of chap. xv., concerning the sons of Judah, and also the history of Caleb in the same chap. v:14. Further, the building of an altar beyond Jordan by the two tribes and a half, chap. xxii:10, sqq., seems to have taken place after the death of Joshua, for in the whole narrative his name is never mentioned, but the people alone held council as to waging war, sent out legates, waited for their return, and finally approved of their answer.

Lastly, from chap. x:14, it is clear that the book was written many generations after the death of Joshua, for it bears witness, there was never any, day like unto, that day, either before or after, that the Lord hearkened to the voice of a man," &c. If, therefore, Joshua wrote any book at all, it was that which is quoted in the work now before us, chap. x:13.

With regard to the book of Judges, I suppose no rational person persuades himself that it was written by the actual Judges. For the conclusion of the whole history contained in chap. ii. clearly shows that it is all the work — of a single historian. Further, inasmuch as the writer frequently tells us that there was then no king in Israel, it is evident that the book was written after the establishment of the monarchy.

The books of Samuel need not detain us long, inasmuch as the narrative in them is continued long after Samuel's death; but I should like to draw attention to the fact that it was written many generations after Samuel's death. For in book i. chap. ix:9, the historian remarks in a, parenthesis, "Beforetime, in Israel, when a man went to inquire of God, thus he spake: Come, and let us go to the seer; for he that is now called a prophet was beforetime called a seer."

Lastly, the books of Kings, as we gather from internal evidence, were compiled from the books of King Solomon (I Kings xi:41), from the chronicles of the kings of Judah (1 Kings xiv:19, 29), and the chronicles of the kings of Israel.

We may, therefore, conclude that all the books we have considered hitherto are compilations, and that the events therein are recorded as having happened in old time. Now, if we turn our attention to the connection and argument of all these books, we shall easily see that they were all written by a single historian, who wished to relate the antiquities of the Jews from their first beginning down to the first destruction of the city. The way in which the several books are connected one with the other is alone enough to show us that they form the narrative of one and the same writer. For as soon as he has related the life of Moses, the historian thus passes on to the story of Joshua: "And it came to pass after that Moses the servant of the Lord was dead, that God spake unto Joshua," &c., so in the same way, after the death of Joshua was concluded, he passes with identically the same transition and connection to the history of the Judges: "And it came to pass after that Joshua was dead, that the children of Israel sought from God," &c. To the book of Judges he adds the story of Ruth, as a sort of appendix, in these words: "Now it came to pass in the days that the judges ruled, that there was a famine in the land."

The first book of Samuel is introduced with a similar phrase; and so is the second book of Samuel. Then, before the history of David is concluded, the historian passes in the same way to the first book of Kings, and, after David's death, to the Second book of Kings.

The putting together, and the order of the narratives, show that they are all the work of one man, writing with a create aim; for the historian begins with relating the first origin of the Hebrew nation, and then sets forth in order the times and the occasions in which Moses put forth his laws, and made his predictions. He then proceeds to relate how the Israelites invaded the promised land in accordance with Moses' prophecy (Deut. vii.); and how, when the land was subdued, they turned their backs on their laws, and thereby incurred many misfortunes (Deut. xxxi:16, 17). He tells how they wished to elect rulers, and how, according as these rulers observed the law, the people flourished or suffered (Deut. xxviii:36); finally, how destruction came upon the nation, even as Moses had foretold. In regard to other matters, which do not serve to confirm the law, the writer either passes over them in silence, or refers the reader to other books for information. All that is set down in the books we have conduces to the sole object of setting forth the words and laws of Moses, and proving them by subsequent events. When we put together these three considerations, namely, the unity of the subject of all the books, the connection between them, and the fact that they are compilations made many generations after the events they relate had taken place, we come to the conclusion, as I have just stated, that they are all the work of a single historian. Who this historian was, it is not so easy to show; but I suspect that he was Ezra, and there are several strong reasons for adopting this hypothesis.

The historian whom we already know to be but one individual brings his history down to the liberation of Jehoiakim, and adds that he himself sat at the king's table all his life — that is, at the table either of Jehoiakim, or of the son of Nebuchadnezzar, for the sense of the passage is ambiguous: hence it follows that he did not live before the time of Ezra. But Scripture does not testify of any except of Ezra (Ezra vii:10), that he "prepared his heart to seek the law of the Lord, and to set it forth, and further that he was a ready scribe in the law of Moses." Therefore, I can not find anyone, save Ezra, to whom to attribute the sacred books.

Further, from this testimony concerning Ezra, we see that he prepared his heart, not only to seek the law of the Lord, but also to set it forth; and, in Nehemiah viii:8, we read that "they read in the book of the law of God distinctly, and gave the sense, and caused them to understand the reading."

As, then, in Deuteronomy, we find not only the book of the law of Moses, or the greater part of it, but also many things inserted for its better explanation, I conjecture that this Deuteronomy is the book of the law of God, written, set forth, and explained by Ezra, which is referred to in the text above quoted. Two examples of the way matters were inserted parenthetically in the text of Deuteronomy, with a view to its fuller explanation, we have already given, in speaking of Aben Ezra's opinion. Many others are found in the course of the work: for instance, in chap. ii:12: "The Horims dwelt also in Seir beforetime; but the children of Esau succeeded them, when they had destroyed them from before them, and dwelt in their stead; as Israel did unto the land of his possession, which the Lord gave unto them." This explains verses 3 and 4 of the same chapter, where it is stated that Mount Seir, which had come to the children of Esau for a possession, did not fall into their hands uninhabited; but that they invaded it, and turned out and destroyed the Horims, who formerly dwelt therein, even as the children of Israel had done unto the Canaanites after the death of Moses.

So, also, verses 6, 7, 8, 9, of the tenth chapter are inserted parenthetically among the words of Moses. Everyone must see that verse 8, which begins, "At that time the Lord separated the tribe of Levi," necessarily refers to verse 5, and not to the death of Aaron, which is only mentioned here by Ezra because Moses, in telling of the golden calf worshipped by the people, stated that he had prayed for Aaron.

He then explains that at the time at which Moses spoke, God had chosen for Himself the tribe of Levi in order that He may point out the reason for their election, and for the fact of their not sharing in the inheritance; after this digression, he resumes the thread of Moses' speech. To these parentheses we must add the preface to the book, and all the passages in which Moses is spoken of in the third person, besides many which we cannot now distinguish, though, doubtless, they would have been plainly recognized by the writer's contemporaries.

If, I say, we were in possession of the book of the law as Moses wrote it, I do not doubt that we should find a great difference in the words of the precepts, the order in which they are given, and the reasons by which they are supported.

A comparison of the decalogue in Deuteronomy with the decalogue in Exodus, where its history is explicitly set forth, will be sufficient to show us a wide discrepancy in all these three particulars, for the fourth commandment is given not only in a different form, but at much greater length, while the reason for its observance differs wholly from that stated in Exodus. Again, the order in which the tenth commandment is explained differs in the two versions. I think that the differences here as elsewhere are the work of Ezra, who explained the law of God to his contemporaries, and who wrote this book of the law of God, before anything else; this I gather from the fact that it contains the laws of the country, of which the people stood in most need, and also because it is not joined to the book which precedes it by any connecting phrase, but begins with the independent statement, "these are the words of Moses." After this task was completed, I think Ezra set himself to give a complete account of the history of the Hebrew nation from the creation of the world to the entire destruction of the city, and in this account he inserted the book of Deuteronomy, and, possibly, he called the first five books by the name of Moses, because his life is chiefly contained therein, and forms their principal subject; for the same reason he called the sixth Joshua, the seventh Judges, the eighth Ruth, the ninth, and perhaps the tenth, Samuel, and, lastly, the eleventh and twelfth Kings. Whether Ezra put the finishing touches to this work and finished it as he intended, we will discuss in the next chapter.

CHAPTER IX

Other questions concerning the same Books: namely, whether they were completely finished by Ezra, and, further, whether the Marginal notes which are found in the Hebrew texts were various readings

How greatly the inquiry we have just made concerning the real writer of the twelve books aids us in attaining a complete understanding of them, may be easily gathered solely from the passages which we have adduced in confirmation of our opinion, and which would be most obscure without it. But besides the question of the writer, there are other points to notice which common superstition forbids the multitude to apprehend. Of these the chief is, that Ezra (whom I will take to be the author of the aforesaid books until some more likely person be suggested) did not put the finishing touches to the narrative contained therein, but merely collected the histories from various writers, and sometimes simply set them down, leaving their examination and arrangement to posterity.

The cause (if it were not untimely death) which prevented him from completing his work in all its portions, I cannot conjecture, but the fact remains most clear, although we have lost the writings of the ancient Hebrew historians, and can only judge from the few fragments which are still extant. For the history of Hezekiah (2 Kings xviii:17), as written in the vision of Isaiah, is related as it is found in the chronicles of the kings of Judah. We read the same story, told with few exceptions,[11], in the same words, in the book of Isaiah which was contained in the chronicles of the kings of Judah (2 Chron. xxxii:32). From this we must conclude that there were various versions of this narrative of Isaiah's, unless,

---

[11] "With few exceptions." One of these exceptions is found in 2 Kings xviii:20, where we read, "Thou sayest (but they are but vain words)," the second person being used. In Isaiah xxxvi:5, we read "I say (but they are but vain words) I have counsel and strength for war," and in the twenty-second verse of the chapter in Kings it is written, "But if ye say," the plural number being used, whereas Isaiah gives the singular. The text in Isaiah does not contain the words found in 2 Kings xxxii:32. Thus there are several cases of various readings where it is impossible to distinguish the best.

indeed, anyone would dream that in this, too, there lurks a mystery. Further, the last chapter of 2 Kings 27-30 is repeated in the last chapter of Jeremiah, v.31-34.

Again, we find 2 Sam. vii. repeated in I Chron. xvii., but the expressions in the two passages are so curiously varied[12], that we can very easily see that these two chapters were taken from two different versions of the history of Nathan.

Lastly, the genealogy of the kings of Idumaea contained in Genesis xxxvi:31, is repeated in the same words in 1 Chron. i., though we know that the author of the latter work took his materials from other historians, not from the twelve books we have ascribed to Ezra. We may therefore be sure that if we still possessed the writings of the historians, the matter would be made clear; however, as we have lost them, we can only examine the writings still extant, and from their order and connection, their various repetitions, and, lastly, the contradictions in dates which they contain, judge of the rest.

These, then, or the chief of them, we will now go through. First, in the story of Judah and Tamar (Gen. xxxviii.) the historian thus begins: "And it came to pass at that time that Judah went down from his brethren." This time cannot refer to what immediately precedes[13], but must necessarily refer to something else, for from the time when Joseph was sold into Egypt to the time when the patriarch Jacob, with all his family, set out thither, cannot be reckoned as more than twenty-two years, for Joseph, when he was sold by his brethren, was seventeen years old, and when he was summoned by Pharaoh from prison was thirty; if to this we add the seven years of plenty and two of famine, the total amounts to twenty-two years. Now, in so short a period, no one can suppose that so many things happened as are described; that Judah had three children, one after the other, from one wife, whom he married at the beginning of the period; that the eldest of these, when he was old enough, married Tamar, and that after he died his next brother succeeded to her; that, after all this, Judah,

---

[12] "The expressions in the two passages are so varied." For instance we read in 2 Sam. vii:6, "But I have walked in a tent and in a tabernacle." Whereas in 1 Chron. xvii:5, "but have gone from tent to tent and from one tabernacle to another." In 2 Sam. vii:10, we read, "to afflict them," whereas in 1 Chron. vii:9, we find a different expression. I could point out other differences still greater, but a single reading of the chapters in question will suffice to make them manifest to all who are neither blind nor devoid of sense.

[13] "This time cannot refer to what immediately precedes." It is plain from the context that this passage must allude to the time when Joseph was sold by his brethren. But this is not all. We may draw the same conclusion from the age of Judah, who was than twenty-two years old at most, taking as basis of calculation his own history just narrated. It follows, indeed, from the last verse of Gen. xxx., that Judah was born in the tenth of the years of Jacob's servitude to Laban, and Joseph in the fourteenth. Now, as we know that Joseph was seventeen years old when sold by his brethren, Judah was then not more than twenty-one. Hence, those writers who assert that Judah's long absence from his father's house took place before Joseph was sold, only seek to delude themselves and to call in question the Scriptural authority which they are anxious to protect.

without knowing it, had intercourse with his daughter-inlaw, and that she bore him twins, and, finally, that the eldest of these twins became a father within the aforesaid period. As all these events cannot have taken place within the period mentioned in Genesis, the reference must necessarily be to something treated of in another book: and Ezra in this instance simply related the story, and inserted it without examination among his other writings.

However, not only this chapter but the whole narrative of Joseph and Jacob is collected and set forth from various histories, inasmuch as it is quite inconsistent with itself. For in Gen. xlvii. we are told that Jacob, when he came at Joseph's bidding to salute Pharaoh, was 130 years old. If from this we deduct the twenty-two years which he passed sorrowing for the absence of Joseph and the seventeen years forming Joseph's age when he was sold, and, lastly, the seven years for which Jacob served for Rachel, we find that he was very advanced in life, namely, eighty four, when he took Leah to wife, whereas Dinah was scarcely seven years old when she was violated by Shechem,[14]. Simeon and Levi were aged respectively eleven and twelve when they spoiled the city and slew all the males therein with the sword.

There is no need that I should go through the whole Pentateuch. If anyone pays attention to the way in which all the histories and precepts in these five books are set down promiscuously and without order, with no regard for dates; and further, how the same story is often repeated, sometimes in a different version, he will easily, I say, discern that all the materials were promiscuously collected and heaped together, in order that they might at some subsequent time be more readily examined and reduced to order. Not only these five books,

---

[14] "Dinah was scarcely seven years old when she was violated by Schechem." The opinion held by some that Jacob wandered about eight or ten years between Mesopotamia and Bethel, savours of the ridiculous; if respect for Aben Ezra, allows me to say so. For it is clear that Jacob had two reasons for haste: first, the desire to see his old parents; secondly, and chiefly to perform, the vow made when he fled from his brother (Gen. xxviii:10 and xxxi:13, and xxxv:1). We read (Gen. xxxi:3), that God had commanded him to fulfill his vow, and promised him help for returning to his country. If these considerations seem conjectures rather than reasons, I will waive the point and admit that Jacob, more unfortunate than Ulysses, spent eight or ten years or even longer, in this short journey. At any rate it cannot be denied that Benjamin was born in the last year of this wandering, that is by the reckoning of the objectors, when Joseph was sixteen or seventeen years old, for Jacob left Laban seven years after Joseph's birth. Now from the seventeenth year of Joseph's age till the patriarch went into Egypt, not more than twenty-two years elapsed, as we have shown in this chapter. Consequently Benjamin, at the time of the journey to Egypt, was twenty-three or twenty-four at the most. He would therefore have been a grandfather in the flower of his age (Gen. xlvi:21, cf. Numb. xxvi:38, 40, and 1 Chron. viii;1), for it is certain that Bela, Benjamin's eldest son, had at that time, two sons, Addai and Naa-man. This is just as absurd as the statement that Dinah was violated at the age of seven, not to mention other impossibilities which would result from the truth of the narrative. Thus we see that unskillful endeavours to solve difficulties, only raise fresh ones, and make confusion worse confounded.

but also the narratives contained in the remaining seven, going down to the destruction of the city, are compiled in the same way. For who does not see that in Judges ii:6 a new historian is being quoted, who had also written of the deeds of Joshua, and that his words are simply copied? For after our historian has stated in the last chapter of the book of Joshua that Joshua died and was buried, and has promised, in the first chapter of Judges, to relate what happened after his death, in what way, if he wished to continue the thread of his history, could he connect the statement here made about Joshua with what had gone before?

So, too, 1 Sam. 17, 18, are taken from another historian, who assigns a cause for David's first frequenting Saul's court very different from that given in chap. xvi. of the same book. For he did not think that David came to Saul in consequence of the advice of Saul's servants, as is narrated in chap. xvi., but that being sent by chance to the camp by his father on a message to his brothers, he was for the first time remarked by Saul on the occasion of his victory, over Goliath the Philistine, and was retained at his court.

I suspect the same thing has taken place in chap. xxvi. of the same book, for the historian there seems to repeat the narrative given in chap. xxiv. according to another man's version. But I pass over this, and go on to the computation of dates.

In I Kings, chap. vi., it is said that Solomon built the Temple in the four hundred and eightieth year after the exodus from Egypt; but from the historians themselves we get a much longer period, for:

	Years
Moses governed the people in the desert	40
Joshua, who lived 110 years, did not, according to Josephus and others' opinion rule more than	26
Cusban Rishathaim held the people in subjection	8
Othniel, son of Kenag, was judge for	[15]40

---

[15] "Othniel, son of Kenag, was judge for forty years." Rabbi Levi Ben Gerson and others believe that these forty years which the Bible says were passed in freedom, should be counted from the death of Joshua, and consequently include the eight years during which the people were subject to Kushan Rishathaim, while the following eighteen years must be added on to the eighty years of Ehud's and Shamgar's judgeships. In this case it would be necessary to reckon the other years of subjection among those said by the Bible to have been passed in freedom. But the Bible expressly notes the number of years of subjection, and the number of years of freedom, and further declares (Judges ii:18) that the Hebrew state was prosperous during the whole time of the judges. Therefore it is evident that Levi Ben Gerson (certainly a very learned man), and those who follow him, correct rather than interpret the Scriptures.

The same fault is committed by those who assert, that Scripture, by this general calculation of years, only intended to mark the period of the regular administration of the Hebrew state, leaving

Eglon, King of Moab, governed the people	18
Ehucl and Shamgar were judges	80
Jachin, King of Canaan, held the people in subjection	20
The people was at peace subsequently for	40
It was under subjection to Median	7
It obtained freedom under Gideon for	40
It fell under the rule of Abimelech	3
Tola, son of Puah, was judge	23
Jair was judge	22
The people was in subjection to the Philistines and Ammonites	18
Jephthah was judge	6
Ibzan, the Bethlehemite, was judge	7
Elon, the Zabulonite	10
Abclon, the Pirathonite	8
The people was again subject to the Philistines	40
Samson was judge	[16]20
Eli was judge	40
The people again fell into subjection to the Philistines, till they were delivered by Samuel	20
David reigned	40
Solomon reigned before he built the temple	4

All these periods added together make a total of 580 years. But to these must be added the years during which the Hebrew republic flourished after the death of Joshua, until it was conquered by Cushan Rishathaim, which I take to be very numerous, for I cannot bring myself to believe that immediately after the death of Joshua all those who had witnessed his miracles died simultaneously, nor that

---

out the years of anarchy and subjection as periods of misfortune and interregnum. Scripture certainly passes over in silence periods of anarchy, but does not, as they dream, refuse to reckon them or wipe them out of the country's annals. It is clear that Ezra, in 1 Kings vi., wished to reckon absolutely all the years since the flight from Egypt. This is so plain, that no one versed in the Scriptures can doubt it. For, without going back to the precise words of the text, we may see that the genealogy of David given at the end of the book of Ruth, and I Chron. ii., scarcely accounts for so great a number of years. For Nahshon, who was prince of the tribe of Judah (Numb. vii;11), two years after the Exodus, died in the desert, and his son Salmon passed the Jordan with Joshua. Now this Salmon, according to the genealogy, was David's great-grandfather. Deducting, then, from the total of 480 years, four years for Solomon's reign, seventy for David's life, and forty for the time passed in the desert, we find that David was born 366 years after the passage of the Jordan. Hence we must believe that David's father, grandfather, great-grandfather, and great-great-grandfather begat children when they were ninety years old.

[16] "Samson was judge for twenty years." Samson was born after the Hebrews had fallen under the dominion of the Philistines.

their successors at one stroke bid farewell to their laws, and plunged from the highest virtue into the depth of wickedness and obstinacy.

Nor, lastly, that Cushan Rishathaim subdued them on the instant; each one of these circumstances requires almost a generation, and there is no doubt that Judges ii:7, 9, 10, comprehends a great many years which it passes over in silence. We must also add the years during which Samuel was judge, the number of which is not stated in Scripture, and also the years during which Saul reigned, which are not clearly shown from his history. It is, indeed, stated in 1 Sam. xiii:1, that he reigned two years, but the text in that passage is mutilated, and the records of his reign lead us to suppose a longer period. That the text is mutilated I suppose no one will doubt who has ever advanced so far as the threshold of the Hebrew language, for it runs as follows: "Saul was in his — year, when he began to reign, and he reigned two years over Israel." Who, I say, does not see that the number of the years of Saul's age when he began to reign has been omitted? That the record of the reign presupposes a greater number of years is equally beyond doubt, for in the same book, chap. xxvii:7, it is stated that David sojourned among the Philistines, to whom he had fled on account of Saul, a year and four months; thus the rest of the reign must have been comprised in a space of eight months, which I think no one will credit. Josephus, at the end of the sixth book of his antiquities, thus corrects the text: Saul reigned eighteen years while Samuel was alive, and two years after his death. However, all the narrative in chap. Xiii. is in complete disagreement with what goes before. At the end of chap. vii. it is narrated that the Philistines were so crushed by the Hebrews that they did not venture, during Samuel's life, to invade the borders of Israel; but in chap. xiii. we are told that the Hebrews were invaded during the life of Samuel by the Philistines, and reduced by them to such a state of wretchedness and poverty that they were deprived not only of weapons with which to defend themselves, but also of the means of making more. I should be at pains enough if I were to try and harmonize all the narratives contained in this first book of Samuel so that they should seem to be all written and arranged by a single historian. But I return to my object. The years, then, during which Saul reigned must be added to the above computation; and, lastly, I have not counted the years of the Hebrew anarchy, for I cannot from Scripture gather their number. I cannot, I say, be certain as to the period occupied by the events related in Judges chap. xvii. on till the end of the book.

It is thus abundantly evident that we cannot arrive at a true computation of years from the histories, and, further, that the histories are inconsistent themselves on the subject. We are compelled to confess that these histories were compiled from various writers without previous arrangement and examination. Not less discrepancy is found between the dates given in the Chronicles of the

Kings of Judah, and those in the Chronicles of the Kings of Israel; in the latter, it is stated that Jehoram, the son of Ahab, began to reign in the second year of the reign of Jehoram, the son of Jehoshaphat (2 Kings i:17), but in the former we read that Jehoram, the son of Jehoshaphat, began to reign in the fifth year of Jehoram, the son of Ahab (2 Kings viii:16). Anyone who compares the narratives in Chronicles with the narratives in the books of Kings, will find many similar discrepancies. These there is no need for me to examine here, and still less am I called upon to treat of the commentaries of those who endeavour to harmonize them. The Rabbis evidently let their fancy run wild. Such commentators as I have, read, dream, invent, and as a last resort, play fast and loose with the language. For instance, when it is said in 2 Chronicles, that Ahab was forty-two years old when he began to reign, they pretend that these years are computed from the reign of Omri, not from the birth of Ahab. If this can be shown to be the real meaning of the writer of the book of Chronicles, all I can say is, that he did not know how to state a fact. The commentators make many other assertions of this kind, which if true, would prove that the ancient Hebrews were ignorant both of their own language, and of the way to relate a plain narrative. I should in such case recognize no rule or reason in interpreting Scripture, but it would be permissible to hypothesize to one's heart's content.

If anyone thinks that I am speaking too generally, and without sufficient warrant, I would ask him to set himself to showing us some fixed plan in these histories which might be followed without blame by other writers of chronicles, and in his efforts at harmonizing and interpretation, so strictly to observe and explain the phrases and expressions, the order and the connections, that we may be able to imitate these also in our writings[17]. If he succeeds, I will at once give him my hand, and he shall be to me as great Apollo; for I confess that after long endeavours I have been unable to discover anything of the kind. I may add that I set down nothing here which I have not long reflected upon, and that, though I was imbued from my boyhood up with the ordinary opinions about the Scriptures, I have been unable to withstand the force of what I have urged.

However, there is no need to detain the reader with this question, and drive him to attempt an impossible task; I merely mentioned the fact in order to throw light on my intention.

I now pass on to other points concerning the treatment of these books. For we must remark, in addition to what has been shown, that these books were not guarded by posterity with such care that no faults crept in. The ancient scribes draw attention to many doubtful readings, and some mutilated passages, but not to all that exist: whether the faults are of sufficient importance to greatly

---

[17] Otherwise, they rather correct than explain Scripture.

embarrass the reader I will not now discuss. I am inclined to think that they are of minor moment to those, at any rate, who read the Scriptures with enlightenment: and I can positively, affirm that I have not noticed any fault or various reading in doctrinal passages sufficient to render them obscure or doubtful.

There are some people, however, who will not admit that there is any corruption, even in other passages, but maintain that by some unique exercise of providence God has preserved from corruption every word in the Bible: they say that the various readings are the symbols of profoundest mysteries, and that mighty secrets lie hid in the twenty-eight hiatus which occur, nay, even in the very form of the letters.

Whether they are actuated by folly and anile devotion, or whether by arrogance and malice so that they alone may be held to possess the secrets of God, I know not: this much I do know, that I find in their writings nothing which has the air of a Divine secret, but only childish lucubrations. I have read and known certain Kabbalistic triflers, whose insanity provokes my unceasing as astonishment. That faults have crept in will, I think, be denied by no sensible person who reads the passage about Saul, above quoted (1 Sam. xiii:1) and also 2 Sam. vi:2: "And David arose and went with all the people that were with him from Judah, to bring up from thence the ark of God."

No one can fail to remark that the name of their destination, viz., Kirjath-jearim[18], has been omitted: nor can we deny that 2 Sam. xiii:37, has been tampered with and mutilated. "And Absalom fled, and went to Talmai, the son of Ammihud, king of Geshur. And he mourned for his son every day. So Absalom fled, and went to Geshur, and was there three years." I know that I have remarked other passages of the same kind, but I cannot recall them at the moment.

That the marginal notes which are found continually in the Hebrew Codices are doubtful readings will, I think, be evident to everyone who has noticed that they often arise from the great similarity, of some of the Hebrew letters, such for instance, as the similarity between Kaph and Beth, Jod and Van, Daleth and Reth, &c. For example, the text in 2 Sam. v:24, runs "in the time when thou hearest," and similarly in Judges xxi:22, "And it shall be when their fathers or

---

[18] "Kirjath-jearim." Kirjath-jearim is also called Baale of Judah. Hence Kimchi and others think that the words Baale Judah, which I have translated "the people of Judah," are the name of a town. But this is not so, for the word Baale is in the plural. Moreover, comparing this text in Samuel with I Chron. Xiii:5, we find that David did not rise up and go forth out of Baale, but that he went thither. If the author of the book of Samuel had meant to name the place whence David took the ark, he would, if he spoke Hebrew correctly, have said, "David rose up, and set forth from Baale Judah, and took the ark from thence."

their brothers come unto us often," the marginal version is "come unto us to complain."

So also many various readings have arisen from the use of the letters named mutes, which are generally not sounded in pronunciation, and are taken promiscuously, one for the other. For example, in Levit. xxv:29, it is written, "The house shall be established which is not in the walled city," but the margin has it, "which is in a walled city."

Though these matters are self-evident, it is necessary, to answer the reasonings of certain Pharisees, by which they endeavour to convince us that the marginal notes serve to indicate some mystery, and were added or pointed out by the writers of the sacred books. The first of these reasons, which, in my, opinion, carries little weight, is taken from the practice of reading the Scriptures aloud.

If, it is urged, these notes were added to show various readings which could not be decided upon by posterity, why has custom prevailed that the marginal readings should always be retained? Why has the meaning which is preferred been set down in the margin when it ought to have been incorporated in the text, and not relegated to a side note?

The second reason is more specious, and is taken from the nature of the case. It is admitted that faults have crept into the sacred writings by chance and not by design; but they say that in the five books the word for a girl is, with one exception, written without the letter "he," contrary to all grammatical rules, whereas in the margin it is written correctly according to the universal rule of grammar. Can this have happened by mistake? Is it possible to imagine a clerical error to have been committed every, time the word occurs? Moreover, it would have been easy, to supply the emendation. Hence, when these readings are not accidental or corrections of manifest mistakes, it is supposed that they must have been set down on purpose by the original writers, and have a meaning. However, it is easy to answer such arguments; as to the question of custom having prevailed in the reading of the marginal versions, I will not spare much time for its consideration: I know not the promptings of superstition, and perhaps the practice may have arisen from the idea that both readings were deemed equally good or tolerable, and therefore, lest either should be neglected, one was appointed to be written, and the other to be read. They feared to pronounce judgment in so weighty a matter lest they should mistake the false for the true, and therefore they would give preference to neither, as they must necessarily have done if they had commanded one only to be both read and written. This would be especially the case where the marginal readings were not written down in the sacred books: or the custom may have originated because some things though rightly written down were desired to be read otherwise according to the marginal version, and therefore the general rule was made that the marginal version should be followed in reading the Scriptures. The cause which induced the scribes to expressly prescribe certain passages to be read in the marginal version, I will now touch on, for not all the marginal notes are various readings, but some mark expressions which have passed out of common use, obsolete words and terms which current decency did not allow to be read in a public assembly. The ancient writers, without any evil intention, employed no courtly paraphrase, but called things by their plain names. Afterwards, through the spread of evil thoughts and luxury, words which could be used by the ancients without offence, came to be considered obscene. There was no need for this cause to change the text of Scripture. Still, as a concession to the popular weakness, it became the custom to substitute more decent terms for words denoting sexual intercourse, exereta, &c., and to read them as they were given in the margin.

At any rate, whatever may have been the origin of the practice of reading Scripture according to the marginal version, it was not that the true interpretation is contained therein. For besides that, the Rabbins in the Talmud often differ from the Massoretes, and give other readings which they approve of, as I will shortly show, certain things are found in the margin which appear less warranted by the uses of the Hebrew language. For example, in 2 Samuel xiv:22, we read, "In that the king hath fulfilled the request of his servant," a construction plainly regular, and agreeing with that in chap. xvi. But the margin has it "of thy servant," which does not agree with the person of the verb. So, too, chap. xvi:25 of the same book, we find, "As if one had inquired at the oracle of God," the margin adding "someone" to stand as a nominative to the verb. But the correction is not apparently warranted, for it is a common practice, well known to grammarians in the Hebrew language, to use the third person singular of the active verb impersonally.

The second argument advanced by the Pharisees is easily answered from what has just been said, namely, that the scribes besides the various readings called attention to obsolete words. For there is no doubt that in Hebrew as in other languages, changes of use made many words obsolete and antiquated, and such were found by the later scribes in the sacred books and noted by them with a view to the books being publicly read according to custom. For this reason the word nahgar is always found marked because its gender was originally common, and it had the same meaning as the Latin juvenis (a young person). So also the Hebrew capital was anciently called Jerusalem, not Jerusalaim. As to the pronouns himself and herself, I think that the later scribes changed vau into jod (a very frequent change in Hebrew) when they wished to express the feminine gender, but that the ancients only distinguished the two genders by a change of vowels. I may also remark that the irregular tenses of certain verbs differ in the ancient and modern forms, it being formerly considered a mark of elegance to employ certain letters agreeable to the ear.

In a word, I could easily multiply proofs of this kind if I were not afraid of abusing the patience of the reader. Perhaps I shall be asked how I became acquainted with the fact that all these expressions are obsolete. I reply that I have found them in the most ancient Hebrew writers in the Bible itself, and that they have not been imitated by subsequent authors, and thus they are recognized as antiquated, though the language in which they occur is dead. But perhaps someone may press the question why, if it be true, as I say, that the marginal notes of the Bible generally mark various readings, there are never more than two readings of a passage, that in the text and that in the margin, instead of three or more; and further, how the scribes can have hesitated between two readings, one of which is evidently contrary to grammar, and the other a plain correction.

The answer to these questions also is easy: I will premise that it is almost certain that there once were more various readings than those now recorded. For instance, one finds many in the Talmud which the Massoretes have neglected, and are so different one from the other that even the superstitious editor of the Bomberg Bible confesses that he cannot harmonize them. "We cannot say anything," he writes, "except what we have said above, namely, that the Talmud is generally in contradiction to the Massorete." So that we are nor bound to hold that there never were more than two readings of any passage, yet I am willing to admit, and indeed I believe that more than two readings are never found: and for the following reasons:—(I.) The cause of the differences of reading only admits of two, being generally the similarity of certain letters, so that the question resolved itself into which should be written Beth, or Kaf, Jod or Vau, Daleth or Reth: cases which are constantly occurring, and frequently yielding a fairly good meaning whichever alternative be adopted. Sometimes, too, it is a question whether a syllable be long or short, quantity being determined by the letters called mutes. Moreover, we never asserted that all the marginal versions, without exception, marked various readings; on the contrary, we have stated that many were due to motives of decency or a desire to explain obsolete words. (II.) I am inclined to attribute the fact that more than two readings are never found to the paucity of exemplars, perhaps not more than two or three, found by the scribes. In the treatise of the scribes, chap. vi., mention is made of three only, pretended to have been found in the time of Ezra, in order that the marginal versions might be attributed to him.

However that may be, if the scribes only had three codices we may easily imagine that in a given passage two of them would be in accord, for it would be extraordinary if each one of the three gave a different reading of the same text.

The dearth of copies after the time of Ezra will surprise no one who has read the 1st chapter of Maccabees, or Josephus's "Antiquities," Bk. 12, chap. 5. Nay, it appears wonderful considering the fierce and daily persecution, that even these few should have been preserved. This will, I think, be plain to even a cursory reader of the history of those times.

We have thus discovered the reasons why there are never more than two readings of a passage in the Bible, but this is a long way from supposing that we may therefore conclude that the Bible was purposely written incorrectly in such passages in order to signify some mystery. As to the second argument, that some passages are so faultily written that they are at plain variance with all grammar, and should have been corrected in the text and not in the margin, I attach little weight to it, for I am not concerned to say what religious motive the scribes may have had for acting as they did: possibly they did so from candour, wishing to transmit the few exemplars of the Bible which they had found exactly in their original state, marking the differences they discovered in the margin, not as doubtful readings, but as simple variants. I have myself called them doubtful readings, because it would be generally impossible to say which of the two versions is preferable.

Lastly, besides these doubtful readings the scribes have (by leaving a hiatus in the middle of a paragraph) marked several passages as mutilated. The Massoretes have counted up such instances, and they amount to eight-and-twenty. I do not know whether any mystery is thought to lurk in the number, at any rate the Pharisees religiously preserve a certain amount of empty space.

One of such hiatus occurs (to give an instance) in Gen. iv:8, where it is written, "And Cain said to his brother . . . . and it came to pass while they were in the field, &c.," a space being left in which we should expect to hear what it was that Cain said.

Similarly there are (besides those points we have noticed) eight-and-twenty hiatus left by the scribes. Many of these would not be recognized as mutilated if it were not for the empty space left. But I have said enough on this subject.

CHAPTER X

An Examination of the remaining books of the Old Testament according to the Preceding Method

I now pass on to the remaining books of the Old Testament. Concerning the two books of Chronicles I have nothing particular or important to remark, except that they were certainly written after the time of Ezra, and possibly after the restoration of the Temple by Judas Maccabaeus[19]. For in chap. ix. of the first book we find a reckoning of the families who were the first to live in Jerusalem, and in verse 17 the names of the porters, of which two recur in Nehemiah. This shows that the books were certainly compiled after the rebuilding of the city. As to their actual writer, their authority, utility, and doctrine, I come to no conclusion. I have always been astonished that they have been included in the Bible by men who shut out from the canon the books of Wisdom, Tobit, and the others styled apocryphal. I do not aim at disparaging their authority, but as they are universally received I will leave them as they are.

The Psalms were collected and divided into five books in the time of the second temple, for Ps. lxxxviii. was published, according to Philo-Judaeus, while king Jehoiachin was still a prisoner in Babylon; and Ps. lxxxix. when the same

---

[19] "After the restoration of the Temple by Judas Maccaboeus." This conjecture, if such it be, is founded on the genealogy of King Jeconiah, given in 1 Chron. iii., which finishes at the sons of Elioenai, the thirteenth in direct descent from him: whereon we must observe that Jeconiah, before his captivity, had no children; but it is probable that he had two while he was in prison, if we may draw any inference from the names he gave them. As to his grandchildren, it is evident that they were born after his deliverance, if the names be any guide, for his grandson, Pedaiah (a name meaning God hath delivered me), who, according to this chapter, was the father of Zerubbabel, was born in the thirty-seventh or thirty-eighth year of Jeconiah's life, that is thirty-three years before the restoration of liberty to the Jews by Cyrus. Therefore Zerubbabel, to whom Cyrus gave the principality of Judaea, was thirteen or fourteen years old. But we need not carry the inquiry so far: we need only read attentively the chapter of 1 Chron., already quoted, where (v. 17, sqq.) mention is made of all the posterity of Jeconiah, and compare it with the Septuagint version to see clearly that these books were not published, till after Maccabaeus had restored the Temple, the sceptre no longer belonging to the house of Jeconiah.

king obtained his liberty: I do not think Philo would have made the statement unless either it had been the received opinion in his time, or else had been told him by trustworthy persons.

The Proverbs of Solomon were, I believe, collected at the same time, or at least in the time of King Josiah; for in chap. xxv:1, it is written, "These are also proverbs of Solomon which the men of Hezekiah, king of Judah, copied out." I cannot here pass over in silence the audacity of the Rabbis who wished to exclude from the sacred canon both the Proverbs and Ecclesiastes, and to put them both in the Apocrypha. In fact, they would actually have done so, if they had not lighted on certain passages in which the law of Moses is extolled. It is, indeed, grievous to think that the settling of the sacred canon lay in the hands of such men; however, I congratulate them, in this instance, on their suffering us to see these books in question, though I cannot refrain from doubting whether they have transmitted them in absolute good faith; but I will not now linger on this point.

I pass on, then, to the prophetic books. An examination of these assures me that the prophecies therein contained have been compiled from other books, and are not always set down in the exact order in which they were spoken or written by the prophets, but are only such as were collected here and there, so that they are but fragmentary.

Isaiah began to prophecy in the reign of Uzziah, as the writer himself testifies in the first verse. He not only prophesied at that time, but furthermore wrote the history of that king (see 2 Chron. xxvi:22) in a volume now lost. That which we possess, we have shown to have been taken from the chronicles of the kings of Judah and Israel.

We may add that the Rabbis assert that this prophet prophesied in the reign of Manasseh, by whom he was eventually put to death, and, although this seems to be a myth, it yet shows that they did not think that all Isaiah's prophecies are extant.

The prophecies of Jeremiah, which are related historically are also taken from various chronicles; for not only are they heaped together confusedly, without any account being taken of dates, but also the same story is told in them differently in different passages. For instance, in chap. xxi. we are told that the cause of Jeremiah's arrest was that he had prophesied the destruction of the city to Zedekiah who consulted him. This narrative suddenly passes, in chap xxii., to the prophet's remonstrances to Jehoiakim (Zedekiah's predecessor), and the prediction he made of that king's captivity; then, in chap. xxv., come the revelations granted to the prophet previously, that is in the fourth year of Jehoiakim, and, further on still, the revelations received in the first year of the same reign. The continuator of Jeremiah goes on heaping prophecy upon prophecy without any regard to dates, until at last, in chap. xxxviii. (as if the intervening chapters had been a parenthesis), he takes up the thread dropped in chap. xxi.

In fact, the conjunction with which chap. xxxviii. begins, refers to the 8th, 9th, and 10th verses of chap. xxi. Jeremiah's last arrest is then very differently described, and a totally separate cause is given for his daily retention in the court of the prison.

We may thus clearly see that these portions of the book have been compiled from various sources, and are only from this point of view comprehensible. The prophecies contained in the remaining chapters, where Jeremiah speaks in the first person, seem to be taken from a book written by Baruch, at Jeremiah's dictation. These, however, only comprise (as appears from chap. xxxvi:2) the prophecies revealed to the prophet from the time of Josiah to the fourth year of Jehoiakim, at which period the book begins. The contents of chap. xlv:2, on to chap. li:59, seem taken from the same volume.

That the book of Ezekiel is only a fragment, is clearly indicated by the first verse. For anyone may see that the conjunction with which it begins, refers to something already said, and connects what follows therewith. However, not only this conjunction, but the whole text of the discourse implies other writings. The fact of the present work beginning the thirtieth year shows that the prophet is continuing, not commencing a discourse; and this is confirmed by the writer, who parenthetically states in verse 3, "The word of the Lord came often unto Ezekiel the priest, the son of Buzi, in the land of the Chaldeans," as if to say that the prophecies which he is about to relate are the sequel to revelations formerly received by Ezekiel from God. Furthermore, Josephus, 11 Antiq." x:9, says that Ezekiel prophesied that Zedekiah should not see Babylon, whereas the book we now have not only contains no such statement, but contrariwise asserts in chap. xvii. that he should be taken to Babylon as a captive,[20].

Of Hosea I cannot positively state that he wrote more than is now extant in the book bearing his name, but I am astonished at the smallness of the quantity, we possess, for the sacred writer asserts that the prophet prophesied for more than eighty years.

We may assert, speaking generally, that the compiler of the prophetic books neither collected all the prophets, nor all the writings of those we have; for of the prophets who are said to have prophesied in the reign of Manasseh and of whom general mention is made in 2 Chron. xxxiii:10, 18, we have, evidently, no

---

[20] "Zedekiah should be taken to Babylon." No one could then have suspected that the prophecy of Ezekiel contradicted that of Jeremiah, but the suspicion occurs to everyone who reads the narrative of Josephus. The event proved that both prophets were in the right.

prophecies extant; neither have we all the prophecies of the twelve who give their names to books. Of Jonah we have only, the prophecy concerning the Ninevites, though he also prophesied to the children of Israel, as we learn in 2 Kings xiv:25.

The book and the personality of Job have caused much controversy. Some think that the book is the work of Moses, and the whole narrative merely allegorical. Such is the opinion of the Rabbins recorded in the Talmud, and they are supported by, Maimonides in his "More Nebuchim." Others believe it to be a true history, and some suppose that Job lived in the time of Jacob, and was married to his daughter Dinah. Aben Ezra, however, as I have already stated, affirms, in his commentaries, that the work is a translation into Hebrew from some other language: I could wish that he could advance more cogent arguments than he does, for we might then conclude that the Gentiles also had sacred books. I myself leave the matter undecided, but I conjecture Job to have been a Gentile, and a man of very stable character, who at first prospered, then was assailed with terrible calamities, and finally, was restored to great happiness. (He is thus named, among others, by Ezekiel, xiv:12.) I take it that the constancy of his mind amid the vicissitudes of his fortune occasioned many men to dispute about God's providence, or at least caused the writer of the book in question to compose his dialogues; for the contents, and also the style, seem to emanate far less from a man wretchedly ill and lying among ashes, than from one reflecting at ease in his study. I should also be inclined to agree with Aben Ezra that the book is a translation, for its poetry seems akin to that of the Gentiles; thus the Father of Gods summons a council, and Momus, here called Satan, criticizes the Divine decrees with the utmost freedom. But these are mere conjectures without any solid foundation.

I pass on to the book of Daniel, which, from chap. viii. onwards, undoubtedly contains the writing of Daniel himself. Whence the first seven chapters are derived I cannot say; we may, however, conjecture that, as they were first written in Chaldean, they are taken from Chaldean chronicles. If this could be proved, it would form a very striking proof of the fact that the sacredness of Scripture depends on our understanding of the doctrines therein signified, and not on the words, the language, and the phrases in which these doctrines are conveyed to us; and it would further show us that books which teach and speak of whatever is highest and best are equally sacred, whatever be the tongue in which they are written, or the nation to which they belong.

We can, however, in this case only remark that the chapters in question were written in Chaldee, and yet are as sacred as the rest of the Bible.

The first book of Ezra is so intimately connected with the book of Daniel that both are plainly recognizable as the work of the same author, writing of Jewish history from the time of the first captivity onwards. I have no hesitation in joining to this the book of Esther, for the conjunction with which it begins can refer to nothing else. It cannot be the same work as that written by Mordecai, for, in chap. ix:20-22, another person relates that Mordecai wrote letters, and tells us their contents; further, that Queen Esther confirmed the days of Purim in their times appointed, and that the decree was written in the book that is (by a Hebraism), in a book known to all then living, which, as Aben Ezra and the rest confess, has now perished. Lastly, for the rest of the acts of Mordecai, the historian refers us to the chronicles of the kings of Persia. Thus there is no doubt that this book was written by the same person as he who recounted the history of Daniel and Ezra, and who wrote Nehemiah,[21], sometimes called the second book of Ezra. We may, then, affirm that all these books are from one hand; but we have no clue whatever to the personality of the author. However, in order to determine whence he, whoever he was, had gained a knowledge of the histories which he had, perchance, in great measure himself written, we may remark that the governors or chiefs of the Jews, after the restoration of the Temple, kept scribes or historiographers, who wrote annals or chronicles of them. The chronicles of the kings are often quoted in the books of Kings, but the chronicles of the chiefs and priests are quoted for the first time in Nehemiah xii:23, and again in 1 Macc. xvi:24. This is undoubtedly the book referred to as containing the decree of Esther and the acts of Mordecai; and which, as we said with Aben Ezra, is now lost. From it were taken the whole contents of these four books, for no other authority is quoted by their writer, or is known to us.

That these books were not written by either Ezra or Nehemiah is plain from Nehemiah xii:9, where the descendants of the high priest, Joshua are traced down to Jaddua, the sixth high priest, who went to meet Alexander the Great, when the Persian empire was almost subdued (Josephus, "Ant." ii. 108), or who, according to Philo-Judaeus, was the sixth and last high priest under the Persians. In the same chapter of Nehemiah, verse 22, this point is clearly brought out: "The Levites in the days of Eliashib, Joiada, and Johanan, and Jaddua, were recorded chief of the fathers: also the priests, to the reign of Darius the Persian" — that is to say, in the chronicles; and, I suppose, no one thinks,[22], that the lives

---

[21] "And who wrote Nehemiah." That the greater part of the book of Nehemiah was taken from the work composed by the prophet Nehemiah himself, follows from the testimony of its author. (See chap. i.). But it is obvious that the whole of the passage contained between chap. viii. and chap. xii. verse 26, together with the two last verses of chap. xii., which form a sort of parenthesis to Nehemiah's words, were added by the historian himself, who outlived Nehemiah.

[22] "I suppose no one thinks" that Ezra was the uncle of the first high priest, named Joshua (see Ezra vii., and 1 Chron. vi:14), and went to Jerusalem from Babylon with Zerubbabel (see Nehemiah xii:1). But it appears that when he saw, that the Jews were in a state of anarchy, he returned to Babylon, as also did others (Nehem. i;2), and remained there till the reign of Artaxerxes, when his requests were granted and he went a second time to Jerusalem. Nehemiah also went to Jerusalem

of Nehemiah and Ezra were so prolonged that they outlived fourteen kings of Persia. Cyrus was the first who granted the Jews permission to rebuild their Temple: the period between his time and Darius, fourteenth and last king of Persia, extends over 230 years. I have, therefore, no doubt that these books were written after Judas Maccabaeus had restored the worship in the Temple, for at that time false books of Daniel, Ezra, and Esther were published by evil-disposed persons, who were almost certainly Sadducees, for the writings were never recognized by the Pharisees, so far as I am aware; and, although certain myths in the fourth book of Ezra are repeated in the Talmud, they must not be set down to the Pharisees, for all but the most ignorant admit that they have been added by some trifler: in fact, I think, someone must have made such additions with a view to casting ridicule on all the traditions of the sect.

Perhaps these four books were written out and published at the time I have mentioned with a view to showing the people that the prophecies of Daniel had been fulfilled, and thus kindling their piety, and awakening a hope of future deliverance in the midst of their misfortunes. In spite of their recent origin, the books before us contain many errors, due, I suppose, to the haste with which they were written. Marginal readings, such as I have mentioned in the last chapter, are found here as elsewhere, and in even greater abundance; there are, moreover, certain passages which can only be accounted for by supposing some such cause as hurry.

However, before calling attention to the marginal readings, I will remark that, if the Pharisees are right in supposing them to have been ancient, and the work of the original scribes, we must perforce admit that these scribes (if there were more than one) set them down because they found that the text from which they were copying was inaccurate, and did yet not venture to alter what was written by their predecessors and superiors. I need not again go into the subject at length, and will, therefore, proceed to mention some discrepancies not noticed in the margin.

I. Some error has crept into the text of the second chapter of Ezra, for in verse 64 we are told that the total of all those mentioned in the rest of the chapter amounts to 42,360; but, when we come to add up the several items we get as result only 29,818. There must, therefore, be an error, either in the total, or in the details. The total is probably correct, for it would most likely be well known to all as a noteworthy thing; but with the details, the case would be

---

with Zerubbabel in the time of Cyrus (Ezra ii:2 and 63, cf. x:9, and Nehemiah x:1). The version given of the Hebrew word, translated "ambassador," is not supported by any authority, while it is certain that fresh names were given to those Jews who frequented the court. Thus Daniel was named Balteshazzar, and Zerubbabel Sheshbazzar (Dan. i:7). Nehemiah was called Atirsata, while in virtue of his office he was styled governor, or president. (Nehem. v. 24, xii:26.)

different. If, then, any error had crept into the total, it would at once have been remarked, and easily corrected. This view is confirmed by Nehemiah vii., where this chapter of Ezra is mentioned, and a total is given in plain correspondence thereto; but the details are altogether different — some are larger, and some less, than those in Ezra, and altogether they amount to 31,089. We may, therefore, conclude that both in Ezra and in Nehemiah the details are erroneously given. The commentators who attempt to harmonize these evident contradictions draw on their imagination, each to the best of his ability; and while professing adoration for each letter and word of Scripture, only succeed in holding up the sacred writers to ridicule, as though they knew not how to write or relate a plain narrative. Such persons effect nothing but to render the clearness of Scripture obscure. If the Bible could everywhere be interpreted after their fashion, there would be no such thing as a rational statement of which the meaning could be relied on. However, there is no need to dwell on the subject; only I am convinced that if any historian were to attempt to imitate the proceedings freely attributed to the writers of the Bible, the commentators would cover him with contempt. If it be blasphemy to assert that there are any errors in Scripture, what name shall we apply to those who foist into it their own fancies, who degrade the sacred writers till they seem to write confused nonsense, and who deny the plainest and most evident meanings? What in the whole Bible can be plainer than the fact that Ezra and his companions, in the second chapter of the book attributed to him, have given in detail the reckoning of all the Hebrews who set out with them for Jerusalem? This is proved by the reckoning being given, not only of those who told their lineage, but also of those who were unable to do so. Is it not equally clear from Nehemiah vii:5, that the writer merely there copies the list given in Ezra? Those, therefore, who explain these pas sages otherwise, deny the plain meaning of Scripture — nay, they deny Scripture itself. They think it pious to reconcile one passage of Scripture with another — a pretty piety, forsooth, which accommodates the clear passages to the obscure, the correct to the faulty, the sound to the corrupt.

Far be it from me to call such commentators blasphemers, if their motives be pure: for to err is human. But I return to my subject.

Besides these errors in numerical details, there are others in the genealogies, in the history, and, I fear also in the prophecies. The prophecy of Jeremiah (chap. xxii.), concerning Jechoniah, evidently does not agree with his history, as given in I Chronicles iii:17-19, and especially with the last words of the chapter, nor do I see how the prophecy, "thou shalt die in peace," can be applied to Zedekiah, whose eyes were dug out after his sons had been slain before him. If prophecies are to be interpreted by their issue, we must make a change of name, and read Jechoniah for Zedekiah, and vice versa

This, however, would be too paradoxical a proceeding; so I prefer to leave the matter unexplained, especially as the error, if error there be, must be set down to the historian, and not to any fault in the authorities.

Other difficulties I will not touch upon, as I should only weary the reader, and, moreover, be repeating the remarks of other writers. For R. Selomo, in face of the manifest contradiction in the above-mentioned genealogies, is compelled to break forth into these words (see his commentary on 1 Chron. viii.): "Ezra (whom he supposes to be the author of the book of Chronicles) gives different names and a different genealogy to the sons of Benjamin from those which we find in Genesis, and describes most of the Levites differently from Joshua, because he found original discrepancies." And, again, a little later: "The genealogy of Gibeon and others is described twice in different ways, from different tables of each genealogy, and in writing them down Ezra adopted the version given in the majority of the texts, and when the authority was equal he gave both." Thus granting that these books were compiled from sources originally incorrect and uncertain.

In fact the commentators, in seeking to harmonize difficulties, generally do no more than indicate their causes: for I suppose no sane person supposes that the sacred historians deliberately wrote with the object of appearing to contradict themselves freely. Perhaps I shall be told that I am overthrowing the authority of Scripture, for that, according to me, anyone may suspect it of error in any passage; but, on the contrary, I have shown that my object has been to prevent the clear and uncorrupted passages being accommodated to and corrupted by the faulty ones; neither does the fact that some passages are corrupt warrant us in suspecting all. No book ever was completely free from faults, yet I would ask, who suspects all books to be everywhere faulty? Surely no one, especially when the phraseology is clear and the intention of the author plain.

I have now finished the task I set myself with respect to the books of the Old Testament. We may easily conclude from what has been said, that before the time of the Maccabees there was no canon of sacred books,[23] but that those

---

[23] "Before the time of the Maccabees there was no canon of sacred books." The synagogue styled "the great" did not begin before the subjugation of Asia by the Macedonians. The contention of Maimonides, Rabbi Abraham, Ben-David, and others, that the presidents of this synagogue were Ezra, Daniel, Nehemiah, Haggai, Zechariah, &c., is a pure fiction, resting only on rabbinical tradition. Indeed they assert that the dominion of the Persians only lasted thirty-four years, and this is their chief reason for maintaining that the decrees of the "great synagogue," or synod (rejected by the Sadducees, but accepted by the Pharisees) were ratified by the prophets, who received them from former prophets and so in direct succession from Moses, who received them from God Himself. Such is the doctrine which the Pharisees maintain with their wonted obstinacy. Enlightened persons, however, who know the reasons for the convoking of councils, or synods, and

which we now possess were selected from a multitude of others at the period of the restoration of the Temple by the Pharisees (who also instituted the set form of prayers), who are alone responsible for their acceptance. Those, therefore, who would demonstrate the authority of Holy Scripture, are bound to show the authority of each separate book; it is not enough to prove the Divine origin of a single book in order to infer the Divine origin of the rest. In that case we should have to assume that the council of Pharisees was, in its choice of books, infallible, and this could never be proved. I am led to assert that the Pharisees alone selected the books of the Old Testament, and inserted them in the canon, from the fact that in Daniel ii. is proclaimed the doctrine of the Resurrection, which the Sadducees denied; and, furthermore, the Pharisees plainly assert in the Talmud that they so selected them. For in the treatise of Sabbathus, chapter ii., folio 30, page 2, it is written: R. Jehuda, surnamed Rabbi, reports that the experts wished to conceal the book of Ecclesiastes because they found therein words opposed to the law (that is, to the book of the law of Moses). Why did they not hide it? "Because it begins in accordance with the law, and ends according to the law;" and a little further on we read: "They sought also to conceal the book of Proverbs." And in the first chapter of the same treatise, fol. 13, page 2: "Verily, name one man for good, even he who was called Neghunja, the son of Hezekiah: for, save for him, the book of Ezekiel would been concealed, because it agreed not with the words of the law."

It is thus abundantly clear that men expert in the law summoned a council to decide which books should be received into the canon, and which excluded. If any man, therefore, wishes to be certified as to the authority of all the books, let him call a fresh council, and ask every member his reasons.

The time has now come for examining in the same manner the books in the New Testament; but as I learn that the task has been already performed by men highly skilled in science and languages, and as I do not myself possess a knowledge of Greek sufficiently exact for the task; lastly, as we have lost the originals of those books which were written in Hebrew, I prefer to decline the undertaking. However, I will touch on those points which have most bearing on my subject in the following chapter.

---

are no strangers to the differences between Pharisees and Sadducees, can easily divine the causes which led to the assembling of this great synagogue. It is very certain that no prophet was there present, and that the decrees of the Pharisees, which they style their traditions, derive all their authority from it.

CHAPTER XI

An Inquiry whether the Apostles wrote their Epistles as Apostles and Prophets, or merely as Teachers; and an explanation of what is meant by an Apostle

No reader of the New Testament can doubt that the Apostles were prophets; but as a prophet does not always speak by revelation, but only, at rare intervals, as we showed at the end of Chap. I., we may fairly inquire whether the Apostles wrote their Epistles as prophets, by revelation and express mandate, as Moses, Jeremiah, and others did, or whether only as private individuals or teachers, especially as Paul, in Corinthians xiv:6, mentions two sorts of preaching.

If we examine the style of the Epistles, we shall find it totally different from that employed by the prophets.

The prophets are continually asserting that they speak by the command of God: "Thus saith the Lord," "The Lord of hosts saith," "The command of the Lord," &c.; and this was their habit not only in assemblies of the prophets, but also in their epistles containing revelations, as appears from the epistle of Elijah to Jehoram, 2 Chron. xxi:12, which begins, "Thus saith the Lord."

In the Apostolic Epistles we find nothing of the sort. Contrariwise, in I Cor. vii:40 Paul speaks according to his own opinion and in many passages we come across doubtful and perplexed phrase; such as, "We think, therefore," Rom. iii:28; "Now I think,"[24], Rom. viii:18, and so on. Besides these, other expressions are met with very different from those used by the prophets. For instance, 1 Cor. vii:6, "But I speak this by permission, not by commandment;" "I give

---

[24] "Now I think." The translators render the {Greek} word "I infer", and assert that Paul uses it as synonymous with {a Greek word}. But the former word has, in Greek, the same meaning as the Hebrew word rendered to think, to esteem, to judge. And this signification would be in entire agreement with the Syriac translation. This Syriac translation (if it be a translation, which is very doubtful, for we know neither the time of its appearance, nor the translators and Syriac was the vernacular of the Apostles) renders the text before us in a way well explained by Tremellius as "we think, therefore."

my judgment as one that hath obtained mercy of the Lord to be faithful" (1 Cor. vii:25), and so on in many other passages. We must also remark that in the aforesaid chapter the Apostle says that when he states that he has or has not the precept or commandment of God, he does not mean the precept or commandment of God revealed to himself, but only the words uttered by Christ in His Sermon on the Mount. Furthermore, if we examine the manner in which the Apostles give out evangelical doctrine, we shall see that it differs materially from the method adopted by the prophets. The Apostles everywhere reason as if they were arguing rather than prophesying; the prophecies, on the other hand, contain only dogmas and commands. God is therein introduced not as speaking to reason, but as issuing decrees by His absolute fiat. The authority of the prophets does not submit to discussion, for whosoever wishes to find rational ground for his arguments, by that very wish submits them to everyone's private judgment. This Paul, inasmuch as he uses reason, appears to have done, for he says in 1 Cor. x:15, "I speak as to wise men, judge ye what I say." The prophets, as we showed at the end of Chapter I., did not perceive what was revealed by virtue of their natural reason, and though there are certain passages in the Pentateuch which seem to be appeals to induction, they turn out, on nearer examination, to be nothing but peremptory commands. For instance, when Moses says, Deut. xxxi:27, "Behold, while I am yet alive with you, this day ye have been rebellious against the Lord; and how much more after my death," we must by no means conclude that Moses wished to convince the Israelites by reason that they would necessarily fall away from the worship of the Lord after his death; for the argument would have been false, as Scripture itself shows: the Israelites continued faithful during the lives of Joshua and the elders, and afterwards during the time of Samuel, David, and Solomon. Therefore the words of Moses are merely a moral injunction, in which he predicts rhetorically the future backsliding of the people so as to impress it vividly on their imagination. I say that Moses spoke of himself in order to lend likelihood to his prediction, and not as a prophet by revelation, because in verse 21 of the same chapter we are told that God revealed the same thing to Moses in different words, and there was no need to make Moses certain by argument of God's prediction and decree; it was only necessary that it should be vividly impressed on his imagination, and this could not be better accomplished than by imagining the existing contumacy of the people, of which he had had frequent experience, as likely to extend into the future.

All the arguments employed by Moses in the five books are to be understood in a similar manner; they are not drawn from the armoury of reason, but are merely, modes of expression calculated to instil with efficacy, and present vividly to the imagination the commands of God. However, I do not wish absolutely to deny that the prophets ever argued from revelation; I only maintain that the prophets made more legitimate use of argument in proportion as their knowledge approached more nearly to ordinary knowledge, and by this we know that they possessed a knowledge above the ordinary, inasmuch as they proclaimed absolute dogmas, decrees, or judgments. Thus Moses, the chief of the prophets, never used legitimate argument, and, on the other hand, the long deductions and arguments of Paul, such as we find in the Epistle to the Romans, are in nowise written from supernatural revelation.

The modes of expression and discourse adopted by the Apostles in the Epistles, show very clearly that the latter were not written by revelation and Divine command, but merely by the natural powers and judgment of the authors. They consist in brotherly admonitions and courteous expressions such as would never be employed in prophecy, as for instance, Paul's excuse in Romans xv:15, "I have written the more boldly unto you in some sort, my brethren."

We may arrive at the same conclusion from observing that we never read that the Apostles were commanded to write, but only that they went everywhere preaching, and confirmed their words with signs. Their personal presence and signs were absolutely necessary for the conversion and establishment in religion of the Gentiles; as Paul himself expressly states in Rom. i:11, "But I long to see you, that I may impart to you some spiritual gift, to the end that ye may be established."

It may be objected that we might prove in similar fashion that the Apostles did not preach as prophets, for they did not go to particular places, as the prophets did, by the command of God. We read in the Old Testament that Jonah went to Nineveh to preach, and at the same time that he was expressly sent there, and told that he most preach. So also it is related, at great length, of Moses that he went to Egypt as the messenger of God, and was told at the same time what he should say to the children of Israel and to king Pharaoh, and what wonders he should work before them to give credit to his words. Isaiah, Jeremiah, and Ezekiel were expressly commanded to preach to the Israelites. Lastly, the prophets only preached what we are assured by Scripture they had received from God, whereas this is hardly ever said of the Apostles in the New Testament, when they went about to preach. On the contrary, we find passages expressly implying that the Apostles chose the places where they should preach on their own responsibility, for there was a difference amounting to a quarrel between Paul and Barnabas on the subject (Acts xv:37, 38). Often they wished to go to a place, but were prevented, as Paul writes, Rom. i:13, "Oftentimes I purposed to come to you, but was let hitherto;" and in I Cor. xvi:12, "As touching our brother Apollos, I greatly desired him to come unto you with the brethren, but his will was not at all to come at this time: but he will come when he shall have convenient time."

From these expressions and differences of opinion among the Apostles, and also from the fact that Scripture nowhere testifies of them, as of the ancient prophets, that they went by the command of God, one might conclude that they preached as well as wrote in their capacity of teachers, and not as prophets: but the question is easily solved if we observe the difference between the mission of an Apostle and that of an Old Testament prophet. The latter were not called to preach and prophesy to all nations, but to certain specified ones, and therefore an express and peculiar mandate was required for each of them; the Apostles, on the other hand, were called to preach to all men absolutely, and to turn all men to religion. Therefore, whithersoever they went, they were fulfilling Christ's commandment; there was no need to reveal to them beforehand what they should preach, for they were the disciples of Christ to whom their Master Himself said (Matt. X:19, 20): "But, when they deliver you up, take no thought how or what ye shall speak, for it shall be given you in that same hour what ye shall speak." We therefore conclude that the Apostles were only indebted to special revelation in what they orally preached and confirmed by signs (see the beginning of Chap. 11.); that which they taught in speaking or writing without any confirmatory signs and wonders they taught from their natural knowledge. (See I Cor. xiv:6.) We need not be deterred by the fact that all the Epistles begin by citing the imprimatur of the Apostleship, for the Apostles, as I will shortly show, were granted, not only the faculty of prophecy, but also the authority to teach. We may therefore admit that they wrote their Epistles as Apostles, and for this cause every one of them began by citing the Apostolic imprimatur, possibly with a view to the attention of the reader by asserting that they were the persons who had made such mark among the faithful by their preaching, and had shown bv many marvelous works that they were teaching true religion and the way of salvation. I observe that what is said in the Epistles with regard to the Apostolic vocation and the Holy Spirit of God which inspired them, has reference to their former preaching, except in those passages where the expressions of the Spirit of God and the Holy Spirit are used to signify a mind pure, upright, and devoted to God. For instance, in 1 Cor. vii:40, Paul says: But she is happier if she so abide, after my judgment, and I think also that I have the Spirit of God." By the Spirit of God the Apostle here refers to his mind, as we may see from the context: his meaning is as follows: "I account blessed a widow who does not wish to marry a second husband; such is my opinion, for I have settled to live unmarried, and I think that I am blessed." There are other similar passages which I need not now quote.

As we have seen that the Apostles wrote their Epistles solely by the light of natural reason, we must inquire how they were enabled to teach by natural knowledge matters outside its scope. However, if we bear in mind what we said in Chap. VII. of this treatise our difficulty will vanish: for although the contents of the Bible entirely surpass our understanding, we may safely discourse of them, provided we assume nothing not told us in Scripture: by the same method the Apostles, from what they saw and heard, and from what was revealed to them, were enabled to form and elicit many conclusions which they would have been able to teach to men had it been permissible.

Further, although religion, as preached by the Apostles, does not come within the sphere of reason, in so far as it consists in the narration of the life of Christ, yet its essence, which is chiefly moral, like the whole of Christ's doctrine, can readily, be apprehended by the natural faculties of all.

Lastly, the Apostles had no lack of supernatural illumination for the purpose of adapting the religion they had attested by signs to the understanding of everyone so that it might be readily received; nor for exhortations on the subject: in fact, the object of the Epistles is to teach and exhort men to lead that manner of life which each of the Apostles judged best for confirming them in religion. We may here repeat our former remark, that the Apostles had received not only the faculty of preaching the history, of Christ as prophets, and confirming it with signs, but also authority for teaching and exhorting according as each thought best. Paul (2 Tim. i:11), "Whereunto I am appointed a preacher, and an apostle, and a teacher of the Gentiles;" and again (I Tim. ii:7), "Whereunto I am ordained a preacher and an apostle (I speak the truth in Christ and lie not), a teacher of the Gentiles in faith and verity." These passages, I say, show clearly the stamp both of the apostleship and the teachership: the authority for admonishing whomsoever and wheresoever he pleased is asserted by Paul in the Epistle to Philemon, v:8: "Wherefore, though I might be much bold in Christ to enjoin thee that which is convenient, yet," &c., where we may remark that if Paul had received from God as a prophet what he wished to enjoin Philemon, and had been bound to speak in his prophetic capacity, he would not have been able to change the command of God into entreaties. We must therefore understand him to refer to the permission to admonish which he had received as a teacher, and not as a prophet. We have not yet made it quite clear that the Apostles might each choose his own way of teaching, but only that by virtue of their Apostleship they were teachers as well as prophets; however, if we call reason to our aid we shall clearly see that an authority to teach implies authority to choose the method. It will nevertheless be, perhaps, more satisfactory to draw all our proofs from Scripture; we are there plainly told that each Apostle chose his particular method (Rom. xv: 20): "Yea, so have I strived to preach the gospel, not where Christ was named, lest I should build upon another man's foundation." If all the Apostles had adopted the same method of teaching, and had all built up the Christian religion on the same foundation, Paul would have had no reason to call the work of a fellow-Apostle "another man's foundation," inasmuch as it would have been identical with his own: his calling it another man's proved that each Apostle built up his religious instruction on different foundations, thus resembling other teachers who have each their own method, and prefer instructing quite ignorant people who have never learnt under another master, whether the subject be science, languages, or even the indisputable truths of mathematics. Furthermore, if we go through the Epistles at all attentively, we shall see that the Apostles, while agreeing about religion itself, are at variance as to the foundations it rests on. Paul, in order to strengthen men's religion, and show them that salvation depends solely on the grace of God, teaches that no one can boast of works, but only of faith, and that no one can be justified by works (Rom. iii:27,28); in fact, he preaches the complete doctrine of predestination. James, on the other hand, states that man is justified by works, and not by faith only (see his Epistle, ii:24), and omitting all the disputations of Paul, confines religion to a very few elements.

Lastly, it is indisputable that from these different ground; for religion selected by the Apostles, many quarrels and schisms distracted the Church, even in the earliest times, and doubtless they will continue so to distract it for ever, or at least till religion is separated from philosophical speculations, and reduced to the few simple doctrines taught by Christ to His disciples; such a task was impossible for the Apostles, because the Gospel was then unknown to mankind, and lest its novelty should offend men's ears it had to be adapted to the disposition of contemporaries (2 Cor. ix:19, 20), and built up on the groundwork most familiar and accepted at the time. Thus none of the Apostles philosophized more than did Paul, who was called to preach to the Gentiles; other Apostles preaching to the Jews, who despised philosophy, similarly, adapted themselves to the temper of their hearers (see Gal. ii. 11), and preached a religion free from all philosophical speculations. How blest would our age be if it could witness a religion freed also from all the trammels of superstition!

CHAPTER XII

Of the true original of the Divine Law, and wherefore Scripture is called Sacred, and the Word of God. How that, in so far as it contains the Word of God, it has come down to us uncorrupted

Those who look upon the Bible as a message sent down by God from Heaven to men, will doubtless cry out that I have committed the sin against the Holy Ghost because I have asserted that the Word of God is faulty, mutilated, tampered with, and inconsistent; that we possess it only in fragments, and that the original of the covenant which God made with the Jews has been lost. However, I have no doubt that a little reflection will cause them to desist from their uproar: for not only reason but the expressed opinions of prophets and apostles openly proclaim that God's eternal Word and covenant, no less than true religion, is Divinely inscribed in human hearts, that is, in the human mind, and that this is the true original of God's covenant, stamped with His own seal, namely, the idea of Himself, as it were, with the image of His Godhood.

Religion was imparted to the early Hebrews as a law written down, because they were at that time in the condition of children, but afterwards Moses (Deut. xxx:6) and Jeremiah (xxxi:33) predicted a time coming when the Lord should write His law in their hearts. Thus only the Jews, and amongst them chiefly the Sadducees, struggled for the law written on tablets; least of all need those who bear it inscribed on their hearts join in the contest. Those, therefore, who reflect, will find nothing in what I have written repugnant either to the Word of God or to true religion and faith, or calculated to weaken either one or the other: contrariwise, they will see that I have strengthened religion, as I showed at the end of Chapter X.; indeed, had it not been so, I should certainly have decided to hold my peace, nay, I would even have asserted as a way out of all difficulties that the Bible contains the most profound hidden mysteries; however, as this doctrine has given rise to gross superstition and other pernicious results spoken of at the beginning of Chapter V., I have thought such a course unnecessary, especially as religion stands in no need of superstitious adornments, but is, on the contrary, deprived by such trappings of some of her splendour.

Still, it will be said, though the law of God is written in the heart, the Bible is none the less the Word of God, and it is no more lawful to say of Scripture than of God's Word that it is mutilated and corrupted. I fear that such objectors are too anxious to be pious, and that they are in danger of turning religion into superstition, and worshipping paper and ink in place of God's Word.

I am certified of thus much: I have said nothing unworthy of Scripture or God's Word, and I have made no assertions which I could not prove by most plain argument to be true. I can, therefore, rest assured that I have advanced nothing which is impious or even savours of impiety.

I confess that some profane men, to whom religion is a burden, may, from what I have said, assume a licence to sin, and without any reason, at I confess that some profane men, to whom religion is a burden, may, the simple dictates of their lusts conclude that Scripture is everywhere faulty and falsified, and that therefore its authority is null; but such men are beyond the reach of help, for nothing, as the pro verb has it, can be said so rightly that it cannot be twisted into wrong. Those who wish to give rein to their lusts are at no loss for an excuse, nor were those men of old who possessed the original Scriptures, the ark of the covenant, nay, the prophets and apostles in person among them, any better than the people of today. Human nature, Jew as well as Gentile, has always been the same, and in every age virtue has been exceedingly rare.

Nevertheless, to remove every scruple, I will here show in what sense the Bible or any inanimate thing should be called sacred and Divine; also wherein the law of God consists, and how it cannot be contained in a certain number of books; and, lastly, I will show that Scripture, in so far as it teaches what is necessary for obedience and salvation, cannot have been corrupted. From these considerations everyone will be able to judge that I have neither said anything against the Word of God nor given any foothold to impiety.

A thing is called sacred and Divine when it is designed for promoting piety, and continues sacred so long as it is religiously used: if the users cease to be pious, the thing ceases to be sacred: if it be turned to base uses, that which was formerly sacred becomes unclean and profane. For instance, a certain spot was named by the patriarch Jacob the house of God, because he worshipped God there revealed to him: by the prophets the same spot was called the house of iniquity (see Amos v:5, and Hosea x:5), because the Israelites were wont, at the instigation of Jeroboam, to sacrifice there to idols. Another example puts the matter in the plainest light. Words gain their meaning solely from their usage, and if they are arranged according to their accepted signification so as to move those who read them to devotion, they will become sacred, and the book so written will be sacred also. But if their usage afterwards dies out so that the words have no meaning, or the book becomes utterly neglected, whether from unworthy motives, or because it is no longer needed, then the words and the book will lose both their use and their sanctity: lastly, if these same words be otherwise arranged, or if their customary meaning becomes perverted into its opposite, then both the words and the book containing them become, instead of sacred, impure and profane.

From this it follows that nothing is in itself absolutely sacred, or profane, and unclean, apart from the mind, but only relatively thereto. Thus much is clear from many passages in the Bible. Jeremiah (to select one case out of many) says (chap. vii:4), that the Jews of his time were wrong in calling Solomon's Temple, the Temple of God, for, as he goes on to say in the same chapter, God's name would only be given to the Temple so long as it was frequented by men who worshipped Him, and defended justice, but that, if it became the resort of murderers, thieves, idolaters, and other wicked persons, it would be turned into a den of malefactors.

Scripture, curiously enough, nowhere tells us what became of the Ark of the Covenant, though there is no doubt that it was destroyed, or burnt together with the Temple; yet there was nothing which the Hebrews considered more sacred, or held in greater reverence. Thus Scripture is sacred, and its words Divine so long as it stirs mankind to devotion towards God: but if it be utterly neglected, as it formerly was by the Jews, it becomes nothing but paper and ink, and is left to be desecrated or corrupted: still, though Scripture be thus corrupted or destroyed, we must not say that the Word of God has suffered in like manner, else we shall be like the Jews, who said that the Temple which would then be the Temple of God had perished in the flames. Jeremiah tells us this in respect to the law, for he thus chides the ungodly of his time, "Wherefore, say you we are masters, and the law of the Lord is with us? Surely it has been given in vain, it is in vain that the pen of the scribes " (has been made) — that is, you say falsely that the Scripture is in your power, and that you possess the law of God; for ye have made it of none effect.

So also, when Moses broke the first tables of the law, he did not by any means cast the Word of God from his hands in anger and shatter it — such an action would be inconceivable, either of Moses or of God's Word — he only broke the tables of stone, which, though they had before been holy from containing the covenant wherewith the Jews had bound themselves in obedience to God, had entirely lost their sanctity when the covenant had been violated by the worship of the calf, and were, therefore, as liable to perish as the ark of the covenant. It is thus scarcely to be wondered at, that the original documents of Moses are no longer extant, nor that the books we possess met with the fate we have described, when we consider that the true original of the Divine covenant, the most sacred object of all, has totally perished.

Let them cease, therefore, who accuse us of impiety, inasmuch as we have said nothing against the Word of God, neither have we corrupted it, but let them keep their anger, if they would wreak it justly, for the ancients whose malice desecrated the Ark, the Temple, and the Law of God, and all that was held sacred, subjecting them to corruption. Furthermore, if, according to the saying of the Apostle in 2 Cor. iii:3, they possessed "the Epistle of Christ, written not with ink, but with the Spirit of the living God, not in tables of stone, but in the fleshy tables of the heart," let them cease to worship the letter, and be so anxious concerning it.

I think I have now sufficiently shown in what respect Scripture should be accounted sacred and Divine; we may now see what should rightly be understood by the expression, the Word of the Lord; debar (the Hebrew original) signifies word, speech, command, and thing. The causes for which a thing is in Hebrew said to be of God, or is referred to Him, have been already detailed in Chap. I., and we can therefrom easily gather what meaning Scripture attaches to the phrases, the word, the speech, the command, or the thing of God. I need not, therefore, repeat what I there said, nor what was shown under the third head in the chapter on miracles. It is enough to mention the repetition for the better understanding of what I am about to say — viz., that the Word of the Lord when it has reference to anyone but God Himself, signifies that Divine law treated of in Chap. IV.; in other words, religion, universal and catholic to the whole human race, as Isaiah describes it (chap. i:10), teaching that the true way of life consists, not in ceremonies, but in charity, and a true heart, and calling it indifferently God's Law and God's Word.

The expression is also used metaphorically for the order of nature and destiny (which, indeed, actually depend and follow from the eternal mandate of the Divine nature), and especially for such parts of such order as were foreseen by the prophets, for the prophets did not perceive future events as the result of natural causes, but as the fiats and decrees of God. Lastly, it is employed for the command of any prophet, in so far as he had perceived it by his peculiar faculty or prophetic gift, and not by the natural light of reason; this use springs chiefly from the usual prophetic conception of God as a legislator, which we remarked in Chap. IV. There are, then, three causes for the Bible's being called the Word of God: because it teaches true religion, of which God is the eternal Founder; because it narrates predictions of future events as though they were decrees of God; because its actual authors generally perceived things not by their ordinary natural faculties, but by a power peculiar to themselves, and introduced these things perceived, as told them by God.

Although Scripture contains much that is merely historical and can be perceived by natural reason, yet its name is acquired from its chief subject matter.

We can thus easily see how God can be said to be the Author of the Bible: it is because of the true religion therein contained, and not because He wished to communicate to men a certain number of books. We can also learn from hence the reason for the division into Old and New Testament. It was made because the prophets who preached religion before Christ, preached it as a national law in virtue of the covenant entered into under Moses; while the Apostles who came after Christ, preached it to all men as a universal religion solely in virtue of Christ's Passion: the cause for the division is not that the two parts are different in doctrine, nor that they were written as originals of the covenant, nor, lastly, that the catholic religion (which is in entire harmony with our nature) was new except in relation to those who had not known it: " it was in the world," as John the Evangelist says, " and the world knew it not."

Thus, even if we had fewer books of the Old and New Testament than we have, we should still not be deprived of the Word of God (which, as we have said, is identical with true religion), even as we do not now hold ourselves to be deprived of it, though we lack many cardinal writings such as the Book of the Law, which was religiously guarded in the Temple as the original of the Covenant, also the Book of Wars, the Book of Chronicles, and many others, from whence the extant Old Testament was taken and compiled. The above conclusion may be supported by many reasons.

I. Because the books of both Testaments were not written by express command at one place for all ages, but are a fortuitous collection of the works of men, writing each as his period and disposition dictated. So much is clearly shown by the call of the prophets who were bade to admonish the ungodly of their time, and also by the Apostolic Epistles.

II. Because it is one thing to understand the meaning of Scripture and the prophets, and quite another thing to understand the meaning of God, or the actual truth. This follows from what we said in Chap. II. We showed, in Chap. VI., that it applied to historic narratives, and to miracles: but it by no means applies to questions concerning true religion and virtue.

III. Because the books of the Old Testament were selected from many, and were collected and sanctioned by a council of the Pharisees, as we showed in Chap. X. The books of the New Testament were also chosen from many by councils which rejected as spurious other books held sacred by many. But these councils, both Pharisee and Christian, were not composed of prophets, but only of learned men and teachers. Still, we must grant that they were guided in their choice by a regard for the Word of God; and they must, therefore, have known what the law of God was.

IV. Because the Apostles wrote not as prophets, but as teachers (see last Chapter), and chose whatever method they thought best adapted for those whom they addressed: and consequently, there are many things in the Epistles (as we showed at the end of the last Chapter) which are not necessary to salvation.

V. Lastly, because there are four Evangelists in the New Testament, and it is scarcely credible that God can have designed to narrate the life of Christ four times over, and to communicate it thus to mankind. For though there are some details related in one Gospel which are not in another, and one often helps us to understand another, we cannot thence conclude that all that is set down is of vital importance to us, and that God chose the four Evangelists in order that the life of Christ might be better understood; for each one preached his Gospel in a separate locality, each wrote it down as he preached it, in simple language, in order that the history of Christ might be clearly told, not with any view of explaining his fellow-Evangelists.

If there are some passages which can be better, and more easily understood by comparing the various versions, they are the result of chance, and are not numerous: their continuance in obscurity would have impaired neither the clearness of the narrative nor the blessedness of mankind.

We have now shown that Scripture can only be called the Word of God in so far as it affects religion, or the Divine law; we must now point out that, in respect to these questions, it is neither faulty, tampered with, nor corrupt. By faulty, tampered with, and corrupt, I here mean written so incorrectly, that the meaning cannot be arrived at by a study of the language, nor from the authority of Scripture. I will not go to such lengths as to say that the Bible, in so far as it contains the Divine law, has always preserved the same vowel-points, the same letters, or the same words (I leave this to be proved by, the Massoretes and other worshippers of the letter), I only, maintain that the meaning by, which alone an utterance is entitled to be called Divine, has come down to us uncorrupted, even though the original wording may have been more often changed than we suppose. Such alterations, as I have said above, detract nothing from the Divinity of the Bible, for the Bible would have been no less Divine had it been written in different words or a different language. That the Divine law has in this sense come down to us uncorrupted, is an assertion which admits of no dispute. For from the Bible itself we learn, without the smallest difficulty or ambiguity,, that its cardinal precept is: To love God above all things, and one's neighbour as one's self. This cannot be a spurious passage, nor due to a hasty and mistaken scribe, for if the Bible had ever put forth a different doctrine it would have had to change the whole of its teaching, for this is the corner-stone of religion, without which the whole fabric would fall headlong to the ground. The Bible would not be the work we have been examining, but something quite different.

We remain, then, unshaken in our belief that this has always been the doctrine of Scripture, and, consequently, that no error sufficient to vitiate it can have crept in without being instantly, observed by all; nor can anyone have succeeded in tampering with it and escaped the discovery of his malice.

As this corner-stone is intact, we must perforce admit the same of whatever other passages are indisputably dependent on it, and are also fundamental, as, for instance, that a God exists, that He foresees all things, that He is Almighty, that by His decree the good prosper and the wicked come to naught, and, finally, that our salvation depends solely on His grace.

These are doctrines which Scripture plainly teaches throughout, and which it is bound to teach, else all the rest would be empty and baseless; nor can we be less positive about other moral doctrines, which plainly are built upon this universal foundation — for instance, to uphold justice, to aid the weak, to do no murder, to covet no man's goods, &c. Precepts, I repeat, such as these, human malice and the lapse of ages are alike powerless to destroy, for if any part of them perished, its loss would immediately be supplied from the fundamental principle, especially the doctrine of charity, which is everywhere in both Testaments extolled above all others. Moreover, though it be true that there is no conceivable crime so heinous that it has never been committed, still there is no one who would attempt in excuse for his crimes to destroy, the law, or introduce an impious doctrine in the place of what is eternal and salutary; men's nature is so constituted that everyone (be he king or subject) who has committed a base action, tries to deck out his conduct with spurious excuses, till he seems to have done nothing but what is just and right.

We may conclude, therefore, that the whole Divine law, as taught by Scripture, has come down to us uncorrupted. Besides this there are certain facts which we may be sure have been transmitted in good faith. For instance, the main facts of Hebrew history, which were perfectly well known to everyone. The Jewish people were accustomed in former times to chant the ancient history of their nation in psalms. The main facts, also, of Christ's life and passion were immediately spread abroad through the whole Roman empire. It is therefore scarcely credible, unless nearly everybody, consented thereto, which we cannot suppose, that successive generations have handed down the broad outline of the Gospel narrative otherwise than as they received it.

Whatsoever, therefore, is spurious or faulty can only have reference to details — some circumstances in one or the other history or prophecy designed to stir the people to greater devotion; or in some miracle, with a view of confounding philosophers; or, lastly, in speculative matters after they had become mixed up with religion, so that some individual might prop up his own inventions with a pretext of Divine authority. But such matters have little to do with salvation, whether they be corrupted little or much, as I will show in detail in the next chapter, though I think the question sufficiently plain from what I have said already, especially in Chapter II.

CHAPTER XIII

It is shown that Scripture teaches only very simple Doctrines, such as suffice for Right Conduct

In the second chapter of this treatise we pointed out that the prophets were gifted with extraordinary powers of imagination, but not of understanding; also that God only revealed to them such things as are very simple — not philosophic mysteries, — and that He adapted His communications to their previous opinions. We further showed in Chap. V. that Scripture only transmits and teaches truths which can readily be comprehended by all; not deducing and concatenating its conclusions from definitions and axioms, but narrating quite simply, and confirming its statements, with a view to inspiring belief, by an appeal to experience as exemplified in miracles and history, and setting forth its truths in the style and phraseology which would most appeal to the popular mind (cf. Chap. VI., third division).

Lastly, we demonstrated in Chap. VIII. that the difficulty of understanding Scripture lies in the language only, and not in the abstruseness of the argument.

To these considerations we may add that the Prophets did not preach only to the learned, but to all Jews, without exception, while the Apostles were wont to teach the gospel doctrine in churches where there were public meetings; whence it follows that Scriptural doctrine contains no lofty speculations nor philosophic reasoning, but only very simple matters, such as could be understood by the slowest intelligence.

I am consequently lost in wonder at the ingenuity of those whom I have already mentioned, who detect in the Bible mysteries so profound that they cannot be explained in human language, and who have introduced so many philosophic speculations into religion that the Church seems like an academy, and religion like a science, or rather a dispute.

It is not to be wondered at that men, who boast of possessing supernatural intelligence, should be unwilling to yield the palm of knowledge to philosophers who have only their ordinary, faculties; still I should be surprised if I found them teaching any new speculative doctrine, which was not a commonplace to those Gentile philosophers whom, in spite of all, they stigmatize as blind; for, if one inquires what these mysteries lurking in Scripture may be, one is confronted with nothing but the reflections of Plato or Aristotle, or the like, which it would often be easier for an ignorant man to dream than for the most accomplished scholar to wrest out of the Bible.

However, I do not wish to affirm absolutely that Scripture contains no doctrines in the sphere of philosophy, for in the last chapter I pointed out some of the kind, as fundamental principles; but I go so far as to say that such doctrines are very few and very simple. Their precise nature and definition I will now set forth. The task will be easy, for we know that Scripture does not aim at imparting scientific knowledge, and, therefore, it demands from men nothing but obedience, and censures obstinacy, but not ignorance.

Furthermore, as obedience to God consists solely in love to our neighbour — for whosoever loveth his neighbour, as a means of obeying God, hath, as St. Paul says (Rom. xiii:8), fulfilled the law, — it follows that no knowledge is commended in the Bible save that which is necessary for enabling all men to obey God in the manner stated, and without which they would become rebellious, or without the discipline of obedience.

Other speculative questions, which have no direct bearing on this object, or are concerned with the knowledge of natural events, do not affect Scripture, and should be entirely separated from religion.

Now, though everyone, as we have said, is now quite able to see this truth for himself, I should nevertheless wish, considering that the whole of Religion depends thereon, to explain the entire question more accurately and clearly. To this end I must first prove that the intellectual or accurate knowledge of God is not a gift, bestowed upon all good men like obedience; and, further, that the knowledge of God, required by Him through His prophets from everyone without exception, as needful to be known, is simply a knowledge of His Divine justice and charity. Both these points are easily proved from Scripture. The first plainly follows from Exodus vi:2, where God, in order to show the singular grace bestowed upon Moses, says to him: "And I appeared unto Abraham, unto Isaac, and unto Jacob by the name of El Sadai (A. V. God Almighty); but by my name Jehovah was I not known to them" — for the better understanding of which passage I may remark that El Sadai, in Hebrew, signifies the God who suffices, in that He gives to every man that which suffices for him; and, although Sadai is often used by itself, to signify God, we cannot doubt that the word El (God, {power, might}) is everywhere understood. Furthermore, we must note that Jehovah is the only word found in Scripture with the meaning of the absolute essence of God, without reference to created things. The Jews maintain, for this reason, that this is, strictly speaking, the only name of God; that the rest of the words used are merely titles; and, in truth, the other names of God, whether they be substantives or adjectives, are merely attributive, and belong to Him, in so far as He is conceived of in relation to created things, or manifested through them. Thus El, or Eloah, signifies powerful, as is well known, and only applies to God in respect to His supremacy, as when we call Paul an apostle; the faculties of his power are set forth in an accompanying adjective, as El, great, awful, just, merciful, &c., or else all are understood at once by the use of El in the plural number, with a singular signification, an expression frequently adopted in Scripture.

Now, as God tells Moses that He was not known to the patriarchs by the name of Jehovah, it follows that they were not cognizant of any attribute of God which expresses His absolute essence, but only of His deeds and promises that is, of His power, as manifested in visible things. God does not thus speak to Moses in order to accuse the patriarchs of infidelity, but, on the contrary, as a means of extolling their belief and faith, inasmuch as, though they possessed no extraordinary knowledge of God (such as Moses had), they yet accepted His promises as fixed and certain; whereas Moses, though his thoughts about God were more exalted, nevertheless doubted about the Divine promises, and complained to God that, instead of the promised deliverance, the prospects of the Israelites had darkened.

As the patriarchs did not know the distinctive name of God, and as God mentions the fact to Moses, in praise of their faith and single-heartedness, and in contrast to the extraordinary grace granted to Moses, it follows, as we stated at first, that men are not bound by, decree to have knowledge of the attributes of God, such knowledge being only granted to a few of the faithful: it is hardly worth while to quote further examples from Scripture, for everyone must recognize that knowledge of God is not equal among all good men. Moreover, a man cannot be ordered to be wise any more than he can be ordered to live and exist. Men, women, and children are all alike able to obey by, commandment, but not to be wise. If any tell us that it is not necessary to understand the Divine attributes, but that we must believe them simply, without proof, he is plainly, trifling. For what is invisible and can only, be perceived by the mind, cannot be apprehended by any, other means than proofs; if these are absent the object remains ungrasped; the repetition of what has been heard on such subjects no more indicates or attains to their meaning than the words of a parrot or a puppet speaking without sense or signification.

Before I proceed I ought to explain how it comes that we are often told in Genesis that the patriarchs preached in the name of Jehovah, this being in plain contradiction to the text above quoted. A reference to what was said in Chap. VIII. will readily explain the difficulty.

It was there shown that the writer of the Pentateuch did not always speak of things and places by the names they bore in the times of which he was writing, but by the names best known to his contemporaries. God is thus said in the Pentateuch to have been preached by the patriarchs under the name of Jehovah, not because such was the name by which the patriarchs knew Him, but because this name was the one most reverenced by the Jews.

This point, I say, must necessarily be noticed, for in Exodus it is expressly stated that God was not known to the patriarchs by this name; and in chap. iii:13, it is said that Moses desired to know the name of God. Now, if this name had been already known it would have been known to Moses. We must therefore draw the conclusion indicated, namely, that the faithful patriarchs did not know this name of God, and that the knowledge of God is bestowed and not commanded by the Deity.

It is now time to pass on to our second point, and show that God through His prophets required from men no other knowledge of Himself than is contained in a knowledge of His justice and charity — that is, of attributes which a certain manner of life will enable men to imitate. Jeremiah states this in so many words (xxii:15, 16): "Did not thy father eat, and drink, and do judgment and justice? and then it was well with him. He judged the cause of the poor and needy; then it was well with him: was not this to know Me? saith the Lord."

The words in chap. ix:24 of the same book are equally, clear. "But let him that glorieth glory in this, that he understandeth and knoweth Me, that I am the Lord which exercise loving-kindness, judgment, and righteousness in the earth; for in these things I delight, saith the Lord." The same doctrine maybe gathered from Exod. xxxiv:6, where God revealed to Moses only, those of His attributes which display the Divine justice and charity. Lastly, we may call attention to a passage in John which we shall discuss at more length hereafter; the Apostle explains the nature of God (inasmuch as no one has beheld Him) through charity only, and concludes that he who possesses charity possesses, and in very, truth knows God.

We have thus seen that Moses, Jeremiah, and John sum up in a very short compass the knowledge of God needful for all, and that they state it to consist in exactly what we said, namely, that God is supremely just, and supremely merciful — in other words, the one perfect pattern of the true life.

We may add that Scripture nowhere gives an express definition of God, and does not point out any other of His attributes which should be apprehended save these, nor does it in set terms praise any others. Wherefore we may draw the general conclusion that an intellectual knowledge of God, which takes cognizance of His nature in so far as it actually is, and which cannot by any manner of living be imitated by mankind or followed as an example, has no bearing whatever on true rules of conduct, on faith, or on revealed religion; consequently that men may be in complete error on the subject without incurring the charge of sinfulness.

We need now no longer wonder that God adapted Himself to the existing opinions and imaginations of the prophets, or that the faithful held different ideas of God, as we showed in Chap. II.; or, again, that the sacred books speak very inaccurately of God, attributing to Him hands, feet, eyes, ears, a mind, and motion from one place to another; or that they ascribe to Him emotions, such as jealousy, mercy, &c., or, lastly, that they describe Him as a Judge in heaven sitting on a royal throne with Christ on His right hand. Such expressions are adapted to the understanding of the multitude, it being the object of the Bible to make men not learned but obedient.

In spite of this the general run of theologians, when they come upon any of these phrases which they cannot rationally harmonize with the Divine nature, maintain that they should be interpreted metaphorically, passages they cannot understand they say should be interpreted literally. But if every expression of this kind in the Bible is necessarily to be interpreted and understood metaphorically, Scripture must have been written, not for the people and the unlearned masses, but chiefly for accomplished experts and philosophers.

If it were indeed a sin to hold piously and simply the ideas about God we have just quoted, the prophets ought to have been strictly on their guard against the use of such expressions, seeing the weak-mindedness of the people, and ought, on the other hand, to have set forth first of all, duly and clearly, those attributes of God which are needful to be understood.

This they have nowhere done; we cannot, therefore, think that opinions taken in themselves without respect to actions are either pious or impious, but must maintain that a man is pious or impious in his beliefs only in so far as he is thereby incited to obedience, or derives from them license to sin and rebel.

If a man, by believing what is true, becomes rebellious, his creed is impious; if by believing what is false he becomes obedient, his creed is pious; for the true knowledge of God comes not by commandment, but by Divine gift. God has required nothing from man but a knowledge of His Divine justice and charity, and that not as necessary to scientific accuracy, but to obedience.

CHAPTER XIV

Definitions of Faith, the Faith, and the Foundations of Faith, which is once for all separated from Philosophy

For a true knowledge of faith it is above all things necessary to understand that the Bible was adapted to the intelligence, not only of the prophets, but also of the diverse and fickle Jewish multitude. This will be recognized by all who give any thought to the subject, for they will see that a person who accepted promiscuously everything in Scripture as being the universal and absolute teaching of God, without accurately defining what was adapted to the popular intelligence, would find it impossible to escape confounding the opinions of the masses with the Divine doctrines, praising the judgments and comments of man as the teaching of God, and making a wrong use of Scriptural authority. Who, I say, does not perceive that this is the chief reason why so many sectaries teach contradictory opinions as Divine documents, and support their contentions with numerous Scriptural texts, till it has passed in Belgium into a proverb, geen ketter sonder letter — no heretic without a text? The sacred books were not written by one man, nor for the people of a single period, but by many authors of different temperaments, at times extending from first to last over nearly two thousand years, and perhaps much longer. We will not, however, accuse the sectaries of impiety because they have adapted the words of Scripture to their own opinions; it is thus that these words were adapted to the understanding of the masses originally, and everyone is at liberty so to treat them if he sees that he can thus obey God in matters relating to justice and charity with a more full consent: but we do accuse those who will not grant this freedom to their fellows, but who persecute all who differ from them, as God's enemies, however honourable and virtuous be their lives; while, on the other hand, they cherish those who agree with them, however foolish they may be, as God's elect. Such conduct is as wicked and dangerous to the state as any that can be conceived.

In order, therefore, to establish the limits to which individual freedom should extend, and to decide what persons, in spite of the diversity of their opinions, are to be looked upon as the faithful, we must define faith and its essentials. This task I hope to accomplish in the present chapter, and also to separate faith from philosophy, which is the chief aim of the whole treatise.

In order to proceed duly to the demonstration let us recapitulate the chief aim and object of Scripture; this will indicate a standard by which we may define faith.

We have said in a former chapter that the aim and object of Scripture is only to teach obedience. Thus much, I think, no one can question. Who does not see that both Testaments are nothing else but schools for this object, and have neither of them any aim beyond inspiring mankind with a voluntary obedience? For (not to repeat what I said in the last chapter) I will remark that Moses did not seek to convince the Jews by reason, but bound them by a covenant, by oaths, and by conferring benefits; further, he threatened the people with punishment if they should infringe the law, and promised rewards if they should obey it. All these are not means for teaching knowledge, but for inspiring obedience. The doctrine of the Gospels enjoins nothing but simple faith, namely, to believe in God and to honour Him, which is the same thing as to obey him. There is no occasion for me to throw further light on a question so plain by citing Scriptural texts commending obedience, such as may be found in great numbers in both Testaments. Moreover, the Bible teaches very clearly in a great many passages what everyone ought to do in order to obey God; the whole duty is summed up in love to one's neighbour. It cannot, therefore, be denied that he who by God's command loves his neighbour as himself is truly obedient and blessed according to the law, whereas he who hates his neighbour or neglects him is rebellious and obstinate.

Lastly, it is plain to everyone that the Bible was not written and disseminated only, for the learned, but for men of every age and race; wherefore we may, rest assured that we are not bound by Scriptural command to believe anything beyond what is absolutely necessary, for fulfilling its main precept.

This precept, then, is the only standard of the whole Catholic faith, and by it alone all the dogmas needful to be believed should be determined. So much being abundantly manifest, as is also the fact that all other doctrines of the faith can be legitimately deduced therefrom by reason alone, I leave it to every man to decide for himself how it comes to pass that so many divisions have arisen in the Church: can it be from any other cause than those suggested at the beginning of Chap. VIII.? It is these same causes which compel me to explain the method of determining the dogmas of the faith from the foundation we have discovered, for if I neglected to do so, and put the question on a regular basis, I might justly be said to have promised too lavishly, for that anyone might, by my showing, introduce any doctrine he liked into religion, under the pretext that it was a necessary means to obedience: especially would this be the case in questions respecting the Divine attributes.

In order, therefore, to set forth the whole matter methodically, I will begin with a definition of faith, which on the principle above given, should be as follows:—

Faith consists in a knowledge of God, without which obedience to Him would be impossible, and which the mere fact of obedience to Him implies. This definition is so clear, and follows so plainly from what we have already proved, that it needs no explanation. The consequences involved therein I will now briefly show.

(I.) Faith is not salutary in itself, but only in respect to the obedience it implies, or as James puts it in his Epistle, ii:17, "Faith without works is dead" (see the whole of the chapter quoted).

(II.) He who is truly obedient necessarily possesses true and saving faith; for if obedience be granted, faith must be granted also, as the same Apostle expressly says in these words (ii:18), "Show me thy faith without thy works, and I will show thee my faith by my works." So also John, I Ep. iv:7: "Everyone that loveth is born of God, and knoweth God: he that loveth not, knoweth not God; for God is love." From these texts, I repeat, it follows that we can only judge a man faithful or unfaithful by his works. If his works be good, he is faithful, however much his doctrines may differ from those of the rest of the faithful: if his works be evil, though he may verbally conform, he is unfaithful. For obedience implies faith, and faith without works is dead.

John, in the 13th verse of the chapter above quoted, expressly teaches the same doctrine: "Hereby," he says, "know we that we dwell in Him and He in us, because He hath given us of His Spirit," i.e. love. He had said before that God is love, and therefore he concludes (on his own received principles), that whoso possesses love possesses truly the Spirit of God. As no one has beheld God he infers that no one has knowledge or consciousness of God, except from love towards his neighbour, and also that no one can have knowledge of any of God's attributes, except this of love, in so far as we participate therein.

If these arguments are not conclusive, they, at any rate, show the Apostle's meaning, but the words in chap. ii:3, 4, of the same Epistle are much clearer, for they state in so many words our precise contention: "And hereby we do know that we know Him, if we keep His commandments. He that saith, I know Him, and keepeth not His commandments, is a liar, and the truth is not in him."

From all this, I repeat, it follows that they are the true enemies of Christ who persecute honourable and justice-loving men because they differ from them, and do not uphold the same religious dogmas as themselves: for whosoever loves justice and charity we know, by that very fact, to be faithful: whosoever persecutes the faithful, is an enemy to Christ.

Lastly, it follows that faith does not demand that dogmas should be true as that they should be pious — that is, such as will stir up the heart to obey; though there be many such which contain not a shadow of truth, so long as they be held in good faith, otherwise their adherents are disobedient, for how can anyone, desirous of loving justice and obeying God, adore as Divine what he knows to be alien from the Divine nature? However, men may err from simplicity of mind, and Scripture, as we have seen, does not condemn ignorance, but obstinacy. This is the necessary result of our definition of faith, and all its branches should spring from the universal rule above given, and from the evident aim and object of the Bible, unless we choose to mix our own inventions therewith. Thus it is not true doctrines which are expressly required by the Bible, so much as doctrines necessary for obedience, and to confirm in our hearts the love of our neighbour, wherein (to adopt the words of John) we are in God, and God in us.

As, then, each man's faith must be judged pious or impious only in respect of its producing obedience or obstinacy, and not in respect of its truth; and as no one will dispute that men's dispositions are exceedingly varied, that all do not acquiesce in the same things, but are ruled some by one opinion some by another, so that what moves one to devotion moves another to laughter and contempt, it follows that there can be no doctrines in the Catholic, or universal, religion, which can give rise to controversy among good men. Such doctrines might be pious to some and impious to others, whereas they should be judged solely by their fruits.

To the universal religion, then, belong only such dogmas as are absolutely required in order to attain obedience to God, and without which such obedience would be impossible; as for the rest, each man — seeing that he is the best judge of his own character should adopt whatever he thinks best adapted to strengthen his love of justice. If this were so, I think there would be no further occasion for controversies in the Church.

I have now no further fear in enumerating the dogmas of universal faith or the fundamental dogmas of the whole of Scripture, inasmuch as they all tend (as may be seen from what has been said) to this one doctrine, namely, that there exists a God, that is, a Supreme Being, Who loves justice and charity, and Who must be obeyed by whosoever would be saved; that the worship of this Being consists in the practice of justice and love towards one's neighbour, and that they contain nothing beyond the following doctrines:—

I. That God or a Supreme Being exists, sovereignly just and merciful, the Exemplar of the true life; that whosoever is ignorant of or disbelieves in His existence cannot obey Him or know Him as a Judge.

II. That He is One. Nobody will dispute that this doctrine is absolutely necessary for entire devotion, admiration, and love towards God. For devotion, admiration, and love spring from the superiority of one over all else.

III. That He is omnipresent, or that all things are open to Him, for if anything could be supposed to be concealed from Him, or to be unnoticed by, Him, we might doubt or be ignorant of the equity of His judgment as directing all things.

IV. That He has supreme right and dominion over all things, and that He does nothing under compulsion, but by His absolute fiat and grace. All things are bound to obey Him, He is not bound to obey any.

V. That the worship of God consists only in justice and charity, or love towards one's neighbour.

VI. That all those, and those only, who obey God by their manner of life are saved; the rest of mankind, who live under the sway of their pleasures, are lost. If we did not believe this, there would be no reason for obeying God rather than pleasure.

VII. Lastly, that God forgives the sins of those who repent. No one is free from sin, so that without this belief all would despair of salvation, and there would be no reason for believing in the mercy of God. He who firmly believes that God, out of the mercy and grace with which He directs all things, forgives the sins of men, and who feels his love of God kindled thereby, he, I say, does really, know Christ according to the Spirit, and Christ is in him.

No one can deny that all these doctrines are before all things necessary, to be believed, in order that every man, without exception, may be able to obey God according to the bidding of the Law above explained, for if one of these precepts be disregarded obedience is destroyed. But as to what God, or the Exemplar of the true life, may be, whether fire, or spirit, or light, or thought, or what not, this, I say, has nothing to do with faith any more than has the question how He comes to be the Exemplar of the true life, whether it be because He has a just and merciful mind, or because all things exist and act through Him, and consequently that we understand through Him, and through Him see what is truly just and good. Everyone may think on such questions as he likes,

Furthermore, faith is not affected, whether we hold that God is omnipresent essentially or potentially; that He directs all things by absolute fiat, or by the necessity of His nature; that He dictates laws like a prince, or that He sets them forth as eternal truths; that man obeys Him by virtue of free will, or by virtue of the necessity of the Divine decree; lastly, that the reward of the good and the punishment of the wicked is natural or supernatural: these and such like questions have no bearing on faith, except in so far as they are used as means to give us license to sin more, or to obey God less. I will go further, and maintain that every man is bound to adapt these dogmas to his own way of thinking, and to interpret them according as he feels that he can give them his fullest and most unhesitating assent, so that he may the more easily obey God with his whole heart.

Such was the manner, as we have already pointed out, in which the faith was in old time revealed and written, in accordance with the understanding and opinions of the prophets and people of the period; so, in like fashion, every man is bound to adapt it to his own opinions, so that he may accept it without any hesitation or mental repugnance. We have shown that faith does not so much re quire truth as piety, and that it is only quickening and pious through obedience, consequently no one is faithful save by obedience alone. The best faith is not necessarily possessed by him who displays the best reasons, but by him who displays the best fruits of justice and charity. How salutary and necessary this doctrine is for a state, in order that men may dwell together in peace and concord; and how many and how great causes of disturbance and crime are thereby cut off, I leave everyone to judge for himself!

Before we go further, I may remark that we can, by means of what we have just proved, easily answer the objections raised in Chap. I., when we were discussing God's speaking with the Israelites on Mount Sinai. For, though the voice heard by the Israelites could not give those men any philosophical or mathematical certitude of God's existence, it was yet sufficient to thrill them with admiration for God, as they already knew Him, and to stir them up to obedience: and such was the object of the display. God did not wish to teach the Israelites the absolute attributes of His essence (none of which He then revealed), but to break down their hardness of heart, and to draw them to obedience: therefore He did not appeal to them with reasons, but with the sound of trumpets, thunder, and lightnings.

It remains for me to show that between faith or theology, and philosophy, there is no connection, nor affinity. I think no one will dispute the fact who has knowledge of the aim and foundations of the two subjects, for they are as wide apart as the poles.

Philosophy has no end in view save truth: faith, as we have abundantly proved, looks for nothing but obedience and piety. Again, philosophy is based on axioms which must be sought from nature alone: faith is based on history and language, and must be sought for only in Scripture and revelation, as we showed in Chap. VII. Faith, therefore, allows the greatest latitude in philosophic speculation, allowing us without blame to think what we like about anything, and only condemning, as heretics and schismatics, those who teach opinions which tend to produce obstinacy, hatred, strife, and anger; while, on the other hand, only considering as faithful those who persuade us, as far as their reason and faculties will permit, to follow justice and charity.

Lastly, as what we are now setting forth are the most important subjects of my treatise, I would most urgently beg the reader, before I proceed, to read these two chapters with especial attention, and to take the trouble to weigh them well in his mind: let him take for granted that I have not written with a view to introducing novelties, but in order to do away with abuses, such as I hope I may, at some future time, at last see reformed.

CHAPTER XV

Theology is shown not to be Subservient to Reason, nor Reason to Theology: a Definition of the Reason which enables us to accept the authority of the Bible

Those who know not that philosophy and reason are distinct, dispute whether Scripture should be made subservient to reason, or reason to Scripture: that is, whether the meaning of Scripture should be made to agreed with reason; or whether reason should be made to agree with Scripture: the latter position is assumed by the sceptics who deny the certitude of reason, the former by the dogmatists. Both parties are, as I have shown, utterly in the wrong, for either doctrine would require us to tamper with reason or with Scripture.

We have shown that Scripture does not teach philosophy, but merely obedience, and that all it contains has been adapted to the understanding and established opinions of the multitude. Those, therefore, who wish to adapt it to philosophy, must needs ascribe to the prophets many ideas which they never even dreamed of, and give an extremely forced interpretation to their words: those on the other hand, who would make reason and philosophy subservient to theology, will be forced to accept as Divine utterances the prejudices of the ancient Jews, and to fill and confuse their mind therewith. In short, one party will run wild with the aid of reason, and the other will run wild without the aid of reason.

The first among the Pharisees who openly maintained that Scripture should be made to agree with reason, was Maimonides, whose opinion we reviewed, and abundantly refuted in Chap. VIII.: now, although this writer had much authority among his contemporaries, he was deserted on this question by almost all, and the majority went straight over to the opinion of a certain R. Jehuda Alpakhar, who, in his anxiety to avoid the error of Maimonides, fell into another, which was its exact contrary. He held that reason should be made subservient, and entirely give way to Scripture. He thought that a passage should not be interpreted metaphorically, simply because it was repugnant to reason, but only in the cases when it is inconsistent with Scripture itself — that is, with its clear doctrines. Therefore he laid down the universal rule, that whatsoever Scripture teaches dogmatically, and affirms expressly, must on its own sole authority be admitted as absolutely true: that there is no doctrine in the Bible which directly contradicts the general tenour of the whole: but only some which appear to involve a difference, for the phrases of Scripture often seem to imply something contrary to what has been expressly taught. Such phrases, and such phrases only, we may interpret metaphorically.

For instance, Scripture clearly teaches the unity of God (see Deut. vi:4), nor is there any text distinctly asserting a plurality of gods; but in several passages God speaks of Himself, and the prophets speak of Him, in the plural number; such phrases are simply a manner of speaking, and do not mean that there actually are several gods: they are to be explained metaphorically, not because a plurality of gods is repugnant to reason, but because Scripture distinctly asserts that there is only one.

So, again, as Scripture asserts (as Alpakhar thinks) in Deut. iv:15, that God is incorporeal, we are bound, solely by the authority of this text, and not by reason, to believe that God has no body: consequently we must explain metaphorically, on the sole authority of Scripture, all those passages which attribute to God hands, feet, &c., and take them merely as figures of speech. Such is the opinion of Alpakhar. In so far as he seeks to explain Scripture by Scripture, I praise him, but I marvel that a man gifted with reason should wish to debase that faculty. It is true that Scripture should be explained by Scripture, so long as we are in difficulties about the meaning and intention of the prophets, but when we have elicited the true meaning, we must of necessity make use of our judgment and reason in order to assent thereto. If reason, however, much as she rebels, is to be entirely subjected to Scripture, I ask, are we to effect her submission by her own aid, or without her, and blindly? If the latter, we shall surely act foolishly and injudiciously; if the former, we assent to Scripture under the dominion of reason, and should not assent to it without her. Moreover, I may ask now, is a man to assent to anything against his reason? What is denial if it be not reason's refusal to assent? In short, I am astonished that anyone should wish to subject reason, the greatest of gifts and a light from on high, to the dead letter which may have been corrupted by human malice; that it should be thought no crime to speak with contempt of mind, the true handwriting of God's Word, calling it corrupt, blind, and lost, while it is considered the greatest of crimes to say the same of the letter, which is merely the reflection and image of God's Word. Men think it pious to trust nothing to reason and their own judgment, and impious to doubt the faith of those who have transmitted to us the sacred books. Such conduct is not piety, but mere folly. And, after all, why are they so anxious? What are they afraid of? Do they think that faith and religion cannot be upheld unless — men purposely keep themselves in ignorance, and turn their backs on reason? If this be so, they have but a timid trust in Scripture.

However, be it far from me to say that religion should seek to enslave reason, or reason religion, or that both should not be able to keep their sovereignity in perfect harmony. I will revert to this question presently, for I wish now to discuss Alpakhar's rule.

He requires, as we have stated, that we should accept as true, or reject as false, everything asserted or denied by Scripture, and he further states that Scripture never expressly asserts or denies anything which contradicts its assertions or negations elsewhere. The rashness of such a requirement and statement can escape no one. For (passing over the fact that he does not notice that Scripture consists of different books, written at different times, for different people, by different authors: and also that his requirement is made on his own authority without any corroboration from reason or Scripture) he would be bound to show that all passages which are indirectly contradictory of the rest, can be satisfactorily explained metaphorically through the nature of the language and the context: further, that Scripture has come down to us untampered with. However, we will go into the matter at length.

Firstly, I ask what shall we do if reason prove recalcitrant? Shall we still be bound to affirm whatever Scripture affirms, and to deny whatever Scripture denies? Perhaps it will be answered that Scripture contains nothing repugnant to reason. But I insist that it expressly affirms and teaches that God is jealous (namely, in the decalogue itself, and in Exod. xxxiv:14, and in Deut. iv:24, and in many other places), and I assert that such a doctrine is repugnant to reason. It must, I suppose, in spite of all, be accepted as true. If there are any passages in Scripture which imply that God is not jealous, they must be taken metaphorically as meaning nothing of the kind. So, also, Scripture expressly states (Exod. xix:20, &c.) that God came down to Mount Sinai, and it attributes to Him other movements from place to place, nowhere directly stating that God does not so move. Wherefore, we must take the passage literally, and Solomon's words (I Kings viii:27), "But will God dwell on the earth? Behold the heavens and earth cannot contain thee," inasmuch as they do not expressly state that God does not move from place to place, but only imply it, must be explained away till they have no further semblance of denying locomotion to the Deity. So also we must believe that the sky is the habitation and throne of God, for Scripture expressly says so; and similarly many passages expressing the opinions of the prophets or the multitude, which reason and philosophy, but not Scripture, tell us to be false, must be taken as true if we are io follow the guidance of our author, for according to him, reason has nothing to do with the matter. Further, it is untrue that Scripture never contradicts itself directly, but only by implication. For Moses says, in so many words (Deut. iv:24), "The Lord thy God is a consuming fire," and elsewhere expressly denies that God has any likeness to visible things. (Deut. iv. 12.) If it be decided that the latter passage only contradicts the former by implication, and must be adapted thereto, lest it seem to negative it, let us grant that God is a fire; or rather, lest we should seem to have taken leave of our senses, let us pass the matter over and take another example.

Samuel expressly denies that God ever repents, "for he is not a man that he should repent" (I Sam. xv:29). Jeremiah, on the other hand, asserts that God does repent, both of the evil and of the good which He had intended to do (Jer. xviii:8-10). What? Are not these two texts directly contradictory? Which of the two, then, would our author want to explain metaphorically? Both statements are general, and each is the opposite of the other — what one flatly affirms, the other flatly, denies. So, by his own rule, he would be obliged at once to reject them as false, and to accept them as true.

Again, what is the point of one passage, not being contradicted by another directly, but only by implication, if the implication is clear, and the nature and context of the passage preclude metaphorical interpretation? There are many such instances in the Bible, as we saw in Chap. II. (where we pointed out that the prophets held different and contradictory opinions), and also in Chaps. IX. and X., where we drew attention to the contradictions in the historical narratives. There is no need for me to go through them all again, for what I have said sufficiently exposes the absurdities which would follow from an opinion and rule such as we are discussing, and shows the hastiness of its propounder.

We may, therefore, put this theory, as well as that of Maimonides, entirely out of court; and we may, take it for indisputable that theology is not bound to serve reason, nor reason theology, but that each has her own domain.

The sphere of reason is, as we have said, truth and wisdom; the sphere of theology, is piety and obedience. The power of reason does not extend so far as to determine for us that men may be blessed through simple obedience, without understanding. Theology, tells us nothing else, enjoins on us no command save obedience, and has neither the will nor the power to oppose reason: she defines the dogmas of faith (as we pointed out in the last chapter) only in so far as they may be necessary, for obedience, and leaves reason to determine their precise truth: for reason is the light of the mind, and without her all things are dreams and phantoms.

By theology, I here mean, strictly speaking, revelation, in so far as it indicates the object aimed at by Scripture namely, the scheme and manner of obedience, or the true dogmas of piety and faith. This may truly be called the Word of God, which does not consist in a certain number of books (see Chap. XII.). Theology thus understood, if we regard its precepts or rules of life, will be found in accordance with reason; and, if we look to its aim and object, will be seen to be in nowise repugnant thereto, wherefore it is universal to all men.

As for its bearing on Scripture, we have shown in Chap. VII. that the meaning of Scripture should be gathered from its own history, and not from the history of nature in general, which is the basis of philosophy.

We ought not to be hindered if we find that our investigation of the meaning of Scripture thus conducted shows us that it is here and there repugnant to reason; for whatever we may find of this sort in the Bible, which men may be in ignorance of, without injury to their charity, has, we may be sure, no bearing on theology or the Word of God, and may, therefore, without blame, be viewed by every one as he pleases.

To sum up, we may draw the absolute conclusion that the Bible must not be accommodated to reason, nor reason to the Bible.

Now, inasmuch as the basis of theology — the doctrine that man may be saved by obedience alone — cannot be proved by reason whether it be true or false, we may be asked, Why, then, should we believe it? If we do so without the aid of reason, we accept it blindly, and act foolishly and injudiciously; if, on the other hand, we settle that it can be proved by reason, theology becomes a part of philosophy, and inseparable therefrom. But I make answer that I have absolutely established that this basis of theology cannot be investigated by the natural light of reason, or, at any rate, that no one ever has proved it by such means, and, therefore, revelation was necessary. We should, however, make use of our reason, in order to grasp with moral certainty what is revealed — I say, with moral certainty, for we cannot hope to attain greater certainty, than the prophets: yet their certainty was only, moral, as I showed in Chap. II.

Those, therefore, who attempt to set forth the authority of Scripture with mathematical demonstrations are wholly in error: for the authority, of the Bible is dependent on the authority of the prophets, and can be supported by no stronger arguments than those employed in old time by the prophets for convincing the people of their own authority. Our certainty on the same subject can be founded on no other basis than that which served as foundation for the certainty of the prophets.

Now the certainty of the prophets consisted (as we pointed out) in these elements:— (I.) A distinct and vivid imagination. (II.) A sign. (III.) Lastly, and chiefly, a mind turned to what is just and good. It was based on no other reasons than these, and consequently they cannot prove their authority by any other reasons, either to the multitude whom they addressed orally, nor to us whom they address in writing.

The first of these reasons, namely, the vivid imagination, could be valid only for the prophets; therefore, our certainty concerning revelation must, and ought to be, based on the remaining two — namely, the sign and the teaching.

Such is the express doctrine of Moses, for (in Deut. xviii.) he bids the people obey the prophet who should give a true sign in the name of the Lord, but if he should predict falsely, even though it were in the name of the Lord, he should be put to death, as should also he who strives to lead away the people from the true religion, though he confirm his authority with signs and portents. We may compare with the above Deut. xiii. Whence it follows that a true prophet could be distinguished from a false one, both by his doctrine and by the miracles he wrought, for Moses declares such an one to be a true prophet, and bids the people trust him without fear of deceit. He condemns as false, and worthy, of death, those who predict anything falsely even in the name of the Lord, or who preach false gods, even though their miracles be real.

The only reason, then, which we have for belief in Scripture or the writings of the prophets, is the doctrine we find therein, and the signs by which it is confirmed. For as we see that the prophets extol charity and justice above all things, and have no other object, we conclude that they did not write from unworthy motives, but because they really thought that men might become blessed through obedience and faith: further, as we see that they confirmed their teaching with signs and wonders, we become persuaded that they did not speak at random, nor run riot in their prophecies. We are further strengthened in our conclusion by the fact that the morality they teach is in evident agreement with reason, for it is no accidental coincidence that the Word of God which we find in the prophets coincides with the Word of God written in our hearts. We may, I say, conclude this from the sacred books as certainly as did the Jews of old from the living voice of the prophets: for we showed in Chap. XII. that Scripture has come down to us intact in respect to its doctrine and main narratives.

Therefore this whole basis of theology and Scripture, though it does not admit of mathematical proof, may yet be accepted with the approval of our judgment. It would be folly to refuse to accept what is confirmed by such ample prophetic testimony, and what has proved such a comfort to those whose reason is comparatively weak, and such a benefit to the state; a doctrine, moreover, which we may believe in without the slightest peril or hurt, and should reject simply because it cannot be mathematically proved: it is as though we should admit nothing as true, or as a wise rule of life, which could ever, in any possible way, be called in question; or as though most of our actions were not full of uncertainty and hazards.

I admit that those who believe that theology and philosophy are mutually contradictory, and that therefore either one or the other must be thrust from its throne — I admit, I say, that such persons are not unreasonable in attempting to put theology on a firm basis, and to demonstrate its truth mathematically. Who, unless he were desperate or mad, would wish to bid an incontinent farewell to reason, or to despise the arts and sciences, or to deny reason's certitude? But, in the meanwhile, we cannot wholly absolve them from blame, inasmuch as they invoke the aid of reason for her own defeat, and attempt infallibly to prove her fallible. While they are trying to prove mathematically the authority and truth of theology, and to take away the authority of natural reason, they are in reality only bringing theology under reason's dominion, and proving that her authority has no weight unless natural reason be at the back of it.

If they boast that they themselves assent because of the inward testimony of the Holy Spirit, and that they only invoke the aid of reason because of unbelievers, in order to convince them, not even so can this meet with our approval, for we can easily show that they have spoken either from emotion or vain-glory. It most clearly follows from the last chapter that the Holy Spirit only gives its testimony in favour of works, called by Paul (in Gal. v:22) the fruits of the Spirit, and is in itself really nothing but the mental acquiescence which follows a good action in our souls. No spirit gives testimony concerning the certitude of matters within the sphere of speculation, save only reason, who is mistress, as we have shown, of the whole realm of truth. If then they assert that they possess this Spirit which makes them certain of truth, they speak falsely, and according to the prejudices of the emotions, or else they are in great dread lest they should be vanquished by philosophers and exposed to public ridicule, and therefore they flee, as it were, to the altar; but their refuge is vain, for what altar will shelter a man who has outraged reason? However, I pass such persons over, for I think I have fulfilled my purpose, and shown how philosophy should be separated from theology, and wherein each consists; that neither should be subservient to the other, but that each should keep her unopposed dominion. Lastly, as occasion offered, I have pointed out the absurdities, the inconveniences, and the evils following from the extraordinary confusion which has hitherto prevailed between the two subjects, owing to their not being properly distinguished and separated. Before I go further I would expressly state (though I have said it before) that I consider the utility and the need for Holy Scripture or Revelation to be very great. For as we cannot perceive by the natural light of reason that simple obedience is the path of salvation[25], and are taught by revelation only that it is so by the special grace of God, which our reason cannot attain, it follows that the Bible has brought a very great consolation to mankind. All are able to obey, whereas there are but very few, compared with the aggregate of humanity, who can acquire the habit of virtue under the unaided guidance of reason. Thus if we had not the testimony of Scripture, we should doubt of the salvation of nearly all men.

---

[25] "That simple obedience is the path of salvation." In other words, it is enough for salvation or blessedness, that we should embrace the Divine decrees as laws or commands; there is no need to conceive them as eternal truths. This can be taught us by Revelation, not Reason, as appears from the demonstrations given in Chapter IV.

CHAPTER XVI

Of the Foundations of a State;
of the Natural and Civil Rights of Individuals;
and of the Rights of the Sovereign Power

Hitherto our care has been to separate philosophy from theology, and to show the freedom of thought which such separation insures to both. It is now time to determine the limits to which such freedom of thought and discussion may extend itself in the ideal state. For the due consideration of this question we must examine the foundations of a State, first turning our attention to the natural rights of individuals, and afterwards to religion and the state as a whole.

By the right and ordinance of nature, I merely mean those natural laws wherewith we conceive every individual to be conditioned by nature, so as to live and act in a given way. For instance, fishes are naturally conditioned for swimming, and the greater for devouring the less; therefore fishes enjoy the water, and the greater devour the less by sovereign natural right. For it is certain that nature, taken in the abstract, has sovereign right to do anything, she can; in other words, her right is co-extensive with her power. The power of nature is the power of God, which has sovereign right over all things; and, inasmuch as the power of nature is simply the aggregate of the powers of all her individual components, it follows that every, individual has sovereign right to do all that he can; in other words, the rights of an individual extend to the utmost limits of his power as it has been conditioned. Now it is the sovereign law and right of nature that each individual should endeavour to preserve itself as it is, without regard to anything but itself; therefore this sovereign law and right belongs to every individual, namely, to exist and act according to its natural conditions. We do not here acknowledge any difference between mankind and other individual natural entities, nor between men endowed with reason and those to whom reason is unknown; nor between fools, madmen, and sane men. Whatsoever an individual does by the laws of its nature it has a sovereign right to do, inasmuch as it acts as it was conditioned by nature, and cannot act otherwise. Wherefore among men, so long as they are considered as living under the sway of nature, he who does not yet know reason, or who has not yet acquired the habit of virtue, acts solely according to the laws of his desire with as sovereign a right as he who orders his life entirely by the laws of reason.

That is, as the wise man has sovereign right to do all that reason dictates, or to live according to the laws of reason, so also the ignorant and foolish man has sovereign right to do all that desire dictates, or to live according to the laws of desire. This is identical with the teaching of Paul, who acknowledges that previous to the law — that is, so long as men are considered of as living under the sway of nature, there is no sin.

The natural right of the individual man is thus determined, not by sound reason, but by desire and power. All are not naturally conditioned so as to act according to the laws and rules of reason; nay, on the contrary, all men are born ignorant, and before they can learn the right way of life and acquire the habit of virtue, the greater part of their life, even if they have been well brought up, has passed away. Nevertheless, they are in the meanwhile bound to live and preserve themselves as far as they can by the unaided impulses of desire. Nature has given them no other guide, and has denied them the present power of living according to sound reason; so that they are no more bound to live by the dictates of an enlightened mind, than a cat is bound to live by the laws of the nature of a lion.

Whatsoever, therefore, an individual (considered as under the sway of nature) thinks useful for himself, whether led by sound reason or impelled by the passions, that he has a sovereign right to seek and to take for himself as he best can, whether by force, cunning, entreaty, or any other means; consequently he may regard as an enemy anyone who hinders the accomplishment of his purpose.

It follows from what we have said that the right and ordinance of nature, under which all men are born, and under which they mostly live, only prohibits such things as no one desires, and no one can attain: it does not forbid strife, nor hatred, nor anger, nor deceit, nor, indeed, any of the means suggested by desire.

This we need not wonder at, for nature is not bounded by the laws of human reason, which aims only at man's true benefit and preservation; her limits are infinitely wider, and have reference to the eternal order of nature, wherein man is but a speck; it is by the necessity of this alone that all individuals are conditioned for living and acting in a particular way. If anything, therefore, in nature seems to us ridiculous, absurd, or evil, it is because we only know in part, and are almost entirely ignorant of the order and interdependence of nature as a whole, and also because we want everything to be arranged according to the dictates of our human reason; in reality that which reason considers evil, is not evil in respect to the order and laws of nature as a whole, but only in respect to the laws of our reason.

Nevertheless, no one can doubt that it is much better for us to live according to the laws and assured dictates of reason, for, as we said, they have men's true good for their object. Moreover, everyone wishes to live as far as possible securely beyond the reach of fear, and this would be quite impossible so long as everyone did everything he liked, and reason's claim was lowered to a par with those of hatred and anger; there is no one who is not ill at ease in the midst of enmity, hatred, anger, and deceit, and who does not seek to avoid them as much as he can. When we reflect that men without mutual help, or the aid of reason, must needs live most miserably, as we clearly proved in Chap. V., we shall plainly see that men must necessarily come to an agreement to live together as securely and well as possible if they are to enjoy as a whole the rights which naturally belong to them as individuals, and their life should be no more conditioned by the force and desire of individuals, but by the power and will of the whole body. This end they will be unable to attain if desire be their only guide (for by the laws of desire each man is drawn in a different direction); they must, therefore, most firmly decree and establish that they will be guided in everything by reason (which nobody will dare openly to repudiate lest he should be taken for a madman), and will restrain any desire which is injurious to a man's fellows, that they will do to all as they would be done by, and that they will defend their neighbour's rights as their own.

How such a compact as this should be entered into, how ratified and established, we will now inquire.

Now it is a universal law of human nature that no one ever neglects anything which he judges to be good, except with the hope of gaining a greater good, or from the fear of a greater evil; nor does anyone endure an evil except for the sake of avoiding a greater evil, or gaining a greater good. That is, everyone will, of two goods, choose that which he thinks the greatest; and, of two evils, that which he thinks the least. I say advisedly that which he thinks the greatest or the least, for it does not necessarily follow that he judges right. This law is so deeply implanted in the human mind that it ought to be counted among eternal truths and axioms.

As a necessary consequence of the principle just enunciated, no one can honestly promise to forego the right which he has over all things[26], and in

---

[26] "No one can honestly promise to forego the right which he has over all things." In the state of social life, where general right determines what is good or evil, stratagem is rightly distinguished as of two kinds, good and evil. But in the state of Nature, where every man is his own judge, possessing the absolute right to lay down laws for himself, to interpret them as he pleases, or to abrogate them if he thinks it convenient, it is not conceivable that stratagem should be evil.

general no one will abide by his promises, unless under the fear of a greater evil, or the hope of a greater good. An example will make the matter clearer. Suppose that a robber forces me to promise that I will give him my goods at his will and pleasure. It is plain (inasmuch as my natural right is, as I have shown, co-extensive with my power) that if I can free myself from this robber by stratagem, by assenting to his demands, I have the natural right to do so, and to pretend to accept his conditions. Or again, suppose I have genuinely promised someone that for the space of twenty days I will not taste food or any nourishment; and suppose I afterwards find that was foolish, and cannot be kept without very great injury to myself; as I am bound by natural law and right to choose the least of two evils, I have complete right to break my compact, and act as if my promise had never been uttered. I say that I should have perfect natural right to do so, whether I was actuated by true and evident reason, or whether I was actuated by mere opinion in thinking I had promised rashly; whether my reasons were true or false, I should be in fear of a greater evil, which, by the ordinance of nature, I should strive to avoid by every means in my power.

We may, therefore, conclude that a compact is only made valid by its utility, without which it becomes null and void. It is, therefore, foolish to ask a man to keep his faith with us for ever, unless we also endeavour that the violation of the compact we enter into shall involve for the violator more harm than good. This consideration should have very great weight in forming a state. However, if all men could be easily led by reason alone, and could recognize what is best and most useful for a state, there would be no one who would not forswear deceit, for everyone would keep most religiously to their compact in their desire for the chief good, namely, the shield and buckler of the commonwealth. However, it is far from being the case that all men can always be easily led by reason alone; everyone is drawn away by his pleasure, while avarice, ambition, envy, hatred, and the like so engross the mind that, reason has no place therein. Hence, though men make — promises with all the appearances of good faith, and agree that they will keep to their engagement, no one can absolutely rely on another man's promise unless there is something behind it. Everyone has by nature a right to act deceitfully. and to break his compacts, unless he be restrained by the hope of some greater good, or the fear of some greater evil.

However, as we have shown that the natural right of the individual is only limited by his power, it is clear that by transferring, either willingly or under compulsion, this power into the hands of another, he in so doing necessarily cedes also a part of his right; and further, that the Sovereign right over all men belongs to him who has sovereign power, wherewith he can compel men by force, or restrain them by threats of the universally feared punishment of death; such sovereign right he will retain only so long as he can maintain his power of enforcing his will; otherwise he will totter on his throne, and no one who is stronger than he will be bound unwillingly to obey him.

In this manner a society can be formed without any violation of natural right, and the covenant can always be strictly kept — that is, if each individual hands over the whole of his power to the body politic, the latter will then possess sovereign natural right over all things; that is, it will have sole and unquestioned dominion, and everyone will be bound to obey, under pain of the severest punishment. A body politic of this kind is called a Democracy, which may be defined as a society which wields all its power as a whole. The sovereign power is not restrained by any laws, but everyone is bound to obey it in all things; such is the state of things implied when men either tacitly or expressly handed over to it all their power of self-defence, or in other words, all their right. For if they had wished to retain any right for themselves, they ought to have taken precautions for its defence and preservation; as they have not done so, and indeed could not have done so without dividing and consequently ruining the state, they placed themselves absolutely at the mercy of the sovereign power; and, therefore, having acted (as we have shown) as reason and necessity demanded, they are obliged to fulfil the commands of the sovereign power, however absurd these may be, else they will be public enemies, and will act against reason, which urges the preservation of the state as a primary duty. For reason bids us choose the least of two evils.

Furthermore, this danger of submitting absolutely to the dominion and will of another, is one which may be incurred with a light heart: for we have shown that sovereigns only possess this right of imposing their will, so long as they have the full power to enforce it: if such power be lost their right to command is lost also, or lapses to those who have assumed it and can keep it. Thus it is very rare for sovereigns to impose thoroughly irrational commands, for they are bound to consult their own interests, and retain their power by consulting the public good and acting according to the dictates of reason, as Seneca says, "violenta imperia nemo continuit diu." No one can long retain a tyrant's sway.

In a democracy, irrational commands are still less to be feared: for it is almost impossible that the majority of a people, especially if it be a large one, should agree in an irrational design: and, moreover, the basis and aim of a democracy is to avoid the desires as irrational, and to bring men as far as possible under the control of reason, so that they may live in peace and harmony: if this basis be removed the whole fabric falls to ruin.

Such being the ends in view for the sovereign power, the duty of subjects is, as I have said, to obey its commands, and to recognize no right save that which it sanctions.

It will, perhaps, be thought that we are turning subjects into slaves: for slaves obey commands and free men live as they like; but this idea is based on a misconception, for the true slave is he who is led away by his pleasures and can neither see what is good for him nor act accordingly: he alone is free who lives with free consent under the entire guidance of reason.

Action in obedience to orders does take away freedom in a certain sense, but it does not, therefore, make a man a slave, all depends on the object of the action. If the object of the action be the good of the state, and not the good of the agent, the latter is a slave and does himself no good: but in a state or kingdom where the weal of the whole people, and not that of the ruler, is the supreme law, obedience to the sovereign power does not make a man a slave, of no use to himself, but a subject. Therefore, that state is the freest whose laws are founded on sound reason, so that every member of it may, if he will, be free[27]; that is, live with full consent under the entire guidance of reason.

Children, though they are bound to obey all the commands of their parents, are yet not slaves: for the commands of parents look generally to the children's benefit.

We must, therefore, acknowledge a great difference between a slave, a son, and a subject; their positions may be thus defined. A slave is one who is bound to obey his master's orders, though they are given solely in the master's interest: a son is one who obeys his father's orders, given in his own interest; a subject obeys the orders of the sovereign power, given for the common interest, wherein he is included.

I think I have now shown sufficiently clearly the basis of a democracy: I have especially desired to do so, for I believe it to be of all forms of government the most natural, and the most consonant with individual liberty. In it no one transfers his natural right so absolutely that he has no further voice in affairs, he only hands it over to the majority of a society, whereof he is a unit. Thus all men remain as they were in the state of nature, equals.

This is the only form of government which I have treated of at length, for it is the one most akin to my purpose of showing the benefits of freedom in a state.

I may pass over the fundamental principles of other forms of government, for we may gather from what has been said whence their right arises without going into its origin. The possessor of sovereign power, whether he be one,

---

[27] "Every member of it may, if he will, be free." Whatever be the social state a man finds; himself in, he may be free. For certainly a man is free, in so far as he is led by reason. Now reason (though Hobbes thinks otherwise) is always on the side of peace, which cannot be attained unless the general laws of the state be respected. Therefore the more he is free, the more constantly will he respect the laws of his country, and obey the commands of the sovereign power to which he is subject.

or many, or the whole body politic, has the sovereign right of imposing any commands he pleases: and he who has either voluntarily, or under compulsion, transferred the right to defend him to another, has, in so doing, renounced his natural right and is therefore bound to obey, in all things, the commands of the sovereign power; and will be bound so to do so long as the king, or nobles, or the people preserve the sovereign power which formed the basis of the original transfer. I need add no more.

The bases and rights of dominion being thus displayed, we shall readily be able to define private civil right, wrong, justice, and injustice, with their relations to the state; and also to determine what constitutes an ally, or an enemy, or the crime of treason.

By private civil right we can only mean the liberty every man possesses to preserve his existence, a liberty limited by the edicts of the sovereign power, and preserved only by its authority: for when a man has transferred to another his right of living as he likes, which was only limited by his power, that is, has transferred his liberty and power of self-defence, he is bound to live as that other dictates, and to trust to him entirely for his defence. Wrong takes place when a citizen, or subject, is forced by another to undergo some loss or pain in contradiction to the authority of the law, or the edict of the sovereign power.

Wrong is conceivable only in an organized community: nor can it ever accrue to subjects from any act of the sovereign, who has the right to do what he likes. It can only arise, therefore, between private persons, who are bound by law and right not to injure one another. Justice consists in the habitual rendering to every man his lawful due: injustice consists in depriving a man, under the pretence of legality, of what the laws, rightly interpreted, would allow him. These last are also called equity and iniquity, because those who administer the laws are bound to show no respect of persons, but to account all men equal, and to defend every man's right equally, neither envying the rich nor despising the poor.

The men of two states become allies, when for the sake of avoiding war, or for some other advantage, they covenant to do each other no hurt, but on the contrary, to assist each other if necessity arises, each retaining his independence. Such a covenant is valid so long as its basis of danger or advantage is in force: no one enters into an engagement, or is bound to stand by his compacts unless there be a hope of some accruing good, or the fear of some evil: if this basis be removed the compact thereby becomes void: this has been abundantly shown by experience. For although different states make treaties not to harm one another, they always take every possible precaution against such treaties being broken by the stronger party, and do not rely on the compact, unless there is a sufficiently obvious object and advantage to both parties in observing it. Otherwise they would fear a breach of faith, nor would there be any wrong done thereby: for who in his proper senses, and aware of the right of the sovereign power, would trust in the promises of one who has the will and the power to do what he likes, and who aims solely at the safety and advantage of his dominion? Moreover, if we consult loyalty and religion, we shall see that no one in possession of power ought to abide by his promises to the injury of his dominion; for he cannot keep such promises without breaking the engagement he made with his subjects, by which both he and they are most solemnly bound. An enemy is one who lives apart from the state, and does not recognize its authority either as a subject or as an ally. It is not hatred which makes a man an enemy, but the rights of the state. The rights of the state are the same in regard to him who does not recognize by any compact the state authority, as they are against him who has done the state an injury: it has the right to force him as best it can, either to submit, or to contract an alliance.

Lastly, treason can only be committed by subjects, who by compact, either tacit or expressed, have transferred all their rights to the state: a subject is said to have committed this crime when he has attempted, for whatever reason, to seize the sovereign power, or to place it in different hands. I say, has attempted, for if punishment were not to overtake him till he had succeeded, it would often come too late, the sovereign rights would have been acquired or transferred already.

I also say, has attempted, for whatever reason, to seize the sovereign power, and I recognize no difference whether such an attempt should be followed by public loss or public gain. Whatever be his reason for acting, the crime is treason, and he is rightly condemned: in war, everyone would admit the justice of his sentence. If a man does not keep to his post, but approaches the enemy without the knowledge of his commander, whatever may be his motive, so long as he acts on his own motion, even if he advances with the design of defeating the enemy, he is rightly put to death, because he has violated his oath, and infringed the rights of his commander. That all citizens are equally bound by these rights in time of peace, is not so generally recognized, but the reasons for obedience are in both cases identical. The state must be preserved and directed by the sole authority of the sovereign, and such authority and right have been accorded by universal consent to him alone: if, therefore, anyone else attempts, without his consent, to execute any public enterprise, even though the state might (as we said) reap benefit therefrom, such person has none the less infringed the sovereigns right, and would be rightly punished for treason.

In order that every scruple may be removed, we may now answer the inquiry, whether our former assertion that everyone who has not the practice of reason, may, in the state of nature, live by sovereign natural right, according to the laws of his desires, is not in direct opposition to the law and right of God as revealed. For as all men absolutely (whether they be less endowed with reason or more) are equally bound by the Divine command to love their neighbour as themselves, it may be said that they cannot, without wrong, do injury to anyone, or live according to their desires.

This objection, so far as the state of nature is concerned, can be easily answered, for the state of nature is, both in nature and in time, prior to religion. No one knows by nature that he owes any obedience to God[28], nor can he attain thereto by any exercise of his reason, but solely by revelation confirmed by signs. Therefore, previous to revelation, no one is bound by a Divine law and right of which he is necessarily in ignorance. The state of nature must by no means be confounded with a state of religion, but must be conceived as without either religion or law, and consequently without sin or wrong: this is how we have described it, and we are confirmed by the authority of Paul. It is not only in respect of ignorance that we conceive the state of nature as prior to, and lacking the Divine revealed law and right; but in respect of freedom also, wherewith all men are born endowed.

If men were naturally bound by the Divine law and right, or if the Divine law and right were a natural necessity, there would have been no need for God to make a covenant with mankind, and to bind them thereto with an oath and agreement.

We must, then, fully grant that the Divine law and right originated at the time when men by express covenant agreed to obey God in all things, and ceded, as it were, their natural freedom, transferring their rights to God in the manner described in speaking of the formation of a state.

However, I will treat of these matters more at length presently.

---

[28] "No one knows by nature that he owes any obedience to God." When Paul says that men have in themselves no refuge, he speaks as a man: for in the ninth chapter of the same epistle he expressly teaches that God has mercy on whom He will, and that men are without excuse, only because they are in God's power like clay in the hands of a potter, who out of the same lump makes vessels, some for honour and some for dishonour, not because they have been forewarned. As regards the Divine natural law whereof the chief commandment is, as we have said, to love God, I have called it a law in the same sense, as philosophers style laws those general rules of nature, according to which everything happens. For the love of God is not a state of obedience: it is a virtue which necessarily exists in a man who knows God rightly. Obedience has regard to the will of a ruler, not to necessity and truth. Now as we are ignorant of the nature of God's will, and on the other hand know that everything happens solely by God's power, we cannot, except through revelation, know whether God wishes in any way to be honoured as a sovereign.

Again; we have shown that the Divine rights appear to us in the light of rights or commands, only so long as we are ignorant of their cause: as soon as their cause is known, they cease to be rights, and we embrace them no longer as rights but as eternal truths; in other words, obedience passes into love of God, which emanates from true knowledge as necessarily as light emanates from the sun. Reason then leads us to love God, but cannot lead us to obey Him; for we cannot embrace the commands of God as Divine, while we are in ignorance of their cause, neither can we rationally conceive God as a sovereign laying down laws as a sovereign.

It may be insisted that sovereigns are as much bound by the Divine law as subjects: whereas we have asserted that they retain their natural rights, and may do whatever they like.

In order to clear up the whole difficulty, which arises rather concerning the natural right than the natural state, I maintain that everyone is bound, in the state of nature, to live according to Divine law, in the same way as he is bound to live according to the dictates of sound reason; namely, inasmuch as it is to his advantage, and necessary for his salvation; but, if he will not so live, he may do otherwise at his own risk. He is thus bound to live according to his own laws, not according to anyone else's, and to recognize no man as a judge, or as a superior in religion. Such, in my opinion, is the position of a sovereign, for he may take advice from his fellow-men, but he is not bound to recognize any as a judge, nor anyone besides himself as an arbitrator on any question of right, unless it be a prophet sent expressly by God and attesting his mission by indisputable signs. Even then he does not recognize a man, but God Himself as His judge.

If a sovereign refuses to obey God as revealed in His law, he does so at his own risk and loss, but without violating any civil or natural right. For the civil right is dependent on his own decree; and natural right is dependent on the laws of nature, which latter are not adapted to religion, whose sole aim is the good of humanity, but to the order of nature — that is, to God's eternal decree unknown to us.

This truth seems to be adumbrated in a somewhat obscurer form by those who maintain that men can sin against God's revelation, but not against the eternal decree by which He has ordained all things.

We may be asked, what should we do if the sovereign commands anything contrary to religion, and the obedience which we have expressly vowed to God? should we obey the Divine law or the human law? I shall treat of this question at length hereafter, and will therefore merely say now, that God should be obeyed before all else, when we have a certain and indisputable revelation of His will: but men are very prone to error on religious subjects, and, according to the diversity of their dispositions, are wont with considerable stir to put forward their own inventions, as experience more than sufficiently attests, so that if no one were bound to obey the state in matters which, in his own opinion concern religion, the rights of the state would be dependent on every man's judgment and passions. No one would consider himself bound to obey laws framed against his faith or superstition; and on this pretext he might assume unbounded license. In this way, the rights of the civil authorities would be utterly set at nought, so that we must conclude that the sovereign power, which alone is bound both by Divine and natural right to preserve and guard the laws of the state, should have supreme authority for making any laws about religion which it thinks fit; all are bound to obey its behests on the subject in accordance with their promise which God bids them to keep.

However, if the sovereign power be heathen, we should either enter into no engagements therewith, and yield up our lives sooner than transfer to it any of our rights; or, if the engagement be made, and our rights transferred, we should (inasmuch as we should have ourselves transferred the right of defending ourselves and our religion) be bound to obey them, and to keep our word: we might even rightly be bound so to do, except in those cases where God, by indisputable revelation, has promised His special aid against tyranny, or given us special exemption from obedience. Thus we see that, of all the Jews in Babylon, there were only three youths who were certain of the help of God, and, therefore, refused to obey Nebuchadnezzar. All the rest, with the sole exception of Daniel, who was beloved by the king, were doubtless compelled by right to obey, perhaps thinking that they had been delivered up by God into the hands of the king, and that the king had obtained and preserved his dominion by God's design. On the other hand, Eleazar, before his country had utterly fallen, wished to give a proof of his constancy to his compatriots, in order that they might follow in his footsteps, and go to any lengths, rather than allow their right and power to be transferred to the Greeks, or brave any torture rather than swear allegiance to the heathen. Instances are occurring every day in confirmation of what I here advance. The rulers of Christian kingdoms do not hesitate, with a view to strengthening their dominion, to make treaties with Turks and heathen, and to give orders to their subjects who settle among such peoples not to assume more freedom, either in things secular or religious, than is set down in the treaty, or allowed by the foreign government. We may see this exemplified in the Dutch treaty with the Japanese, which I have already mentioned.

CHAPTER XVII

It is shown that no one can, or need, transfer all his Rights to the Sovereign Power. Of the Hebrew Republic, as it was during the lifetime of Moses, and after his death, till the foundation of the Monarchy; and of its Excellence. Lastly, of the causes why the Theocratic Republic fell, and why it could hardly have continued without Dissension

The theory put forward in the last chapter, of the universal rights of the sovereign power, and of the natural rights of the individual transferred thereto, though it corresponds in many respects with actual practice, and though practice may be so arranged as to conform to it more and more, must nevertheless always remain in many respects purely ideal. No one can ever so utterly transfer to another his power and, consequently, his rights, as to cease to be a man; nor can there ever be a power so sovereign that it can carry out every possible wish. It will always be vain to order a subject to hate what he believes brings him advantage, or to love what brings him loss, or not to be offended at insults, or not to wish to be free from fear, or a hundred other things of the sort, which necessarily follow from the laws of human nature. So much, I think, is abundantly shown by experience: for men have never so far ceded their power as to cease to be an object of fear to the rulers who received such power and right; and dominions have always been in as much danger from their own subjects as from external enemies. If it were really the case, that men could be deprived of their natural rights so utterly as never to have any further influence on affairs[29], except with the permission of the holders of sovereign right, it would then be possible to

---

[29] "If men could lose their natural rights so as to be absolutely unable for the future to oppose the will of the sovereign" Two common soldiers undertook to change the Roman dominion, and did change it. (Tacitus, Hist. i:7.)

maintain with impunity the most violent tyranny, which, I suppose, no one would for an instant admit.

We must, therefore, grant that every man retains some part of his right, in dependence on his own decision, and no one else's.

However, in order correctly to understand the extent of the sovereign's right and power, we must take notice that it does not cover only those actions to which it can compel men by fear, but absolutely every action which it can induce men to perform: for it is the fact of obedience, not the motive for obedience, which makes a man a subject.

Whatever be the cause which leads a man to obey the commands of the sovereign, whether it be fear or hope, or love of his country, or any other emotion — the fact remains that the man takes counsel with himself, and nevertheless acts as his sovereign orders. We must not, therefore, assert that all actions resulting from a man's deliberation with himself are done in obedience to the rights of the individual rather than the sovereign: as a matter of fact, all actions spring from a man's deliberation with himself, whether the determining motive be love or fear of punishment; therefore, either dominion does not exist, and has no rights over its subjects, or else it extends over every instance in which it can prevail on men to decide to obey it. Consequently, every action which a subject performs in accordance with the commands of the sovereign, whether such action springs from love, or fear, or (as is more frequently the case) from hope and fear together, or from reverence. compounded of fear and admiration, or, indeed, any motive whatever, is performed in virtue of his submission to the sovereign, and not in virtue of his own authority.

This point is made still more clear by the fact that obedience does not consist so much in the outward act as in the mental state of the person obeying; so that he is most under the dominion of another who with his whole heart determines to obey another's commands; and consequently the firmest dominion belongs to the sovereign who has most influence over the minds of his subjects; if those who are most feared possessed the firmest dominion, the firmest dominion would belong to the subjects of a tyrant, for they are always greatly feared by their ruler. Furthermore, though it is impossible to govern the mind as completely as the tongue, nevertheless minds are, to a certain extent, under the control of the sovereign, for he can in many ways bring about that the greatest part of his subjects should follow his wishes in their beliefs, their loves, and their hates. Though such emotions do not arise at the express command of the sovereign they often result (as experience shows) from the authority of his power, and from his direction; in other words, in virtue of his right; we may, therefore, without doing violence to our understanding, conceive men who follow the instigation of their sovereign in their beliefs, their loves, their hates, their contempt, and all other emotions whatsoever.

Though the powers of government, as thus conceived, are sufficiently ample, they can never become large enough to execute every possible wish of their possessors. This, I think, I have already shown clearly enough. The method of forming a dominion which should prove lasting I do not, as I have said, intend to discuss, but in order to arrive at the object I have in view, I will touch on the teaching of Divine revelation to Moses in this respect, and we will consider the history and the success of the Jews, gathering therefrom what should be the chief concessions made by sovereigns to their subjects with a view to the security and increase of their dominion.

That the preservation of a state chiefly depends on the subjects' fidelity and constancy in carrying out the orders they receive, is most clearly taught both by reason and experience; how subjects ought to be guided so as best to preserve their fidelity and virtue is not so obvious. All, both rulers and ruled, are men, and prone to follow after their lusts. The fickle disposition of the multitude almost reduces those who have experience of it to despair, for it is governed solely by emotions, not by reason: it rushes headlong into every enterprise, and is easily corrupted either by avarice or luxury: everyone thinks himself omniscient and wishes to fashion all things to his liking, judging a thing to be just or unjust, lawful or unlawful, according as he thinks it will bring him profit or loss: vanity leads him to despise his equals, and refuse their guidance: envy of superior fame or fortune (for such gifts are never equally distributed) leads him to desire and rejoice in his neighbour's downfall. I need not go through the whole list, everyone knows already how much crime. results from disgust at the present — desire for change, headlong anger, and contempt for poverty — and how men's minds are engrossed and kept in turmoil thereby.

To guard against all these evils, and form a dominion where no room is left for deceit; to frame our institutions so that every man, whatever his disposition, may prefer public right to private advantage, this is the task and this the toil. Necessity is often the mother of invention, but she has never yet succeeded in framing a dominion that was in less danger from its own citizens than from open enemies, or whose rulers did not fear the latter less than the former. Witness the state of Rome, invincible by her enemies, but many times conquered and sorely oppressed by her own citizens, especially in the war between Vespasian and Vitellius. (See Tacitus, Hist. bk. iv. for a description of the pitiable state of the city.)

Alexander thought prestige abroad more easy to acquire than prestige at home, and believed that his greatness could be destroyed by his own followers. Fearing such a disaster, he thus addressed his friends: "Keep me safe from internal treachery and domestic plots, and I will front without fear the dangers of battle and of war. Philip was more secure in the battle array than in the theatre: he often escaped from the hands of the enemy, he could not escape from his own subjects. If you think over the deaths of kings, you will count up more who have died by the assassin than by the open foe." (Q. Curtius, chap. vi.)

For the sake of making themselves secure, kings who seized the throne in ancient times used to try to spread the idea that they were descended from the immortal gods, thinking that if their subjects and the rest of mankind did not look on them as equals, but believed them to be gods, they would willingly submit to their rule, and obey their commands. Thus Augustus persuaded the Romans that he was descended from AEneas, who was the son of Venus, and numbered among the gods. "He wished himself to be worshipped in temples, like the gods, with flamens and priests." (Tacitus, Ann. i. 10.)

Alexander wished to be saluted as the son of Jupiter, not from motives of pride but of policy, as he showed by his answer to the invective of Hermolaus: "It is almost laughable," said he, that Hermolaus asked me to contradict Jupiter, by whose oracle I am recognized. Am I responsible for the answers of the gods? It offered me the name of son; acquiescence was by no means foreign to my present designs. Would that the Indians also would believe me to be a god! Wars are carried through by prestige, falsehoods that are believed often gain the force of truth." (Curtius, viii,. Para, 8.) In these few words he cleverly contrives to palm off a fiction on the ignorant, and at the same time hints at the motive for the deception.

Cleon, in his speech persuading the Macedonians to obey their king, adopted a similar device: for after going through the praises of Alexander with admiration, and recalling his merits, he proceeds, "the Persians are not only pious, but prudent in worshipping their kings as gods: for kingship is the shield of public safety," and he ends thus, "I, myself, when the king enters a banquet hall, should prostrate my body on the ground; other men should do the like, especially those who are wise " (Curtius, viii. Para. 66). However, the Macedonians were more prudent — indeed, it is only complete barbarians who can be so openly cajoled, and can suffer themselves to be turned from subjects into slaves without interests of their own. Others, notwithstanding, have been able more easily to spread the belief that kingship is sacred, and plays the part of God on the earth, that it has been instituted by God, not by the suffrage and consent of men; and that it is preserved and guarded by Divine special providence and aid. Similar fictions have been promulgated by monarchs, with the object of strengthening their dominion, but these I will pass over, and in order to arrive at my main purpose, will merely recall and discuss the teaching on the subject of Divine revelation to Moses in ancient times.

We have said in Chap. V. that after the Hebrews came up out of Egypt they were not bound by the law and right of any other nation, but were at liberty to institute any new rites at their pleasure, and to occupy whatever territory they chose. After their liberation from the intolerable bondage of the Egyptians, they were bound by no covenant to any man; and, therefore, every man entered into his natural right, and was free to retain it or to give it up, and transfer it to another. Being, then, in the state of nature, they followed the advice of Moses, in whom they chiefly trusted, and decided to transfer their right to no human being, but only to God; without further delay they all, with one voice, promised to obey all the commands of the Deity, and to acknowledge no right that He did not proclaim as such by prophetic revelation. This promise, or transference of right to God, was effected in the same manner as we have conceived it to have been in ordinary societies, when men agree to divest themselves of their natural rights. It is, in fact, in virtue of a set covenant, and an oath (see Exod. xxxiv:10), that the Jews freely, and not under compulsion or threats, surrendered their rights and transferred them to God. Moreover, in order that this covenant might be ratified and settled, and might be free from all suspicion of deceit, God did not enter into it till the Jews had had experience of His wonderful power by which alone they had been, or could be, preserved in a state of prosperity (Exod. xix:4, 5). It is because they believed that nothing but God's power could preserve them that they surrendered to God the natural power of self-preservation, which they formerly, perhaps, thought they possessed, and consequently they surrendered at the same time all their natural right.

God alone, therefore, held dominion over the Hebrews, whose state was in virtue of the covenant called God's kingdom, and God was said to be their king; consequently the enemies of the Jews were said to be the enemies of God, and the citizens who tried to seize the dominion were guilty of treason against God; and, lastly, the laws of the state were called the laws and commandments of God. Thus in the Hebrew state the civil and religious authority, each consisting solely of obedience to God, were one and the same. The dogmas of religion were not precepts, but laws and ordinances; piety was regarded as the same as loyalty, impiety as the same as disaffection. Everyone who fell away from religion ceased to be a citizen, and was, on that ground alone, accounted an enemy: those who died for the sake of religion, were held to have died for their country; in fact, between civil and religious law and right there was no distinction whatever. {in Biblical Hebrew, there was no word for what we call Religion. Modern Hebrew has selected a word whose root is "knowledge."} For this reason the government could be called a Theocracy, inasmuch as the citizens were not bound by anything save the revelations of God.

However, this state of things existed rather in theory than in practice, for it will appear from what we are about to say, that the Hebrews, as a matter of fact, retained absolutely in their own hands the right of sovereignty: this is shown by the method and plan by which the government was carried on, as I will now explain.

Inasmuch as the Hebrews did not transfer their rights to any other person but, as in a democracy, all surrendered their rights equally, and cried out with one voice, "Whatsoever God shall speak (no mediator or mouthpiece being named) that will we do," it follows that all were equally bound by the covenant, and that all had an equal right to consult the Deity, to accept and to interpret His laws, so that all had an exactly equal share in the government. Thus at first they all approached God together, so that they might learn His commands, but in this first salutation, they were so thoroughly terrified and so astounded to hear God speaking, that they thought their last hour was at hand: full of fear, therefore, they went afresh to Moses, and said, "Lo, we have heard God speaking in the fire, and there is no cause why we should wish to die: surely this great fire will consume us: if we hear again the voice of God, we shall surely die. Thou, therefore, go near, and hear all the words of our God, and thou (not God) shalt speak with us: all that God shall tell us, that will we hearken to and perform."

They thus clearly abrogated their former covenant, and absolutely transferred to Moses their right to consult God and interpret His commands: for they do not here promise obedience to all that God shall tell them, but to all that God shall tell Moses (see Deut. v:20 after the Decalogue, and chap. xviii:15, 16). Moses, therefore, remained the sole promulgator and interpreter of the Divine laws, and consequently also the sovereign judge, who could not be arraigned himself, and who acted among the Hebrews the part, of God; in other words, held the sovereign kingship: he alone had the right to consult God, to give the Divine answers to the people, and to see that they were carried out. I say he alone, for if anyone during the life of Moses was desirous of preaching anything in the name of the Lord, he was, even if a true prophet, considered guilty and a usurper of the sovereign right (Numb. xi:28)[30]. We may here notice, that though the people

---

[30] See Numbers xi. 28. In this passage it is written that two men prophesied in the camp, and that Joshua wished to punish them. This he would not have done, if it had been lawful for anyone to deliver the Divine oracles to the people without the consent of Moses. But Moses thought good to pardon the two men, and rebuked Joshua for exhorting him to use his royal prerogative, at a time when he was so weary of reigning, that he preferred death to holding undivided sway (Numb. xi:14). For he made answer to Joshua, "Enviest thou for my sake? Would God that all the Lord's people were prophets, and that the Lord would put His spirit upon them." That is to say, would God that the right of taking counsel of God were general, and the power were in the hands of the people. Thus Joshua was not mistaken as to the right, but only as to the time for using it, for which he was rebuked by Moses, in the same way as Abishai was rebuked by David for counselling that Shimei, who had undoubtedly been guilty of treason, should be put to death. See 2 Sam. xix:22, 23.

had elected Moses, they could not rightfully elect Moses's successor; for having transferred to Moses their right of consulting God, and absolutely promised to regard him as a Divine oracle, they had plainly forfeited the whole of their right, and were bound to accept as chosen by God anyone proclaimed by Moses as his successor. If Moses had so chosen his successor, who like him should wield the sole right of government, possessing the sole right of consulting God, and consequently of making and abrogating laws, of deciding on peace or war, of sending ambassadors, appointing judges — in fact, discharging all the functions of a sovereign, the state would have become simply a monarchy, only differing from other monarchies in the fact, that the latter are, or should be, carried on in accordance with God's decree, unknown even to the monarch, whereas the Hebrew monarch would have been the only person to whom the decree was revealed. A difference which increases, rather than diminishes the monarch's authority. As far as the people in both cases are concerned, each would be equally subject, and equally ignorant of the Divine decree, for each would be dependent on the monarch's words, and would learn from him alone, what was lawful or unlawful: nor would the fact that the people believed that the monarch was only issuing commands in accordance with God's decree revealed to him, make it less in subjection, but rather more. However, Moses elected no such successor, but left the dominion to those who came after him in a condition which could not be called a popular government, nor an aristocracy, nor a monarchy, but a Theocracy. For the right of interpreting laws was vested in one man, while the right and power of administering the state according to the laws thus interpreted, was vested in another man (see Numb. xxvii:21)[31].

In order that the question may be thoroughly understood, I will duly set forth the administration of the whole state.

First, the people were commanded to build a tabernacle, which should be, as it were, the dwelling of God — that is, of the sovereign authority of the state. This tabernacle was to be erected at the cost of the whole people, not of one man, in order that the place where God was consulted might be public property. The Levites were chosen as courtiers and administrators of this royal abode; while Aaron, the brother of Moses, was chosen to be their chief and second, as it were, to God their King, being succeeded in the office by his legitimate sons.

He, as the nearest to God, was the sovereign interpreter of the Divine laws; he communicated the answers of the Divine oracle to the people, and entreated God's favour for them. If, in addition to these privileges, he had possessed the

---

[31] See Numbers xxvii:21. The translators of the Bible have rendered incorrectly verses 19 and 23 of this chapter. The passage does not mean that Moses gave precepts or advice to Joshua, but that he made or established him chief of the Hebrews. The phrase is very freguent in Scripture (see Exodus, xviii:23; 1 Sam. xiii:15; Joshua i:9; 1 Sam. xxv:80).

right of ruling, he would have been neither more nor less than an absolute monarch; but, in respect to government, he was only a private citizen: the whole tribe of Levi was so completely divested of governing rights that it did not even take its share with the others in the partition of territory. Moses provided for its support by inspiring the common people with great reverence for it, as the only tribe dedicated to God.

Further, the army, formed from the remaining twelve tribes, was commanded to invade the land of Canaan, to divide it into twelve portions, and to distribute it among the tribes by lot. For this task twelve captains were chosen, one from every tribe, and were, together with Joshua and Eleazar, the high priest, empowered to divide the land into twelve equal parts, and distribute it by lot. Joshua was chosen for the chief command of the army, inasmuch as none but he had the right to consult God in emergencies, not like Moses, alone in his tent, or in the tabernacle, but through the high priest, to whom only the answers of God were revealed. Furthermore, he was empowered to execute, and cause the people to obey God's commands, transmitted through the high priests; to find, and to make use of, means for carrying them out; to choose as many, army captains as he liked; to make whatever choice he thought best; to send ambassadors in his own name; and, in short, to have the entire control of the war. To his office there was no rightful successor — indeed, the post was only filled by the direct order of the Deity, on occasions of public emergency. In ordinary times, all the management of peace and war was vested in the captains of the tribes, as I will shortly point out. Lastly, all men between the ages of twenty and sixty were ordered to bear arms, and form a citizen army, owing allegiance, not to its general-inchief, nor to the high priest, but to Religion and to God. The army, or the hosts, were called the army of God, or the hosts of God. For this reason God was called by the Hebrews the God of Armies; and the ark of the covenant was borne in the midst of the army in important battles, when the safety or destruction of the whole people hung upon the issue, so that the people might, as it were, see their King among them, and put forth all their strength.

From these directions, left by Moses to his successors, we plainly see that he chose administrators, rather than despots, to come after him; for he invested no one with the power of consulting God, where he liked and alone, consequently, no one had the power possessed by himself of ordaining and abrogating laws, of deciding on war or peace, of choosing men to fill offices both religious and secular: all these are the prerogatives of a sovereign. The high priest, indeed, had the right of interpreting laws, and communicating the answers of God, but he could not do so when he liked, as Moses could, but only when he was asked by the general-inchief of the army, the council, or some similar authority. The general-inchief and the council could consult God when they liked, but could only receive His answers through the high priest; so that the utterances of God, as reported by the high priest, were not decrees, as they were when reported by Moses, but only answers; they were accepted by Joshua and the council, and only then had the force of commands and decrees {Like the separation of powers in the United States of America.}

The high priest, both in the case of Aaron and of his son Eleazar, was chosen by Moses; nor had anyone, after Moses' death, a right to elect to the office, which became hereditary . The general-inchief of the army was also chosen by Moses, and assumed his functions in virtue of the commands, not of the high priest, but of Moses: indeed, after the death of Joshua, the high priest did not appoint anyone in his place, and the captains did not consult God afresh about a general-inchief, but each retained Joshua's power in respect to the contingent of his own tribe, and all retained it collectively, in respect to the whole army. There seems to have been no need of a general-inchief, except when they were obliged to unite their forces against a common enemy. This occurred most frequently during the time of Joshua, when they had no fixed dwelling. place, and possessed all things in common. After all the tribes had gained their territories by right of conquest, and had divided their allotted gains, they, became separated, having no longer their possessions in common, so that the need for a single commander ceased, for the different tribes should be considered rather in the light of confederated states than of bodies of fellow-citizens. In respect to their God and their religion, they, were fellow-citizens; but, in respect to the rights which one possessed with regard to another, they were only confederated: they, were, in fact, in much the same position (if one excepts the Temple common to all) as the United States of the Netherlands {or United States of America}. The division of property, held in common is only another phrase for the possession of his share by each of the owners singly, and the surrender by the others of their rights over such share. This is why Moses elected captains of the tribes — namely, that when the dominion was divided, each might take care of his own part; consulting God through the high priest on the affairs of his tribe, ruling over his army, building and fortifying cities, appointing judges, attacking the enemies of his own dominion, and having complete control over all civil and military affairs. He was not bound to acknowledge any superior judge save God[32], or a prophet

---

[32] "There was no judge over each of the captains save God." The Rabbis and some Christians equally foolish pretend that the Sanhedrin, called "the great" was instituted by Moses. As a matter of fact, Moses chose seventy colleagues to assist him in governing, because he was not able to bear alone the burden of the whole people; but he never passed any law for forming a college of seventy members; on the contrary he ordered every tribe to appoint for itself, in the cities which God had given it, judges to settle disputes according to the laws which he himself had laid down. In cases where the opinions of the judges differed as to the interpretation of these laws, Moses bade them

whom God should expressly send. If he departed from the worship of God, the rest of the tribes did not arraign him as a subject, but attacked him as an enemy. Of this we have examples in Scripture. When Joshua was dead, the children of Israel (not a fresh general-inchief) consulted God; it being decided that the tribe of Judah should be the first to attack its enemies, the tribe in question contracted a single alliance with the tribe of Simeon, for uniting their forces, and attacking their common enemy, the rest of the tribes not being included in the alliance (Judges i:1, 2, 3). Each tribe separately made war against its own enemies, and, according to its pleasure, received them as subjects or allies, though it had been commanded not to spare them on any conditions, but to destroy them utterly. Such disobedience met with reproof from the rest of the tribes, but did not cause the offending tribe to be arraigned: it was not considered a sufficient reason for proclaiming a civil war, or interfering in one another's affairs. But when the tribe of Benjamin offended against the others, and so loosened the bonds of peace that none of the confederated tribes could find refuge within its borders, they attacked it as an enemy, and gaining the victory over it after three battles, put to death both guilty and innocent, according to the laws of war: an act which they subsequently bewailed with tardy repentance.

These examples plainly confirm what we have said concerning the rights of each tribe. Perhaps we shall be asked who elected the successors to the captains of each tribe; on this point I can gather no positive information in

---

take counsel of the High Priest (who was the chief interpreter of the law), or of the chief judge, to whom they were then subordinate (who had the right of consulting the High Priest), and to decide the dispute in accordance with the answer obtained. If any subordinate judge should assert, that he was not bound by the decision of the High Priest, received either directly or through the chief of his state, such an one was to be put to death (Deut. xvii:9) by the chief judge, whoever he might be, to whom he was a subordinate. This chief judge would either be Joshua, the supreme captain of the whole people, or one of the tribal chiefs who had been entrusted, after the division of the tribes, with the right of consulting the high priest concerning the affairs of his tribe, of deciding on peace or war, of fortifying towns, of appointing inferior judges, &c. Or, again, it might be the king, in whom all or some of the tribes had vested their rights.I could cite many instances in confirmation of what I here advance. I will confine myself to one, which appears to me the most important of all. When the Shilomitish prophet anointed Jeroboam king, he, in so doing, gave him the right of consulting the high priest, of appointing judges, &c. In fact he endowed him with all the rights over the ten tribes, which Rehoboam retained over the two tribes. Consequently Jeroboam could set up a supreme council in his court with as much right as Jehoshaphat could at Jerusalem (2 Chron. xix:8). For it is plain that neither Jeroboam, who was king by God's command, nor Jeroboam's subjects, were bound by the Law of Moses to accept the judgments of Rehoboam, who was not their king. Still less were they under the jurisdiction of the judge, whom Rehoboam had set up in Jerusalem as subordinate to himself. According, therefore, as the Hebrew dominion was divided, so was a supreme council setup in each division. Those who neglect the variations in the constitution of the Hebrew States, and confuse them all together in one, fall into numerous difficulties.

Scripture, but I conjecture that as the tribes were divided into families, each headed by its senior member, the senior of all these heads of families succeeded by right to the office of captain, for Moses chose from among these seniors his seventy coadjutors, who formed with himself the supreme council. Those who administered the government after the death of Joshua were called elders, and elder is a very common Hebrew expression in the sense of judge, as I suppose everyone knows; however, it is not very important for us to make up our minds on this point. It is enough to have shown that after the death of Moses no one man wielded all the power of a sovereign; as affairs were not all managed by one man, nor by a single council, nor by the popular vote, but partly by one tribe, partly by the rest in equal shares, it is most evident that the government, after the death of Moses, was neither monarchic, nor aristocratic, nor popular, but, as we have said, Theocratic. The reasons for applying this name are:

I. Because the royal seat of government was the Temple, and in respect to it alone, as we have shown, all the tribes were fellow-citizens,

II. Because all the people owed allegiance to God, their supreme Judge, to whom only they had promised implicit obedience in all things.

III. Because the general-inchief or dictator, when there was need of such, was elected by none save God alone. This was expressly commanded by Moses in the name of God (Deut. xix:15), and witnessed by the actual choice of Gideon, of Samson, and of Samuel; wherefrom we may conclude that the other faithful leaders were chosen in the same manner, though it is not expressly told us.

These preliminaries being stated, it is now time to inquire the effects of forming a dominion on this plan, and to see whether it so effectually kept within bounds both rulers and ruled, that the former were never tyrannical and the latter never rebellious.

Those who administer or possess governing power, always try to surround their high-handed actions with a cloak of legality, and to persuade the people that they act from good motives; this they are easily able to effect when they are the sole interpreters of the law; for it is evident that they are thus able to assume a far greater freedom to carry out their wishes and desires than if the interpretation if the law is vested in someone else, or if the laws were so self-evident that no one could be in doubt as to their meaning. We thus see that the power of evil-doing was greatly curtailed for the Hebrew captains by the fact that the whole interpretation of the law was vested in the Levites (Deut. xxi:5), who, on their part, had no share in the government, and depended for all their support and consideration on a correct interpretation of the laws entrusted to them. Moreover, the whole people was commanded to come together at a certain place every seven years and be instructed in the law by the high-priest; further, each individual was bidden to read the book of the law through and through continually with scrupulous care. (Deut. xxxi:9, 10, and vi:7.) The captains were thus for their own sakes bound to take great care to administer everything according to the laws laid down, and well known to all, if they, wished to be held in high honour by, the people, who would regard them as the administrators of God's dominion, and as God's vicegerents; otherwise they could not have escaped all the virulence of theological hatred. There was another very important check on the unbridled license of the captains, in the fact, that the army was formed from the whole body, of the citizens, between the ages of twenty and sixty, without exception, and that the captains were not able to hire any foreign soldiery. This I say was very, important, for it is well known that princes can oppress their peoples with the single aid of the soldiery in their pay; while there is nothing more formidable to them than the freedom of citizen soldiers, who have established the freedom and glory of their country, by their valour, their toil, and their blood. Thus Alexander, when he was about to make wax on Darius, a second time, after hearing the advice of Parmenio, did not chide him who gave the advice, but Polysperchon, who was standing by. For, as Curtius says (iv. Para. 13), he did not venture to reproach Parmenio again after having shortly, before reproved him too sharply. This freedom of the Macedonians, which he so dreaded, he was not able to subdue till after the number of captives enlisted in the army, surpassed that of his own people: then, but not till then, he gave rein to his anger so long checked by, the independence of his chief fellow-countrymen.

If this independence of citizen soldiers can restrain the princes of ordinary states who are wont to usurp the whole glory of victories, it must have been still more effectual against the Hebrew captains, whose soldiers were fighting, not for the glory of a prince, but for the glory of God, and who did not go forth to battle till the Divine assent had been given.

We must also remember that the Hebrew captains were associated only by the bonds of religion: therefore, if any one of them had transgressed, and begun to violate the Divine right, he might have been treated by the rest as an enemy and lawfully subdued.

An additional check may be found in the fear of a new prophet arising, for if a man of unblemished life could show by certain signs that he was really a prophet, he ipso facto obtained the sovereign right to rule, which was given to him, as to Moses formerly, in the name of God, as revealed to himself alone; not merely through the high priest, as in the case of the captains. There is no doubt that such an one would easily be able to enlist an oppressed people in his cause, and by trifling signs persuade them of anything he wished: on the other hand, if affairs were well ordered, the captain would be able to make provision in time; that the prophet should be submitted to his approval, and be examined whether he were really of unblemished life, and possessed indisputable signs of his mission: also, whether the teaching he proposed to set forth in the name of the Lord agreed with received doctrines, and the general laws of the country; if his credentials were insufficient, or his doctrines new, he could lawfully be put to death, or else received on the captain's sole responsibility and authority.

Again, the captains were not superior to the others in nobility or birth, but only administered the government in virtue of their age and personal qualities. Lastly, neither captains nor army had any reason for preferring war to peace. The army, as we have stated, consisted entirely of citizens, so that affairs were managed by the same persons both in peace and war. The man who was a soldier in the camp was a citizen in the market-place, he who was a leader in the camp was a judge in the law courts, he who was a general in the camp was a ruler in the state. Thus no one could desire war for its own sake, but only for the sake of preserving peace and liberty; possibly the captains avoided change as far as possible, so as not to be obliged to consult the high priest and submit to the indignity of standing in his presence.

So much for the precautions for keeping the captains within bounds. We must now look for the restraints upon the people: these, however, are very clearly indicated in the very groundwork of the social fabric.

Anyone who gives the subject the slightest attention, will see that the state was so ordered as to inspire the most ardent patriotism in the hearts of the citizens, so that the latter would be very hard to persuade to betray their country, and be ready to endure anything rather than submit to a foreign yoke. After they had transferred their right to God, they thought that their kingdom belonged to God, and that they themselves were God's children. Other nations they looked upon as God's enemies, and regarded with intense hatred (which they took to be piety, see Psalm cxxxix:21, 22): nothing would have been more abhorrent to them than swearing allegiance to a foreigner, and promising him obedience: nor could they conceive any greater or more execrable crime than the betrayal of their country, the kingdom of the God whom they adored.

It was considered wicked for anyone to settle outside of the country, inasmuch as the worship of God by which they were bound could not be carried on elsewhere: their own land alone was considered holy, the rest of the earth unclean and profane.

David, who was forced to live in exile, complained before Saul as follows: "But if they be the children of men who have stirred thee up against me, cursed be they before the Lord; for they have driven me out this day from abiding in the inheritance of the Lord, saying, Go, serve other gods." (I Sam. xxvi:19.) For the same reason no citizen, as we should especially remark, was ever sent into exile: he who sinned was liable to punishment, but not to disgrace.

Thus the love of the Hebrews for their country was not only patriotism, but also piety, and was cherished and nurtured bv daily rites till, like their hatred of other nations, it must have passed into their nature. Their daily worship was not only different from that of other nations (as it might well be, considering that they were a peculiar people and entirely apart from the rest), it was absolutely contrary. Such daily reprobation naturally gave rise to a lasting hatred, deeply implanted in the heart: for of all hatreds none is more deep and tenacious than that which springs from extreme devoutness or piety, and is itself cherished as pious. Nor was a general cause lacking for inflaming such hatred more and more, inasmuch as it was reciprocated; the surrounding nations regarding the Jews with a hatred just as intense.

How great was the effect of all these causes, namely, freedom from man's dominion; devotion to their country; absolute rights over all other men; a hatred not only permitted but pious; a contempt for their fellow-men; the singularity of their customs and religious rites; the effect, I repeat, of all these causes in strengthening the hearts of the Jews to bear all things for their country, with extraordinary constancy and valour, will at once be discerned by reason and attested by experience. Never, so long as the city was standing, could they endure to remain under foreign dominion; and therefore they called Jerusalem "a rebellious city" (Ezra iv:12). Their state after its reestablishment (which was a mere shadow of the first, for the high priests had usurped the rights of the tribal captains) was, with great difficulty, destroyed by the Romans, as Tacitus bears witness (Hist. ii:4):— "Vespasian had closed the war against the Jews, abandoning the siege of Jerusalem as an enterprise difficult and arduous rather from the character of the people and the obstinacy of their superstition, than from the strength left to the besieged for meeting their necessities." But besides these characteristics, which are merely ascribed by an individual opinion, there was one feature peculiar to this state and of great importance in retaining the affections of the citizens, and checking all thoughts of desertion, or abandonment of the country: namely, self-interest, the strength and life of all human action. This was peculiarly engaged in the Hebrew state, for nowhere else did citizens possess their goods so securely, as did the subjects of this community, for the latter possessed as large a share in the land and the fields as did their chiefs, and were owners of their plots of ground in perpetuity; for if any man was compelled by poverty to sell his farm or his pasture, he received it back again intact at the year of jubilee: there were other similar enactments against the possibility of alienating real property.

Again, poverty w as nowhere more endurable than in a country where duty towards one's neighbour, that is, one's fellow-citizen, was practised with the utmost piety, as a means of gaining the favour of God the King. Thus the

Hebrew citizens would nowhere be so well off as in their own country; outside its limits they met with nothing but loss and disgrace.

The following considerations were of weight, not only in keeping them at home, but also in preventing civil war and removing causes of strife; no one was bound to serve his equal, but only to serve God, while charity and love towards fellow-citizens was accounted the highest piety; this last feeling was not a little fostered by the general hatred with which they regarded foreign nations and were regarded by them. Furthermore, the strict discipline of obedience in which they were brought up, was a very important factor; for they were bound to carry on all their actions according to the set rules of the law: a man might not plough when he liked, but only at certain times, in certain years, and with one sort of beast at a time; so, too, he might only sow and reap in a certain method and season — in fact, his whole life was one long school of obedience (see Chap. V. on the use of ceremonies); such a habit was thus engendered, that conformity seemed freedom instead of servitude, and men desired what was commanded rather than what was forbidden. This result was not a little aided by the fact that the people were bound, at certain seasons of the year, to give themselves up to rest and rejoicing, not for their own pleasure, but in order that they might worship God cheerfully.

Three times in the year they feasted before the Lord; on the seventh day of every week they were bidden to abstain from all work and to rest; besides these, there were other occasions when innocent rejoicing and feasting were not only allowed but enjoined. I do not think any better means of influencing men's minds could be devised; for there is no more powerful attraction than joy springing from devotion, a mixture of admiration and love. It was not easy to be wearied by constant repetition, for the rites on the various festivals were varied and recurred seldom. We may add the deep reverence for the Temple which all most religiously fostered, on account of the peculiar rites and duties that they were obliged to perform before approaching thither. Even now, Jews cannot read without horror of the crime of Manasseh, who dared to place au idol in the Temple. The laws, scrupulously preserved in the inmost sanctuary, were objects of equal reverence to the people. Popular reports and misconceptions were, therefore, very little to be feared in this quarter, for no one dared decide on sacred matters, but all felt bound to obey, without consulting their reason, all the commands given by the answers of God received in the Temple, and all the laws which God had ordained.

I think I have now explained clearly, though briefly,, the main features of the Hebrew commonwealth. I must now inquire into the causes which led the people so often to fall away from the law, which brought about their frequent subjection, and, finally, the complete destruction of their dominion. Perhaps I shall be told that it sprang from their hardness of heart; but this is childish, for why should this people be more hard of heart than others; was it by nature?

But nature forms individuals, not peoples; the latter are only distinguishable by the difference of their language, their customs, and their laws; while from the two last — i.e., customs and laws, — it may arise that they have a peculiar disposition, a peculiar manner of life, and peculiar prejudices. If, then, the Hebrews were harder of heart than other nations, the fault lay with their laws or customs.

This is certainly true, in the sense that, if God had wished their dominion to be more lasting, He would have given them other rites and laws, and would have instituted a different form of government. We can, therefore, only say that their God was angry with them, not only, as Jeremiah says, from the building of the city, but even from the founding of their laws.

This is borne witness to by Ezekiel xx:25: "Wherefore I gave them also statutes that were not good, and judgments whereby they should not live; and I polluted them in their own gifts, in that they caused to pass through the fire all that openeth the womb; that I might make them desolate, to the end that they might know that I am the Lord."

In order that we may understand these words, and the destruction of the Hebrew commonwealth, we must bear in mind that it had at first been intended to entrust the whole duties of the priesthood to the firstborn, and not to the Levites (see Numb. viii:17). It was only when all the tribes, except the Levites, worshipped the golden calf, that the firstborn were rejected and defiled, and the Levites chosen in their stead (Deut. x:8). When I reflect on this change, I feel disposed to break forth with the words of Tacitus. God's object at that time was not the safety of the Jews, but vengeance. I am greatly astonished that the celestial mind was so inflamed with anger that it ordained laws, which always are supposed to promote the honour, well-being, and security of a people, with the purpose of vengeance, for the sake of punishment; so that the laws do not seem so much laws — that is, the safeguard of the people — as pains and penalties.

The gifts which the people were obliged to bestow on the Levites and priests — the redemption of the firstborn, the poll-tax due to the Levites, the privilege possessed by the latter of the sole performance of sacred rites — all these, I say, were a continual reproach to the people, a continual reminder of their defilement and rejection. Moreover, we may be sure that the Levites were for ever heaping reproaches upon them: for among so many thousands there must have been many importunate dabblers in theology. Hence the people got into the way of watching the acts of the Levites, who were but human; of accusing the whole body of the faults of one member, and continually murmuring.

Besides this, there was the obligation to keep in idleness men hateful to them, and connected by no ties of blood. Especially would this seem grievous when provisions were dear. What wonder, then, if in times of peace, when striking miracles had ceased, and no men of paramount authority were forthcoming, the irritable and greedy temper of the people began to wax cold, and at length to fall away from a worship, which, though Divine, was also humiliating, and even hostile, and to seek after something fresh; or can we be surprised that the captains, who always adopt the popular course, in order to gain the sovereign power for themselves by enlisting the sympathies of the people, and alienating the high priest, should have yielded to their demands, and introduced a new worship? If the state had been formed according to the original intention, the rights and honour of all the tribes would have been equal, and everything would have rested on a firm basis. Who is there who would willingly violate the religious rights of his kindred? What could a man desire more than to support his own brothers and parents, thus fulfilling the duties of religion? Who would not rejoice in being taught by them the interpretation of the laws, and receiving through them the answers of God?

The tribes would thus have been united by a far closer bond, if all alike had possessed the right to the priesthood. All danger would have been obviated, if the choice of the Levites had not been dictated by anger and revenge. But, as we have said, the Hebrews had offended their God, Who, as Ezekiel says, polluted them in their own gifts by rejecting all that openeth the womb, so that He might destroy them.

This passage is also confirmed by their history. As soon as the people in the wilderness began to live in ease and plenty, certain men of no mean birth began to rebel against the choice of the Levites, and to make it a cause for believing that Moses had not acted by the commands of God, but for his own good pleasure, inasmuch as he had chosen his own tribe before all the rest, and had bestowed the high priesthood in perpetuity on his own brother. They, therefore, stirred up a tumult, and came to him, crying out that all men were equally sacred, and that he had exalted himself above his fellows wrongfully. Moses was not able to pacify them with reasons; but by the intervention of a miracle in proof of the faith, they all perished. A fresh sedition then arose among the whole people, who believed that their champions had not been put to death by the judgment of God, but by the device of Moses. After a great slaughter, or pestilence, the rising subsided from inanition, but in such a manner that all preferred death to life under such conditions.

We should rather say that sedition ceased than that harmony was re-established. This is witnessed by Scripture (Deut. xxxi:21), where God, after predicting to Moses that the people after his death will fall away from the Divine worship, speaks thus: "For I know their imagination which they go about, even now before I have brought them into the land which I sware;" and, a little while after (xxxi:27), Moses says: For I know thy rebellion and thy stiff neck: behold while I am yet alive with you this day, ye have been rebellious against the Lord; and how much more after my death!"

Indeed, it happened according to his words, as we all know. Great changes, extreme license, luxury, and hardness of heart grew up; things went from bad to worse, till at last the people, after being frequently conquered, came to an open rupture with the Divine right, and wished for a mortal king, so that the seat of government might be the Court, instead of the Temple, and that the tribes might remain fellow-citizens in respect to their king, instead of in respect to Divine right and the high priesthood.

A vast material for new seditions was thus produced, eventually resulting in the ruin of the entire state. Kings are above all things jealous of a precarious rule, and can in nowise brook a dominion within their own. The first monarchs, being chosen from the ranks of private citizens, were content with the amount of dignity to which they had risen; but their sons, who obtained the throne by right of inheritance, began gradually to introduce changes, so as to get all the sovereign rights into their own hands. This they were generally unable to accomplish, so long as the right of legislation did not rest with them, but with the high priest, who kept the laws in the sanctuary, and interpreted them to the people. The kings were thus bound to obey the laws as much as were the subjects, and were unable to abrogate them, or to ordain new laws of equal authority; moreover, they were prevented by the Levites from administering the affairs of religion, king and subject being alike unclean. Lastly, the whole safety of their dominion depended on the will of one man, if that man appeared to be a prophet; and of this they had seen an example, namely, how completely Samuel had been able to command Saul, and how easily, because of a single disobedience, he had been able to transfer the right of sovereignty to David. Thus the kings found a dominion within their own, and wielded a precarious sovereignty.

In order to surmount these difficulties, they allowed other temples to be dedicated to the gods, so that there might be no further need of consulting the Levites; they also sought out many who prophesied in the name of God, so that they might have creatures of their own to oppose to the true prophets. However, in spite of all their attempts, they never attained their end. For the prophets, prepared against every emergency, waited for a favourable opportunity, such as the beginning of a new reign, which is always precarious, while the memory of the previous reign remains green. At these times they could easily pronounce by Divine authority that the king was tyrannical, and could produce a champion of distinguished virtue to vindicate the Divine right, and lawfully to claim dominion, or a share in it. Still, not even so could the prophets effect much. They could, indeed, remove a tyrant; but there were reasons which prevented them from doing more than setting up, at great cost of civil bloodshed, another tyrant in his stead. Of discords and civil wars there was no end, for the causes for the violation of Divine right remained always the same, and could only be removed by a complete remodelling of the state.

We have now seen how religion was introduced into the Hebrew commonwealth, and how the dominion might have lasted for ever, if the just wrath of the Lawgiver had allowed it. As this was impossible, it was bound in time to perish. I am now speaking only of the first commonwealth, for the second was a mere shadow of the first, inasmuch as the people were bound by the rights of the Persians to whom they were subject. After the restoration of freedom, the high priests usurped the rights of the secular chiefs, and thus obtained absolute dominion. The priests were inflamed with an intense desire to wield the powers of the sovereignty and the high priesthood at the same time. I have, therefore, no need to speak further of the second commonwealth. Whether the first, in so far as we deem it to have been durable, is capable of imitation, and whether it would be pious to copy it as far as possible, will appear from what fellows. I wish only to draw attention, as a crowning conclusion, to the principle indicated already — namely, that it is evident, from what we have stated in this chapter, that the Divine right, or the right of religion, originates in a compact: without such compact, none but natural rights exist. The Hebrews were not bound by their religion to evince any pious care for other nations not included in the compact, but only for their own fellow-citizens.

CHAPTER XVIII

From the Commonwealth of the Hebrews, and their History, certain Political Doctrines are Deduced

Although the commonwealth of the Hebrews, as we have conceived it, might have lasted for ever, it would be impossible to imitate it at the present day, nor would it be advisable so to do. If a people wished to transfer their rights to God it would be necessary to make an express covenant with Him, and for this would be needed not only the consent of those transferring their rights, but also the consent of God. God, however, has revealed through his Apostles that the covenant of God is no longer written in ink, or on tables of stone, but with the Spirit of God in the fleshy tables of the heart.

Furthermore, such a form of government would only be available for those who desire to have no foreign relations, but to shut themselves up within their own frontiers, and to live apart from the rest of the world; it would be useless to men who must have dealings with other nations; so that the cases where it could be adopted are very few indeed.

Nevertheless, though it could not be copied in its entirety, it possessed many excellent features which might be brought to our notice, and perhaps imitated with advantage. My intention, however, is not to write a treatise on forms of government, so I will pass over most of such points in silence, and will only touch on those which bear upon my purpose.

God's kingdom is not infringed upon by the choice of an earthly ruler endowed with sovereign rights; for after the Hebrews had transferred their rights to God, they conferred the sovereign right of ruling on Moses, investing him with the sole power of instituting and abrogating laws in the name of God, of choosing priests, of judging, of teaching, of punishing — in fact, all the prerogatives of an absolute monarch.

Again, though the priests were the interpreters of the laws, they had no power to judge the citizens, or to excommunicate anyone: this could only be done by the judges and chiefs chosen from among the people. A consideration of the successes and the histories of the Hebrews will bring to light other considerations worthy of note. To wit:

I. That there were no religious sects, till after the high priests, in the second commonwealth, possessed the authority to make decrees, and transact the business of government. In order that such authority might last for ever, the high priests usurped the rights of secular rulers, and at last wished to be styled kings. The reason for this is ready to hand; in the first commonwealth no decrees could bear the name of the high priest, for he had no right to ordain laws, but only to give the answers of God to questions asked by the captains or the councils: he had, therefore, no motive for making changes in the law, but took care, on the contrary, to administer and guard what had already been received and accepted. His only means of preserving his freedom in safety against the will of the captains lay in cherishing the law intact. After the high priests had assumed the power of carrying on the government, and added the rights of secular rulers to those they already possessed, each one began both in things religious and in things secular, to seek for the glorification of his own name, settling everything by sacerdotal authority, and issuing every day, concerning ceremonies, faith, and all else, new decrees which he sought to make as sacred and authoritative as the laws of Moses. Religion thus sank into a degrading superstition, while the true meaning and interpretation of the laws became corrupted. Furthermore, while the high priests were paving their way to the secular rule just after the restoration, they attempted to gain popular favour by assenting to every demand; approving whatever the people did, however impious, and accommodating Scripture to the very depraved current morals. Malachi bears witness to this in no measured terms: he chides the priests of his time as despisers of the name of God, and then goes on with his invective as follows (Mal ii:7, 8): "For the priest's lips should keep knowledge, and they should seek the law at his mouth: for he is the messenger of the Lord of hosts. But ye are departed out of the way; ye have caused many to stumble at the law, ye have corrupted the covenant of Levi, saith the Lord of hosts." He further accuses them of interpreting the laws according to their own pleasure, and paying no respect to God but only to persons. It is certain that the high priests were never so cautious in their conduct as to escape the remark of the more shrewd among the people, for the latter were at length emboldened to assert that no laws ought to be kept save those that were written, and that the decrees which the Pharisees (consisting, as Josephus says in his " Amtiquities," chiefly, of the common people), were deceived into calling the traditions of the fathers, should not be observed at all. However this may be, we can in nowise doubt that flattery of the high priest, the corruption of religion and the laws, and the enormous increase of the extent of the last-named, gave very great and frequent occasion for disputes and altercations impossible to allay. When men begin to quarrel with all the ardour of superstition, and the magistracy to back up one side or the other, they can never come to a compromise, but are bound to split into sects.

II. It is worthy of remark that the prophets, who were in a private station of life, rather irritated than reformed mankind by their freedom of warning, rebuke, and censure; whereas the kings, by their reproofs and punishments, could always produce an effect. The prophets were often intolerable even to pious kings, on account of the authority they assumed for judging whether an action was right or wrong, or for reproving the kings themselves if they dared to transact any business, whether public or private, without prophetic sanction. King Asa who, according to the testimony of Scripture, reigned piously, put the prophet Hanani into a prison-house because he had ventured freely to chide and reprove him for entering into a covenant with the king of Armenia.

Other examples might be cited, tending to prove that religion gained more harm than good by such freedom, not to speak of the further consequence, that if the prophets had retained their rights, great civil wars would have resulted.

III. It is remarkable that during all the period, during which the people held the reins of power, there was only one civil war, and that one was completely extinguished, the conquerors taking such pity on the conquered, that they endeavoured in every way to reinstate them in their former dignity and power. But after that the people, little accustomed to kings, changed its first form of government into a monarchy, civil war raged almost continuously; and battles were so fierce as to exceed all others recorded; in one engagement (taxing our faith to the utmost) five hundred thousand Israelites were slaughtered by the men of Judah, and in another the Israelites slew great numbers of the men of Judah (the figures are not given in Scripture), almost razed to the ground the walls of Jerusalem, and sacked the Temple in their unbridled fury. At length, laden with the spoils of their brethren, satiated with blood, they took hostages, and leaving the king in his well-nigh devastated kingdom, laid down their arms, relying on the weakness rather than the good faith of their foes. A few years after, the men of Judah, with recruited strength, again took the field, but were a second time beaten by the Israelites, and slain to the number of a hundred and twenty thousand, two hundred thousand of their wives and children were led into captivity, and a great booty again seized. Worn out with these and similar battles set forth at length in their histories, the Jews at length fell a prey to their enemies.

Furthermore, if we reckon up the times during which peace prevailed under each form of government, we shall find a great discrepancy. Before the monarchy forty years and more often passed, and once eighty years (an almost unparalleled period), without any war, foreign or civil. After the kings acquired sovereign power, the fighting was no longer for peace and liberty, but for glory; accordingly we find that they all, with the exception of Solomon (whose virtue and wisdom would be better displayed in peace than in war) waged war, and finally a fatal desire for power gained ground, which, in many cases, made the path to the throne a bloody one.

Lastly, the laws, during the rule of the people, remained uncorrupted and were studiously observed. Before the monarchy there were very, few prophets to admonish the people, but after the establishment of kings there were a great number at the same time. Obadiah saved a hundred from death and hid them away, lest they should be slain with the rest. The people, so far as we can see, were never deceived by false prophets till after the power had been vested in kings, whose creatures many of the prophets were. Again, the people, whose heart was generally proud or humble according to its circumstances, easily corrected itself under misfortune, turned again to God, restored His laws, and so freed itself from all peril; but the kings, whose hearts were always equally puffed up, and who could not be corrected without humiliation, clung pertinaciously to their vices, even till the last overthrow of the city.

We may now clearly see from what I have said:—

I. How hurtful to religion and the state is the concession to ministers of religion of any power of issuing decrees or transacting the business of government: how, on the contrary, far greater stability is afforded, if the said ministers are only allowed to give answers to questions duly put to them, and are, as a rule, obliged to preach and practise the received and accepted doctrines.

II How dangerous it is to refer to Divine right matters merely speculative and subject or liable to dispute. The most tyrannical governments are those which make crimes of opinions, for everyone has an inalienable right over his thoughts — nay, such a state of things leads to the rule of popular passion.

Pontius Pilate made concession to the passion of the Pharisees in consenting to the crucifixion of Christ, whom he knew to be innocent. Again, the Pharisees, in order to shake the position of men richer than themselves, began to set on foot questions of religion, and accused the Sadducees of impiety, and, following their example, the vilest — hypocrites, stirred, as they pretended, by the same holy wrath which they called zeal for the Lord, persecuted men whose unblemished character and distinguished virtue had excited the popular hatred, publicly denounced their opinions, and inflamed the fierce passions of the people against them.

This wanton licence being cloaked with the specious garb of religion could not easily be repressed, especially when the sovereign authorities introduced a sect of which they, were not the head; they were then regarded not as interpreters of Divine right, but as sectarians — that is, as persons recognizing the right of Divine interpretation assumed by the leaders of the sect. The authority of the magistrates thus became of little account in such matters in comparison with the authority of sectarian leaders before whose interpretations kings were obliged to bow.

To avoid such evils in a state, there is no safer way, than to make piety and religion to consist in acts only — that is, in the practice of justice and charity, leaving everyone's judgment in other respects free. But I will speak of this more at length presently.

III. We see how necessary it is, both in the interests of the state and in the interests of religion, to confer on the sovereign power the right of deciding what is lawful or the reverse. If this right of judging actions could not be given to the very prophets of God without great injury, to the state and religion, how much less should it be entrusted to those who can neither foretell the future nor work miracles! But this again I will treat of more fully hereafter.

IV. Lastly,, we see how disastrous it is for a people unaccustomed to kings, and possessing a complete code of laws, to set up a monarchy. Neither can the subjects brook such a sway, nor the royal authority submit to laws and popular rights set up by anyone inferior to itself. Still less can a king be expected to defend such laws, for they were not framed to support his dominion, but the dominion of the people, or some council which formerly ruled, so that in guarding the popular rights the king would seem to be a slave rather than a master. The representative of a new monarchy will employ all his zeal in attempting to frame new laws, so as to wrest the rights of dominion to his own use, and to reduce the people till they find it easier to increase than to curtail the royal prerogative. I must not, however, omit to state that it is no less dangerous to remove a monarch, though he is on all hands admitted to be a tyrant. For his people are accustomed to royal authority and will obey no other, despising and mocking at any less august control.

It is therefore necessary, as the prophets discovered of old, if one king be removed, that he should be replaced by another, who will be a tyrant from necessity rather than choice. For how will he be able to endure the sight of the hands of the citizens reeking with royal blood, and to rejoice in their regicide as a glorious exploit? Was not the deed perpetrated as an example and warning for himself?

If he really wishes to be king, and not to acknowledge the people as the judge of kings and the master of himself, or to wield a precarious sway, he must avenge the death of his predecessor, making an example for his own sake, lest the people should venture to repeat a similar crime. He will not, however, be able easily to avenge the death of the tyrant by the slaughter of citizens unless he defends the cause of tyranny and approves the deeds of his predecessor, thus following in his footsteps.

Hence it comes to pass that peoples have often changed their tyrants, but never removed them or changed the monarchical form of government into any other.

The English people furnish us with a terrible example of this fact. They sought how to depose their monarch under the forms of law, but when he had been removed, they were utterly unable to change the form of government, and after much bloodshed only brought it about, that a new monarch should be hailed under a different name (as though it had been a mere question of names); this new monarch could only consolidate his power by completely destroying the royal stock, putting to death the king's friends, real or supposed, and disturbing with war the peace which might encourage discontent, in order that the populace might be engrossed with novelties and divert its mind from brooding over the slaughter of the king. At last, however, the people reflected that it had accomplished nothing for the good of the country beyond violating the rights of the lawful king and changing everything for the worse. It therefore decided to retrace its steps as soon as possible, and never rested till it had seen a complete restoration of the original state of affairs.

It may perhaps be objected that the Roman people was easily able to remove its tyrants, but I gather from its history a strong confirmation of my contention. Though the Roman people was much more than ordinarily capable of removing their tyrants and changing their form of government, inasmuch as it held in its own hands the power of electing its king and his successor, said being composed of rebels and criminals had not long been used to the royal yoke (out of its six kings it had put to death three), nevertheless it could accomplish nothing beyond electing several tyrants in place of one, who kept it groaning under a continual state of war, both foreign and civil, till at last it changed its government again to a form differing from monarchy, as in England, only in name.

As for the United States of the Netherlands, they have never, as we know, had a king, but only counts, who never attained the full rights of dominion. The States of the Netherlands evidently acted as principals in the settlement made by them at the time of the Earl of Leicester's mission: they always reserved for themselves the authority to keep the counts up to their duties, and the power to preserve this authority and the liberty of the citizens. They had ample means of vindicating their rights if their rulers should prove tyrannical, and could impose such restraints that nothing could be done without their consent and approval.

Thus the rights of sovereign power have always been vested in the States, though the last count endeavoured to usurp them. It is therefore little likely that the States should give them up, especially as they have just restored their original dominion, lately almost lost.

These examples, then, confirm us in our belief, that every dominion should retain its original form, and, indeed, cannot change it without danger of the utter ruin of the whole state. Such are the points I have here thought worthy of remark.

CHAPTER XIX

It is shown that the Right over matters Spiritual lies wholly with the Sovereign, and that the outward forms of Religion should be in accordance with Public Peace, if we would obey God aright

When I said that the possessors of sovereign power have rights over everything, and that all rights are dependent on their decree, I did not merely mean temporal rights, but also spiritual rights; of the latter, no less than the former, they ought to be the interpreters and the champions. I wish to draw special attention to this point, and to discuss it fully in this chapter, because many persons deny that the right of deciding religious questions belongs to the sovereign power, and refuse to acknowledge it as the interpreter of Divine right. They accordingly assume full licence to accuse and arraign it, nay, even to excommunicate it from the Church, as Ambrosius treated the Emperor Theodosius in old time. However, I will show later on in this chapter that they take this means of dividing the government, and paving the way to their own ascendancy. I wish, however, first to point out that religion acquires its force as law solely from the decrees of the sovereign. God has no special kingdom among men except in so far as He reigns through temporal rulers. Moreover, the rites of religion and the outward observances of piety should be in accordance with the public peace and well-being, and should therefore be determined by the sovereign power alone. I speak here only of the outward observances of piety and the external rites of religion, not of piety, itself, nor of the inward worship of God, nor the means by which the mind is inwardly led to do homage to God in singleness of heart.

Inward worship of God and piety in itself are within the sphere of everyone's private rights, and cannot be alienated (as I showed at the end of Chapter VII.). What I here mean by the kingdom of God is, I think, sufficiently clear from what has been said in Chapter XIV. I there showed that a man best fulfils Gods law who worships Him, according to His command, through acts of justice and charity; it follows, therefore, that wherever justice and charity have the force of law and ordinance, there is God's kingdom.

I recognize no difference between the cases where God teaches and commands the practice of justice and charity through our natural faculties, and those where He makes special revelations; nor is the form of the revelation of importance so long as such practice is revealed and becomes a sovereign and supreme law to men. If, therefore, I show that justice and charity can only acquire the force of right and law through the rights of rulers, I shall be able readily to arrive at the conclusion (seeing that the rights of rulers are in the possession of the sovereign), that religion can only acquire the force of right by means of those who have the right to command, and that God only rules among men through the instrumentality of earthly potentates. It follows from what has been said, that the practice of justice and charity only acquires the force of law through the rights of the sovereign authority; for we showed in Chapter XVI. that in the state of nature reason has no more rights than desire, but that men living either by the laws of the former or the laws of the latter, possess rights co-extensive with their powers.

For this reason we could not conceive sin to exist in the state of nature, nor imagine God as a judge punishing man's transgressions; but we supposed all things to happen according to the general laws of universal nature, there being no difference between pious and impious, between him that was pure (as Solomon says) and him that was impure, because there was no possibility either of justice or charity.

In order that the true doctrines of reason, that is (as we showed in Chapter IV.), the true Divine doctrines might obtain absolutely the force of law and right, it was necessary that each individual should cede his natural right, and transfer it either to society as a whole, or to a certain body of men, or to one man. Then, and not till then, does it first dawn upon us what is justice and what is injustice, what is equity and what is iniquity.

Justice, therefore, and absolutely all the precepts of reason, including love towards one's neighbour, receive the force of laws and ordinances solely through the rights of dominion, that is (as we showed in the same chapter) solely on the decree of those who possess the right to rule. Inasmuch as the kingdom of God consists entirely in rights applied to justice and charity or to true religion, it follows that (as we asserted) the kingdom of God can only exist among men through the means of the sovereign powers; nor does it make any difference whether religion be apprehended by our natural faculties or by revelation: the argument is sound in both cases, inasmuch as religion is one and the same, and is equally revealed by God, whatever be the manner in which it becomes known to men.

Thus, in order that the religion revealed by the prophets might have the force of law among the Jews, it was necessary that every man of them should yield up his natural right, and that all should, with one accord, agree that they would only obey such commands as God should reveal to them through the prophets. Just as we have shown to take place in a democracy, where men with one consent agree to live according to the dictates of reason. Although the Hebrews furthermore transferred their right to God, they were able to do so rather in theory than in practice, for, as a matter of fact (as we pointed out above) they absolutely retained the right of dominion till they transferred it to Moses, who in his turn became absolute king, so that it was only through him that God reigned over the Hebrews. For this reason (namely, that religion only acquires the force of law by means of the sovereign power) Moses was not able to punish those who, before the covenant, and consequently while still in possession of their rights, violated the Sabbath (Exod. xvi:27), but was able to do so after the covenant (Numb. xv:36), because everyone had then yielded up his natural rights, and the ordinance of the Sabbath had received the force of law.

Lastly, for the same reason, after the destruction of the Hebrew dominion, revealed religion ceased to have the force of law; for we cannot doubt that as soon as the Jews transferred their right to the king of Babylon, the kingdom of God and the Divine right forthwith ceased. For the covenant wherewith they promised to obey all the utterances of God was abrogated; God's kingdom, which was based thereupon, also ceased. The Hebrews could no longer abide thereby, inasmuch as their rights no longer belonged to them but to the king of Babylon, whom (as we showed in Chapter XVI.) they were bound to obey in all things. Jeremiah (chap. xxix:7) expressly admonishes them of this fact: "And seek the peace of the city, whither I have caused you to be carried away captives, and pray unto the Lord for it; for in the peace thereof shall ye have peace." Now, they could not seek the peace of the City as having a share in its government, but only as slaves, being, as they were, captives; by obedience in all things, with a view to avoiding seditions, and by observing all the laws of the country, however different from their own. It is thus abundantly evident that religion among the Hebrews only acquired the form of law through the right of the sovereign rule; when that rule was destroyed, it could no longer be received as the law of a particular kingdom, but only as the universal precept of reason. I say of reason, for the universal religion had not yet become known by revelation. We may therefore draw the general conclusion that religion, whether revealed through our natural faculties or through prophets, receives the force of a command solely through the decrees of the holders of sovereign power; and, further, that God has no special kingdom among men, except in so far as He reigns through earthly potentates.

We may now see in a clearer light what was stated in Chapter IV., namely, that all the decrees of God involve eternal truth and necessity, so that we cannot conceive God as a prince or legislator giving laws to mankind. For this reason the Divine precepts, whether revealed through our natural faculties, or through prophets, do not receive immediately from God the force of a command, but only from those, or through the mediation of those, who possess the right of ruling and legislating. It is only through these latter means that God rules among men, and directs human affairs with justice and equity.

This conclusion is supported by experience, for we find traces of Divine justice only in places where just men bear sway; elsewhere the same lot (to repeat, again Solomon's words) befalls the just and the unjust, the pure and the impure: a state of things which causes Divine Providence to be doubted by many who think that God immediately reigns among men, and directs all nature for their benefit.

As, then, both reason and experience tell us that the Divine right is entirely dependent on the decrees of secular rulers, it follows that secular rulers are its proper interpreters. How this is so we shall now see, for it is time to show that the outward observances of religion, and all the external practices of piety should be brought into accordance with the public peace and well-being if we would obey God rightly. When this has been shown we shall easily understand how the sovereign rulers are the proper interpreters of religion and piety.

It is certain that duties towards one's country are the highest that man can fulfil; for, if government be taken away, no good thing can last, all falls into dispute, anger and anarchy reign unchecked amid universal fear. Consequently there can be no duty towards our neighbour which would not become an offence if it involved injury to the whole state, nor can there be any offence against our duty towards our neighbour, or anything but loyalty in what we do for the sake of preserving the state. For instance: it is in the abstract my duty when my neighbour quarrels with me and wishes to take my cloak, to give him my coat also; but if it be thought that such conduct is hurtful to the maintenance of the state, I ought to bring him to trial, even at the risk of his being condemned to death.

For this reason Manlius Torquatus is held up to honour, inasmuch as the public welfare outweighed with him his duty towards his children. This being so, it follows that the public welfare is the sovereign law to which all others, Divine and human, should be made to conform. Now, it is the function of the sovereign only to decide what is necessary for the public welfare and the safety of the state, and to give orders accordingly; therefore it is also the function of the sovereign only to decide the limits of our duty towards our neighbour — in other words, to determine how we should obey God. We can now clearly understand how the sovereign is the interpreter of religion, and further, that no one can obey God rightly, if the practices of his piety do not conform to the public welfare; or, consequently, if he does not implicitly obey all the commands of the sovereign. For as by God's command we are bound to do our duty to all men without exception, and to do no man an injury, we are also bound not to help one man at another's loss, still less at a loss to the whole state. Now, no private citizen can know what is good for the state, except he learn it through the sovereign power, who alone has the right to transact public business: therefore no one can rightly practise piety or obedience to God, unless he obey the sovereign power's commands in all things. This proposition is confirmed by the facts of experience. For if the sovereign adjudge a man to be worthy of death or an enemy, whether he be a citizen or a foreigner, a private individual or a separate ruler, no subject is allowed to give him assistance. So also though the Jews were bidden to love their fellow-citizens as themselves (Levit. xix:17, 18), they were nevertheless bound, if a man offended against the law, to point him out to the judge (Levit. v:1, and Deut. xiii:8, 9), and, if he should be condemned to death, to slay him (Deut. xvii:7).

Further, in order that the Hebrews might preserve the liberty they had gained, and might retain absolute sway over the territory they had conquered, it was necessary, as we showed in Chapter XVII., that their religion should be adapted to their particular government, and that they should separate themselves from the rest of the nations: wherefore it was commanded to them, "Love thy neighbour and hate thine enemy" (Matt. v:43), but after they had lost their dominion and had gone into captivity in Babylon, Jeremiah bid them take thought for the safety of the state into which they had been led captive; and Christ when He saw that they would be spread over the whole world, told them to do their duty by all men without exception; all of which instances show that religion has always been made to conform to the public welfare. Perhaps someone will ask: By what right, then, did the disciples of Christ, being private citizens, preach a new religion? I answer that they did so by the right of the power which they had received from Christ against unclean spirits (see Matt. x:1). I have already stated in Chapter XVI. that all are bound to obey a tyrant, unless they have received from God through undoubted revelation a promise of aid against him; so let no one take example from the Apostles unless he too has the power of working miracles. The point is brought out more clearly by Christ's command to His disciples, "Fear not those who kill the body" (Matt. x:28). If this command were imposed on everyone, governments would be founded in vain, and Solomon's words (Prov. xxiv:21), "My son, fear God and the king," would be impious, which they certainly are not; we must therefore admit that the authority which Christ gave to His disciples was given to them only, and must not be taken as an example for others.

I do not pause to consider the arguments of those who wish to separate secular rights from spiritual rights, placing the former under the control of the sovereign, and the latter under the control of the universal Church; such pretensions are too frivolous to merit refutation. I cannot however, pass over in silence the fact that such persons are woefully deceived when they seek to support their seditious opinions (I ask pardon for the somewhat harsh epithet) by the example of the Jewish high priest, who, in ancient times, had the right of administering the sacred offices. Did not the high priests receive their right by the decree of Moses (who, as I have shown, retained the sole right to rule), and could they not by the same means be deprived of it? Moses himself chose not only Aaron, but also his son Eleazar, and his grandson Phineas, and bestowed on them the right of administering the office of high priest. This right was retained by the high priests afterwards, but none the less were they delegates of Moses — that is, of the sovereign power. Moses, as we have shown, left no successor to his dominion, but so distributed his prerogatives, that those who came after him seemed, as it were, regents who administer the government when a king is absent but not dead.

In the second commonwealth the high priests held their right absolutely, after they had obtained the rights of principality in addition. Wherefore the rights of the high priesthood always depended on the edict of the sovereign, and the high priests did not possess them till they became sovereigns also. Rights in matters spiritual always remained under the control of the kings absolutely (as I will show at the end of this chapter), except in the single particular that they were not allowed to administer in person the sacred duties in the Temple, inasmuch as they were not of the family of Aaron, and were therefore considered unclean, a reservation which would have no force in a Christian community.

We cannot, therefore, doubt that the daily sacred rites (whose performance does not require a particular genealogy but only a special mode of life, and from which the holders of sovereign power are not excluded as unclean) are under the sole control of the sovereign power; no one, save by the authority or concession of such sovereign, has the right or power of administering them, of choosing others to administer them, of defining or strengthening the foundations of the Church and her doctrines; of judging on questions of morality or acts of piety; of receiving anyone into the Church or excommunicating him therefrom, or, lastly, of providing for the poor.

These doctrines are proved to be not only true (as we have already pointed out), but also of primary necessity for the preservation of religion and the state. We all know what weight spiritual right and authority carries in the popular mind: how everyone hangs on the lips, as it were, of those who possess it. We may even say that those who wield such authority have the most complete sway over the popular mind.

Whosoever, therefore, wishes to take this right away from the sovereign power, is desirous of dividing the dominion; from such division, contentions, and strife will necessarily spring up, as they did of old between the Jewish kings and high priests, and will defy all attempts to allay them. Nay, further, he who strives to deprive the sovereign power of such authority, is aiming (as we have said), at gaining dominion for himself. What is left for the sovereign power to decide on, if this right be denied him? Certainly nothing concerning either war or peace, if he has to ask another man's opinion as to whether what he believes to be beneficial would be pious or impious. Everything would depend on the verdict of him who had the right of deciding and judging what was pious or impious, right or wrong.

When such a right was bestowed on the Pope of Rome absolutely, he gradually acquired complete control over the kings, till at last he himself mounted to the summits of dominion; however much monarchs, and especially the German emperors, strove to curtail his authority, were it only by a hairsbreadth, they effected nothing, but on the contrary by their very endeavours largely increased it. That which no monarch could accomplish with fire and sword, ecclesiastics could bring about with a stroke of the pen; whereby we may easily see the force and power at the command of the Church, and also how necessary it is for sovereigns to reserve such prerogatives for themselves.

If we reflect on what was said in the last chapter we shall see that such reservation conduced not a little to the increase of religion and piety; for we observed that the prophets themselves, though gifted with Divine efficacy, being merely private citizens, rather irritated than reformed the people by their freedom of warning, reproof, and denunciation, whereas the kings by warnings and punishments easily bent men to their will. Furthermore, the kings themselves, not possessing the right in question absolutely, very often fell away from religion and took with them nearly the whole people. The same thing has often happened from the same cause in Christian states.

Perhaps I shall be asked, "But if the holders of sovereign power choose to be wicked, who will be the rightful champion of piety? Should the sovereigns still be its interpreters? "I meet them with the counter-question, "But if ecclesiastics (who are also human, and private citizens, and who ought to mind only their own affairs), or if others whom it is proposed to entrust with spiritual authority, choose to be wicked, should they still be considered as piety's rightful interpreters?" It is quite certain that when sovereigns wish to follow their own pleasure, whether they have control over spiritual matters or not, the whole state, spiritual and secular, will go to ruin, and it will go much faster if private citizens seditiously assume the championship of the Divine rights.

Thus we see that not only is nothing gained by denying such rights to sovereigns, but on the contrary, great evil ensues. For (as happened with the

Jewish kings who did not possess such rights absolutely) rulers are thus driven into wickedness, and the injury and loss to the state become certain and inevitable, instead of uncertain and possible. Whether we look to the abstract truth, or the security of states, or the increase of piety, we are compelled to maintain that the Divine right, or the right of control over spiritual matters, depends absolutely on the decree of the sovereign, who is its legitimate interpreter and champion. Therefore the true ministers of God's word are those who teach piety to the people in obedience to the authority of the sovereign rulers by whose decree it has been brought into conformity with the public welfare.

There remains for me to point out the cause for the frequent disputes on the subject of these spiritual rights in Christian states; whereas the Hebrews, so far as I know, never, had any doubts about the matter. It seems monstrous that a question so plain and vitally important should thus have remained undecided, and that the secular rulers could never obtain the prerogative without controversy, nay, nor without great danger of sedition and injury to religion. If no cause for this state of things were forthcoming, I could easily persuade myself that all I have said in this chapter is mere theorizing, or a kind of speculative reasoning which can never be of any practical use. However, when we reflect on the beginnings of Christianity the cause at once becomes manifest. The Christian religion was not taught at first by kings, but by private persons, who, against the wishes of those in power, whose subjects they, were, were for a long time accustomed to hold meetings in secret churches, to institute and perform sacred rites, and on their own authority to settle and decide on their affairs without regard to the state, When, after the lapse of many years, the religion was taken up by the authorities, the ecclesiastics were obliged to teach it to the emperors themselves as they had defined it: wherefore they easily gained recognition as its teachers and interpreters, and the church pastors were looked upon as vicars of God. The ecclesiastics took good care that the Christian kings should not assume their authority, by prohibiting marriage to the chief ministers of religion and to its highest interpreter. They furthermore elected their purpose by multiplying the dogmas of religion to such an extent and so blending them with philosophy that their chief interpreter was bound to be a skilled philosopher and theologian, and to have leisure for a host of idle speculations: conditions which could only be fulfilled by a private individual with much time on his hands.

Among the Hebrews things were very differently arranged: for their Church began at the same time as their dominion, and Moses, their absolute ruler, taught religion to the people, arranged their sacred rites, and chose their spiritual ministers. Thus the royal authority carried very great weight with the people, and the kings kept a firm hold on their spiritual prerogatives.

Although, after the death of Moses, no one held absolute sway, yet the power of deciding both in matters spiritual and matters temporal was in the hands of the secular chief, as I have already pointed out. Further, in order that it might be taught religion and piety, the people was bound to consult the supreme judge no less than the high priest (Deut. xvii:9, 11). Lastly, though the kings had not as much power as Moses, nearly the whole arrangement and choice of the sacred ministry depended on their decision. Thus David arranged the whole service of the Temple (see 1 Chron. xxviii:11, 12, &c.); from all the Levites he chose twenty-four thousand for the sacred psalms; six thousand of these formed the body from which were chosen the judges and proctors, four thousand were porters, and four thousand to play on instruments (see 1 Chron. xxiii:4, 5). He further divided them into companies (of whom he chose the chiefs), so that each in rotation, at the allotted time, might perform the sacred rites. The priests he also divided into as many companies; I will not go through the whole catalogue, but refer the reader to 2 Chron. viii:13, where it is stated, "Then Solomon offered burnt offerings to the Lord . . . . . after a certain rate every day, offering according to the commandments of Moses;" and in verse 14, "And he appointed, according to the order of David his father, the courses of the priests to their service . . . . . . for so had David the man of God commanded." Lastly, the historian bears witness in verse 15: "And they departed not from the commandment of the king unto the priests and Levites concerning any matter, or concerning the treasuries."

From these and other histories of the kings it is abundantly evident, that the whole practice of religion and the sacred ministry depended entirely on the commands of the king.

When I said above that the kings had not the same right as Moses to elect the high priest, to consult God without intermediaries, and to condemn the prophets who prophesied during their reign; I said so simply because the prophets could, in virtue of their mission, choose a new king and give absolution for regicide, not because they could call a king who offended against the law to judgment, or could rightly act against him[33].

Wherefore if there had been no prophets who, in virtue of a special revelation, could give absolution for regicide, the kings would have possessed absolute rights over all matters both spiritual and temporal. Consequently the rulers of modern times, who have no prophets and would not rightly be bound in any case to receive them (for they are not subject to Jewish law), have absolute possession of the spiritual prerogative, although they are not celibates, and they will always retain it, if they will refuse to allow religious dogmas to be unduly multiplied or confounded with philosophy.

---

[33] I must here bespeak special attention for what was said in Chap. XVI. concerning rights.

CHAPTER XX

That in a Free State every man may Think what he Likes, and Say what he Thinks

If men's minds were as easily controlled as their tongues, every king would sit safely on his throne, and government by compulsion would cease; for every subject would shape his life according to the intentions of his rulers, and would esteem a thing true or false, good or evil, just or unjust, in obedience to their dictates. However, we have shown already (Chapter XVII.) that no man's mind can possibly lie wholly at the disposition of another, for no one can willingly transfer his natural right of free reason and judgment, or be compelled so to do. For this reason government which attempts to control minds is accounted tyrannical, and it is considered an abuse of sovereignty and a usurpation of the rights of subjects, to seek to prescribe what shall be accepted as true, or rejected as false, or what opinions should actuate men in their worship of God. All these questions fall within a man's natural right, which he cannot abdicate even with his own consent.

I admit that the judgment can be biassed in many ways, and to an almost incredible degree, so that while exempt from direct external control it may be so dependent on another man's words, that it may fitly be said to be ruled by him; but although this influence is carried to great lengths, it has never gone so far as to invalidate the statement, that every man's understanding is his own, and that brains are as diverse as palates.

Moses, not by fraud, but by Divine virtue, gained such a hold over the popular judgment that he was accounted superhuman, and believed to speak and act through the inspiration of the Deity; nevertheless, even he could not escape murmurs and evil interpretations. How much less then can other monarchs avoid them! Yet such unlimited power, if it exists at all, must belong to a monarch, and least of all to a democracy, where the whole or a great part of the people wield authority collectively. This is a fact which I think everyone can explain for himself.

However unlimited, therefore, the power of a sovereign may be, however implicitly it is trusted as the exponent of law and religion, it can never prevent men from forming judgments according to their intellect, or being influenced by any given emotion. It is true that it has the right to treat as enemies all men whose opinions do not, on all subjects, entirely coincide with its own; but we are not discussing its strict rights, but its proper course of action. I grant that it has the right to rule in the most violent manner, and to put citizens to death for very trivial causes, but no one supposes it can do this with the approval of sound judgment. Nay, inasmuch as such things cannot be done without extreme peril to itself, we may even deny that it has the absolute power to do them, or, consequently, the absolute right; for the rights of the sovereign are limited by his power.

Since, therefore, no one can abdicate his freedom of judgment and feeling; since every man is by indefeasible natural right the master of his own thoughts, it follows that men thinking in diverse and contradictory fashions, cannot, without disastrous results, be compelled to speak only according to the dictates of the supreme power. Not even the most experienced, to say nothing of the multitude, know how to keep silence. Men's common failing is to confide their plans to others, though there be need for secrecy, so that a government would be most harsh which deprived the individual of his freedom of saying and teaching what he thought; and would be moderate if such freedom were granted. Still we cannot deny that authority may be as much injured by words as by actions; hence, although the freedom we are discussing cannot be entirely denied to subjects, its unlimited concession would be most baneful; we must, therefore, now inquire, how far such freedom can and ought to be conceded without danger to the peace of the state, or the power of the rulers; and this, as I said at the beginning of Chapter XVI., is my principal object. It follows, plainly, from the explanation given above, of the foundations of a state, that the ultimate aim of government is not to rule, or restrain, by fear, nor to exact obedience, but contrariwise, to free every man from fear, that he may live in all possible security; in other words, to strengthen his natural right to exist and work — without injury to himself or others.

No, the object of government is not to change men from rational beings into beasts or puppets, but to enable them to develope their minds and bodies in security, and to employ their reason unshackled; neither showing hatred, anger, or deceit, nor watched with the eyes of jealousy and injustice. In fact, the true aim of government is liberty.

Now we have seen that in forming a state the power of making laws must either be vested in the body of the citizens, or in a portion of them, or in one man. For, although mens free judgments are very diverse, each one thinking that he alone knows everything, and although complete unanimity of feeling and speech is out of the question, it is impossible to preserve peace, unless individuals abdicate their right of acting entirely on their own judgment. Therefore, the individual justly cedes the right of free action, though not of free reason and judgment; no one can act against the authorities without danger to the state, though his feelings and judgment may be at variance therewith; he may even speak against them, provided that he does so from rational conviction, not from fraud, anger, or hatred, and provided that he does not attempt to introduce any change on his private authority.

For instance, supposing a man shows that a law is repugnant to sound reason, and should therefore be repealed; if he submits his opinion to the judgment of the authorities (who, alone, have the right of making and repealing laws), and meanwhile acts in nowise contrary to that law, he has deserved well of the state, and has behaved as a good citizen should; but if he accuses the authorities of injustice, and stirs up the people against them, or if he seditiously strives to abrogate the law without their consent, he is a mere agitator and rebel.

Thus we see how an individual may declare and teach what he believes, without injury to the authority of his rulers, or to the public peace; namely, by leaving in their hands the entire power of legislation as it affects action, and by doing nothing against their laws, though he be compelled often to act in contradiction to what he believes, and openly feels, to be best.

Such a course can be taken without detriment to justice and dutifulness, nay, it is the one which a just and dutiful man would adopt. We have shown that justice is dependent on the laws of the authorities, so that no one who contravenes their accepted decrees can be just, while the highest regard for duty, as we have pointed out in the preceding chapter, is exercised in maintaining public peace and tranquillity; these could not be preserved if every man were to live as he pleased; therefore it is no less than undutiful for a man to act contrary to his country's laws, for if the practice became universal the ruin of states would necessarily follow.

Hence, so long as a man acts in obedience to the laws of his rulers, he in nowise contravenes his reason, for in obedience to reason he transferred the right of controlling his actions from his own hands to theirs. This doctrine we can confirm from actual custom, for in a conference of great and small powers, schemes are seldom carried unanimously, yet all unite in carrying out what is decided on, whether they voted for or against. But I return to my proposition.

From the fundamental notions of a state, we have discovered how a man may exercise free judgment without detriment to the supreme power: from the same premises we can no less easily determine what opinions would be seditious. Evidently those which by their very nature nullify the compact by which the right of free action was ceded. For instance, a man who holds that the supreme power has no rights over him, or that promises ought not to be kept, or that everyone should live as he pleases, or other doctrines of this nature in direct opposition to the above-mentioned contract, is seditious, not so much from his actual opinions and judgment, as from the deeds which they involve; for he who maintains such theories abrogates the contract which tacitly, or openly, he made with his rulers. Other opinions which do not involve acts violating the contract, such as revenge, anger, and t he like, are not seditious, unless it be in some. corrupt state, where superstitious and ambitious persons, unable to endure men of learning, are so popular with the multitude that their word is more valued than the law.

However, I do not deny that there are some doctrines which, while they are apparently only concerned with abstract truths and falsehoods, are yet propounded and published with unworthy motives. This question we have discussed in Chapter XV., and shown that reason should nevertheless remain unshackled. If we hold to the principle that a man's loyalty to the state should be judged, like his loyalty to God, from his actions only — namely, from his charity towards his neighbours; we cannot doubt that the best government will allow freedom of philosophical speculation no less than of religious belief. I confess that from such freedom inconveniences may sometimes arise, but what question was ever settled so wisely that no abuses could possibly spring therefrom? He who seeks to regulate everything by law, is more likely to arouse vices than to reform them. It is best to grant what cannot be abolished, even though it be in itself harmful. How many evils spring from luxury, envy, avarice, drunkenness, and the like, yet these are tolerated — vices as they are — because they cannot be prevented by legal enactments. How much more then should free thought be granted, seeing that it is in itself a virtue and that it cannot be crushed! Besides, the evil results can easily be checked, as I will show, by the secular authorities, not to mention that such freedom is absolutely necessary for progress in science and the liberal arts: for no man follows such pursuits to advantage unless his judgment be entirely free and unhampered.

But let it be granted that freedom may be crushed, and men be so bound down, that they do not dare to utter a whisper, save at the bidding of their rulers; nevertheless this can never be carried to the pitch of making them think according to authority, so that the necessary consequences would be that men would daily be thinking one thing and saying another, to the corruption of good faith, that mainstay of government, and to the fostering of hateful flattery and perfidy, whence spring stratagems, and the corruption of every good art.

It is far from possible to impose uniformity of speech, for the more rulers strive to curtail freedom of speech, the more obstinately are they resisted; not indeed by the avaricious, the flatterers, and other numskulls, who think supreme salvation consists in filling their stomachs and gloating over their money-bags, but by those whom good education, sound morality, and virtue have rendered more free. Men, as generally constituted, are most prone to resent the branding as criminal of opinions which they believe to be true, and the proscription as wicked of that which inspires them with piety towards God and man; hence they are ready to forswear the laws and conspire against the authorities, thinking it not shameful but honourable to stir up seditions and perpetuate any sort of crime with this end in view. Such being the constitution of human nature, we see that laws directed against opinions affect the generous minded rather than the wicked, and are adapted less for coercing criminals than for irritating the upright; so that they cannot be maintained without great peril to the state.

Moreover, such laws are almost always useless, for those who hold that the opinions proscribed are sound, cannot possibly obey the law; whereas those who already reject them as false, accept the law as a kind of privilege, and make such boast of it, that authority is powerless to repeal it, even if such a course be subsequently desired.

To these considerations may be added what we said in Chapter XVIII. in treating of the history of the Hebrews. And, lastly, how many schisms have arisen in the Church from the attempt of the authorities to decide by law the intricacies of theological controversy! If men were not allured by the hope of getting the law and the authorities on their side, of triumphing over their adversaries in the sight of an applauding multitude, and of acquiring honourable distinctions, they would not strive so maliciously, nor would such fury sway their minds. This is taught not only by reason but by daily examples, for laws of this kind prescribing what every man shall believe and forbidding anyone to speak or write to the contrary, have often been passed, as sops or concessions to the anger of those who cannot tolerate men of enlightenment, and who, by such harsh and crooked enactments, can easily turn the devotion of the masses into fury and direct it against whom they will. How much better would it be to restrain popular anger and fury, instead of passing useless laws, which can only be broken by those who love virtue and the liberal arts, thus paring down the state till it is too small to harbour men of talent. What greater misfortune for a state can be conceived then that honourable men should be sent like criminals into exile, because they hold diverse opinions which they cannot disguise? What, I say, can be more hurtful than that men who have committed no crime or wickedness should, simply because they are enlightened, be treated as enemies and put to death, and that the scaffold, the terror of evil-doers, should become the arena where the highest examples of tolerance and virtue are displayed to the people with all the marks of ignominy that authority can devise?

He that knows himself to be upright does not fear the death of a criminal, and shrinks from no punishment; his mind is not wrung with remorse for any disgraceful deed: he holds that death in a good cause is no punishment, but an honour, and that death for freedom is glory.

What purpose then is served by the death of such men, what example in proclaimed? the cause for which they die is unknown to the idle and the foolish, hateful to the turbulent, loved by the upright. The only lesson we can draw from such scenes is to flatter the persecutor, or else to imitate the victim.

If formal assent is not to be esteemed above conviction, and if governments are to retain a firm hold of authority and not be compelled to yield to agitators, it is imperative that freedom of judgment should be granted, so that men may live together in harmony, however diverse, or even openly contradictory their opinions may be. We cannot doubt that such is the best system of government and open to the fewest objections, since it is the one most in harmony with human nature. In a democracy (the most natural form of government, as we have shown in Chapter XVI.) everyone submits to the control of authority over his actions, but not over his judgment and reason; that is, seeing that all cannot think alike, the voice of the majority has the force of law, subject to repeal if circumstances bring about a change of opinion. In proportion as the power of free judgment is withheld we depart from the natural condition of mankind, and consequently the government becomes more tyrannical.

In order to prove that from such freedom no inconvenience arises, which cannot easily be checked by the exercise of the sovereign power, and that men's actions can easily be kept in bounds, though their opinions be at open variance, it will be well to cite an example. Such an one is not very, far to seek. The city of Amsterdam reaps the fruit of this freedom in its own great prosperity and in the admiration of all other people. For in this most flourishing state, and most splendid city, men of every, nation and religion live together in the greatest harmony, and ask no questions before trusting their goods to a fellow-citizen, save whether he be rich or poor, and whether he generally acts honestly, or the reverse. His religion and sect is considered of no importance: for it has no effect before the judges in gaining or losing a cause, and there is no sect so despised that its followers, provided that they harm no one, pay every man his due, and live uprightly, are deprived of the protection of the magisterial authority.

On the other hand, when the religious controversy between Remonstrants and Counter-Remonstrants began to be taken up by politicians and the States, it grew into a schism, and abundantly showed that laws dealing with religion and seeking to settle its controversies are much more calculated to irritate than to reform, and that they give rise to extreme licence: further, it was seen that schisms do not originate in a love of truth, which is a source of courtesy and gentleness, but rather in an inordinate desire for supremacy, From all these considerations it is clearer than the sun at noonday, that the true schismatics are those who condemn other men's writings, and seditiously stir up the quarrelsome masses against their authors, rather than those authors themselves, who generally write only for the learned, and appeal solely to reason. In fact, the real disturbers of the peace are those who, in a free state, seek to curtail the liberty of judgment which they are unable to tyrannize over.

I have thus shown:—

I. That it is impossible to deprive men of the liberty of saying what they think.

II. That such liberty can be conceded to every man without injury to the rights and authority of the sovereign power, and that every man may retain it without injury to such rights, provided that he does not presume upon it to the extent of introducing any new rights into the state, or acting in any way contrary, to the existing laws.

III. That every man may enjoy this liberty without detriment to the public peace, and that no inconveniences arise therefrom which cannot easily be checked.

IV. That every man may enjoy it without injury to his allegiance.

V. That laws dealing with speculative problems are entirely useless.

VI. Lastly, that not only may such liberty be granted without prejudice to the public peace, to loyalty, and to the rights of rulers, but that it is even necessary, for their preservation. For when people try to take it away, and bring to trial, not only the acts which alone are capable of offending, but also the opinions of mankind, they only succeed in surrounding their victims with an appearance of martyrdom, and raise feelings of pity and revenge rather than of terror.

Uprightness and good faith are thus corrupted, flatterers and traitors are encouraged, and sectarians triumph, inasmuch as concessions have been made to their animosity, and they have gained the state sanction for the doctrines of which they are the interpreters. Hence they arrogate to themselves the state authority and rights, and do not scruple to assert that they have been directly chosen by God, and that their laws are Divine, whereas the laws of the state are human, and should therefore yield obedience to the laws of God — in other words, to their own laws.

Everyone must see that this is not a state of affairs conducive to public welfare.

Wherefore, as we have shown in Chapter XVIII., the safest way for a state is to lay down the rule that religion is comprised solely in the exercise of charity and justice, and that the rights of rulers in sacred, no less than in secular matters, should merely have to do with actions, but that every man should think what he likes and say what he thinks.

I have thus fulfilled the task I set myself in this treatise.

It remains only to call attention to the fact that I have written nothing which I do not most willingly submit to the examination and approval of my country's rulers; and that I am willing to retract anything which they shall decide to be repugnant to the laws, or prejudicial to the public good.

I know that I am a man, and as a man liable to error, but against error I have taken scrupulous care, and have striven to keep in entire accordance with the laws of my country, with loyalty, and with morality.